# REINVENTING
# AUSTRALIA

# REINVENTING AUSTRALIA

## The mind and mood of Australia in the 90s

# HUGH MACKAY

Angus&Robertson
An imprint of HarperCollins*Publishers*

## An Angus & Robertson Publication

Angus&Robertson, an imprint of
HarperCollins*Publishers*
25 Ryde Road, Pymble, Sydney, NSW 2073, Australia
31 View Road, Glenfield, Auckland 10, New Zealand

First published in Australia in 1993
Original edition reprinted three times
This updated edition 1993
Reprinted 1993

National Library of Australia
Cataloguing-in-Publication data:

Mackay, Hugh.
  Reinventing Australia:
  The mind and mood of Australia in the 90s.

  Includes index.
  ISBN 0 207 18314 7.

  1. National characteristics, Australian.
  2. Australia – Social conditions – 1990– .
  3. Australia – Social life and customs – 1990–  . I. Title.
306.0994

Typeset by Midland Typesetters, Maryborough
Printed in Australia by The Griffin Paperbacks, Adelaide

12 11 10 9 8 7 6
97 96 95 94 93

# Preface

This is a book about attitudes. *Reinventing Australia* is not intended to be a comprehensive assessment of Australian society nor a series of brave predictions about how the Australian way of life will change. It is simply an account of how Australians' attitudes are changing under the influence of the events of the past 20 years—a period of relentless social, cultural, economic, political and technological change.

The analysis is based on a long-term social research program, *The Mackay Report*, which has been continuously probing Australians' attitudes, values, motivations, fears, hopes and dreams since 1979. In that time, over 60 individual reports have been published and many of them are quoted in the pages of this book. A complete list of the reports appears in the Appendix, together with a description of the research methods used in the program.

I know that many Australians will recognise themselves in these pages. Thousands of people have participated in the group discussions and individual interviews on which the research is based, and I am grateful to all of them for the time they have so generously given to the program. Their willing participation makes this kind of social research possible; their frankness and openness gives it its integrity.

Being admitted into people's homes to listen to their conversations about everything from love and marriage to work and politics is a wonderful privilege. I hope that my attempt to discern some of the underlying patterns in all those conversations might help to relieve a little of the anxiety and insecurity reported by so many contemporary Australians: understanding what's happening to us is the beginning of being able to do something about it.

The book is full of questions. It will have served its purpose if some readers decide that some of those questions are worth pursuing.

HUGH MACKAY

# Acknowledgements

I have already acknowledged in the Preface the debt which I owe to the thousands of respondents who have taken part in the social research program, *The Mackay Report*, on which this book is based. Social research of this kind cannot proceed without the cooperation of people who are prepared to discuss their thoughts and feelings and, although we go to great lengths to make the process as easy and natural as possible, it is nevertheless an intrusion into their time and privacy.

As a researcher, I am fortunate to have received tuition, support and encouragement from four mentors: Ian McNair, who taught me to be strict about research method and respectful towards data; Robert McLaughlin, who rescued me from the study of economics and encouraged me to experience the joys of psychology and philosophy; Peter Kenny, who introduced me to the possibilities of qualitative research and taught me the art of interpretation; Keith Cousins, who encouraged my early attempts to make qualitative research 'respectable' in the business community and who, in the mid-Sixties, supported the establishment of Australia's first commercial group of qualitative research specialists.

Max Suich and David Dale have both created significant opportunities for me to present some of the results of my research to the community (who, after all, have supplied me with all my raw data). In 1980, Max Suich invited me to write a weekly column in *The National Times* and it was he who first suggested that I should attempt an overview of the mind and mood of the Australian community, thus sowing the seed for this book. During 1991–92, as part of David Dale's 2BL breakfast program, I had a weekly radio conversation with David about social issues arising from my research. I am grateful to both of them for their continuing interest in my research and for stimulating me to be more adventurous in exploring the implications of my findings.

I must also acknowledge the support of professional colleagues who have worked with me in data collection, analysis and interpretation. In particular, I would like to mention the contribution of Adele Mackay who collaborated with me on the original design of *The Mackay Report* and worked with me during the early years of its development, and Elizabeth Turnock, who has worked continuously on the project since 1981. The other members of the present research team are Prue Parkhill, Margie Beaumont and Maree MacCallum.

Finally, my thanks to the organisations whose annual subscriptions to *The Mackay Report* fund the whole research program. While they receive a commercial benefit from our regular reports, their continuing support has helped to create a unique body of information about Australian society.

# Contents

# 1

# THE BIG ANGST

I t is a grey, autumnal morning in Adelaide. I'm knocking at the door of a well-established brick house in a leafy middle-class suburb. The garden, like all the others in this street, is well kept and there is a general air of domestic contentment. There's even a dog sleeping on the front porch. Nothing in the scene points to what I am about to hear.

I'm looking forward, as I always do, to listening to a group of Australians (in this case, women in their forties) talking about the things that are on their minds. I'm anticipating a pleasant hour or so of animated conversation, probably touching on five or six different topics ranging from children to politics. The women are at home on a week-day morning, so they are not entirely typical of contemporary Australian women: I expect them to be a little more relaxed than the group of working mothers on the previous evening whose whole discussion was about the difficulties of balancing their full-time jobs with the responsibilities of running a household; or the recent group of men in Sydney who became so angry about the women's movement that they had to close the door so the wife of the host wouldn't be able to hear what they were saying from the next room. (She heard anyway, she told me as I was leaving, but said she'd heard it all before.)

A well-spoken but rather timid woman answers the door with a cigarette in her hand and I follow her into a large sitting room furnished with a leather lounge suite. A huge TV set is in one corner; there's a bookcase filled with a mixture of books and videos; posters on the wall; gas fire burning. Cups of tea and coffee are being passed around; home-made biscuits are on a plate on the pine coffee table. The women are relaxed with each other, casually dressed in jeans or track suits, deep in conversation about an outbreak of vandalism at the local primary school. Unemployed teenagers are being blamed.

One of the women has a heavy cold and mentions that she's having a 'sickie'. I am offered a cup of tea and I settle into a comfortable chair and explain the purpose of my visit. They listen rather impatiently to my description of the research project I am working on and the way I would like them to handle the discussion: no agenda, just a free-flowing chat about whatever you've been thinking and talking about over the past few days; relaxed and informal; no rules; I wouldn't be leading the discussion, just listening.

Smiles all round. A moment of hesitation before the conversation resumes its previous momentum. Everything normal. Normal?

'Guilt! Guilt! Guilt!' says the woman with the heavy cold, suddenly. 'That's what I've been feeling for the last week. I've only had my job for about six months, but you'd think I'd abandoned my family. Guilt! That's what they try to make me feel and they succeed. My husband's the worst. He hardly has to say anything to make me feel guilty. Last night he just mentioned that I'd forgotten to get something for one of the kids' school projects. Why didn't *he* get it? Why always *me*? And why do I feel guilty every time? Every time! I *know* why, because deep down I think I should be at home being a good little wife and mother. Just like my mother was. And I *did* like her being there when I came home from school. I admit it. But she was a doormat to my father and I'm buggered if I'm going to end up like that. I'm *buggered* if I am. They can just put up with it. I've got a life, too.'

The other women are leaning forward, eyes shining. The room is full of energy.

'I know *exactly* what you mean,' says a second woman,

and gives a similar account of how unjust she felt it was that she was constantly being made to feel guilty—mainly by her own mother—about doing what she believed was absolutely the right thing.

Another woman with a part-time job chimes in with some suggestions for how to train children more effectively to pull their weight with the household chores: 'I do this all on my own since Bob left. I'd go round the twist if the kids didn't help. Even so, I have to re-train them every time they come back from a weekend with Bob and his bimbo. Grrrr. He indulges them dreadfully, but they still hate going there. They can't *stand* her. I know how they feel.'

The conversation swings round to husbands—present and past—and there is shrieking agreement between two of the women that men are fundamentally, irrevocably *hopeless*—except for one thing, and they're not always so wonderful for that, either. (I shrink into my chair, but I needn't have worried: they've forgotten I am there.) Another woman insists that *her* husband is an angel in disguise. 'Heavy disguise, sometimes,' she admits.

The vandalism at the school comes up again, in the context of one of the women reporting having recently had a VCR stolen—for the second time—and her jewellery drawer gone through: 'They didn't think anything was worth taking—I was quite offended.'

Off again, on the subject of men and holidays: 'Never rent a house. It's no holiday at all, but they can't understand that.'

'Oh, we can't go anywhere at present. John thinks he's about to be retrenched. The strain is nearly killing him. I tell him he'd be better off resigning but of course he won't.'

Later, the hostess mentions that she is thinking of looking for a part-time job. She begins tentatively, looking for reactions. She speaks of her frustration at getting no fulfilment from being home all day with her children now at school, and a husband who really does think of her as an unpaid servant. One of the other women thinks she is mad, and says so: wasn't there too much stress involved in trying to get a job in the present climate? What would you do?

'I don't know yet,' she says, 'but I've got to do something. Look at this.' She produces some fragments of a china bowl and explains that she'd smashed it a couple of days ago in a moment of frustrated rage. She hasn't told her husband yet. She knows he won't understand. Everyone compliments her on her biscuits. Someone suggests she should do a Uni course of some kind. Or Tai Chi.

The conversation surges on: problems with in-laws following a divorce; children's disrespect for parents ('maybe we should try sending them to Sunday School . . . God, no, Sunday is the only day we can sleep in'); the pace of life; being a chauffeur for kids with sport, ballet and music lessons; the depressing sight of For Lease signs in several local shop windows; Australia as a republic ('might as well'); stories about racial tension in Sydney ('must be awful'); grudging sympathy for stressed husbands; the desperate need to be understood; declining moral standards . . . can't even trust the TV stations to stick to 'safe' material in children's viewing times . . .

The tone is negative, but the energy level remains high. These women are angry, not depressed. There's a recurring theme: 'I'm sure my own mother had an easier time than I'm having.'

'Parenting wasn't so complicated then. Kids these days reckon they have rights.'

'Sometimes, I honestly think I'm losing my grip.'

'So do I. We know we're doing too much, but we don't know what to do about it. It's sort of expected of you . . . I don't think I really *want* to change, anyway. I couldn't go back to the old way.'

'There must be a better way. I don't like what's happening to our kids. Money has become too important.'

'I wish I had more control over my life.'

'I'll tell you how I feel—I feel as if I'm making it all up as I go along. Everything keeps changing so much.'

Largely by accident, Australians in the last quarter of the 20th century have become a nation of pioneers; some heroically, some reluctantly, some painfully. We have been plunged into a period of unprecedented social, cultural, political, economic and technological change in which the Australian way of life is being radically redefined.

Everything from the roles of men and women, through marriage and the family to the structure of the labour market, the party political process, the Constitution and the racial and cultural composition of our society is being questioned. Whether we realise it or not, *all* Australians are becoming New Australians as we struggle partly to adapt to the changes going on around us, and partly to shape them to our own liking.

In the process, Australian society has come to the threshold of a new maturity, with the prospect of achieving an identity and an ethos all its own. Finally evolving into something more than a mere amalgam of inherited cultures, dumped here with successive waves of immigrants, Australian society is only now starting to face the truth about itself and its potential, and is beginning to outgrow its comfortable myths and legends.

This is a demanding process. As we move through the

1990s, the anxiety, stress and insecurity which have become characteristic of Australians may well be the sign that a cultural revolution is occurring. If a new sense of national identity is indeed emerging, then the widespread sense of *loss* of identity may be the darkness before the dawn.

The work of the pioneer is always stressful. When we are virtually all pioneers, the stress becomes a drain on the emotional resources of our society rather than a pain endured in private. So apparent is our national malaise that it has become fashionable to talk about the Age of Anxiety. For people given to applying labels to decades, the 1980s was popularly described as 'The Anxious Eighties' and there is no doubt that the decade lived up to the promise of that rather depressing label.

Australia has not been alone in all this. All around the Western world, social commentators have been struck by the rising level of anxiety over the past 20 years, by the extent to which people report stress as a central feature of their lives, and by the feelings of insecurity which sap the energy of so many people—especially young people. Some commentators, following the path of Jung, talk about a kind of generalised angst which has gripped Western society's collective unconscious; New Age philosophers interpret signs of stress as evidence of the increasing disharmony between urban life and the natural order; theologians smile knowingly; medical authorities simply speak of a virtual epidemic of anxiety and of a widespread need to be tranquilised.

However we might describe it, the evidence of that epidemic is all around us. Sometimes it reveals itself only fleetingly and through clenched teeth:

A man steps off an escalator in a Sydney department store

and, briefly disorientated, looks around for a moment before deciding whether to take the next escalator up. In that moment of indecision, he is standing in the pathway of a grim-faced woman who is intent on reaching her destination in the shortest possible time. She is put off her stride by the sight of this indecisive figure, and she has to divert a step or two out of her way to move around him. She does so with an elaborate sigh of impatience and a muttered expression of anger. Realising that he has inconvenienced her, the man steps aside and apologises, but the woman is embarrassed by the apology and, in her embarrassment, becomes even angrier. Head down, she rushes off to her destination.

Sometimes, the evidence of stress is far more open and explicit:

An office worker is driving home through the peak-hour traffic. There appears to be more traffic than usual and progress is slow. He can feel the tension building up inside him, because he is already running late and he promised his wife that he would collect their daughter from her music lesson on his way home from work. The timing is pretty tight because his wife will already be at home preparing the dinner, as their son has to be taken to soccer training later in the evening. For the last three weeks, this man has been late to collect his daughter from music; tonight, he is determined to get there on time. Approaching a red light, he loses concentration for a moment and, falling behind in his line of traffic, allows a driver from the adjoining lane to cut in ahead of him. He has to brake sharply to avoid hitting the intruder and he suddenly loses his temper. When the traffic stops for the red light, he leaps out of his car, runs forward and drives his fist through the open window of the offending vehicle, just missing the jaw of its astonished driver. A furious shouting match ensues but, before things can escalate into a more serious scuffle, the light turns green and he dashes back to his own car and they both move off with the traffic. He tells no-one about the incident and, reflecting on it later in the evening, he can scarcely believe what he has done.

Sometimes, life in the Age of Anxiety develops into an all-too-familiar pattern:

A married couple appear to have everything they want. They live in their own home with a mortgage they can afford; they have two young children who are healthy and happy; they have an affectionate relationship; they both hold secure and satisfying jobs. And yet, almost every night of their lives, arguments break out about things which, in retrospect, always seem too trivial to explain the intensity of the anger which they direct at each other. Sometimes the arguments are about one partner having spent money without consulting the other; sometimes they are about the sharing of domestic responsibilities; sometimes they are about relationships with members of the extended family—especially in-laws; sometimes they are about lack of sexual responsiveness. Almost always, the arguments seem to start because one partner interprets a remark made by the other as being 'below the belt'. Gradually, they are coming to realise that their nightly arguments are a symptom of a larger difficulty: they realise that they are both permanently tense and that their reactions to minor irritation are born of that deeper tension, but they have not yet worked out what to do about it.

Sometimes, the signs of anxiety are painfully obvious and potentially damaging:

A working mother is struggling to get herself and her children ready for the day. Everyone seems to be dragging the chain, and her major concern is that the youngest child will not be ready in time to be collected by the woman who takes him to the child-minding centre. He is a rather cranky four year-old and he is suffering from a cold which is causing him to sniff in a way which is increasingly irritating to his mother. The older two children finally get themselves ready for school and leave the house with barely enough time to catch the school bus. One of them fails to say goodbye to his mother, and her anger mounts. She realises that she will not be ready when the child-minder arrives in another few minutes, and the four year old continues to sniff. Suddenly, she snaps. Feeling angry with herself for not having her life under better control, angry with her husband for having to do shift work which allows him to sleep through the daily horror of the morning routine, angry with her boss for not making more allowance for the fact that she has a family as well as a job, angry with her older son for not having kissed her goodbye and now, unreasonably, feeling that that was one sniff too many, she lashes out and hits the boy across the shoulder. He looks at her in bewilderment and she hits him again. After three or four blows, he begins to cry and, at that moment, the child-minder knocks at the front door. The mother looks at her son and realises that, with one of the blows, she has scratched his face with her fingernails. Full of remorse, she gathers him into her arms and carries him, in a sobbing bundle, to the front door. Weeping herself by now, she thrusts the boy into the arms of the child-minder, with garbled explanations about the tears, the running nose and the bleeding cut. She forgets to say goodbye to her son. She slams the door. She looks at her watch and realises that she will be lucky to get to work on time. 'Why does everything have to be so hard?' she asks herself. It is a question she has been asking herself for years.

The problem is that, all over Australia, people feel themselves to be operating on a short fuse. Little things which might, in previous generations, have been quite easily tolerated and absorbed as part of the ups and downs of daily life, now seem to assume bigger proportions. The general level of anxiety in the community is such that it only requires a small spark to ignite feelings of irritation, helplessness, frustration, anger or violence.

One way of explaining this is to suggest that many Australians are suffering from the Last Straw syndrome, a condition in which so much stress and anxiety is being experienced that even quite minor upsets can feel like one thing too many.

There's an analogy in the field of environmental pollution. Environmental scientists tell us that when the background level of pollution is high, allergic reactions to specific irritants—dust, pollen, chemicals, perfumes—are more widespread. It is as though our bodies' ability to cope with pollution is stretched by the demands of the total environment and we are correspondingly more vulnerable to the effects of smaller irritations which, on their own, may not have affected us. So it is with stress.

People who are suffering from the Last Straw syndrome are often puzzled by their own outbreaks of anger; often feel that the descent into a pit of despair was not really justified by the event which precipitated it; often find themselves resolving that they are going to get their lives back under control before they do something drastic or foolish in response to one of those 'last straws'.

Certainly, in the field of domestic violence and child abuse, the Last Straw syndrome seems to be taking a heavy toll. People whose emotional and physical resources are already depleted by deep feelings of insecurity and anxiety may find that relatively minor domestic irritations (an argument over money, a crying baby, the breakdown of an appliance at an inconvenient time) can push them over the edge.

Drug abuse is, for many Australians, a symptom of the same syndrome. People who take refuge in over-consumption of tranquilisers, alcohol or any other mind-altering drugs, are usually seeking short-term relief from the stress created by long-term anxiety and from the pressure which builds up in people who are tired of trying to cope with a sustained sense of inadequacy.

Australians commonly describe 'stress' as their major health problem and—whether accurately or not—attribute many symptoms of illness to the increased stress in their lives: hypertension, sleeplessness, allergies, frequent headaches, respiratory disorders, vague feelings of restlessness . . . such symptoms are often taken to be a sign that The Big Angst is among us.

Some large organisations are now providing counselling or other forms of special treatment to help their employees cope with the fact that stress at work can be the last straw for people whose domestic lives are also characterised by stress.

Many marketing organisations are reporting a rise in

customer complaints. Why, they ask, are our customers more inclined to complain now, when we are more careful than ever about quality control? The answer is that their customers are suffering from the Last Straw syndrome: a minor difficulty with a product or service, which might previously have passed unremarked, may now be the basis for a customer complaint.

Crankiness and irritability are the most obvious and widespread manifestations of the Last Straw syndrome. On the roads, at the bank or the supermarket, at work, on the sporting field, or in personal relationships, Australians are increasingly intolerant of minor stress because their emotional resources are depleted by the task of coping with major stress. One of the sad symptoms of the level of anxiety in the Australian community emerged in The Mackay Report on *The Australian Dream* (1990): because Australians are so preoccupied with the problems of trying to cope with their present circumstances, they have temporarily abandoned any serious consideration of what the future might hold. The Australian dream machine more or less ground to a halt at the beginning of the 1990s, because people had come to feel that survival was a real issue and that it was time to batten down the hatches rather than worry too much about setting a new course.

That same report suggested that one of the things which most inhibits Australians' ability to dream of a better future is their fear that Australia is becoming a more violent society. Whereas it was once regarded as characteristic of life in Australia that our cities and suburbs were safe at virtually any time of day or night, today's Australians believe that this is no longer true. Parents report that they are uneasy about their children travelling alone on public transport, or even going to the beach with a group of other children. They resent the steps which they feel that they have to take to ensure their own security and the security of their children. Teenagers, too, frequently complain about the lengths to which they have to go to ensure their safety when they are travelling alone or in small groups— especially at night.

Such anxieties are well justified by official statistics about the rising rate of crime in Australia. According to the NSW Bureau of Crime Statistics and Research, the *rate* of serious assault in Australia has increased five-fold in the past 20 years. Even allowing for some variations in the official definition of 'serious assault' in that time, the picture is dramatic and alarming. These figures have nothing to do with population increase: they reveal that Australians are now five times as likely to be seriously assaulted as they were 20 years ago. (The rate for serious assault jumped from 21 per 100,000 in 1973–74 to 100 per 100,000 in 1988–89.)

Some people might argue that the murder rate is the ultimate indication of a violent society, and point to the fact that the murder rate in Australia has remained relatively stable throughout the twentieth century. But that is a misleading argument: murder, after all, is unlikely to be the outcome of relatively unfocussed anxiety. Murder is almost always directed at an absolutely specific target. The more general and widespread crimes of assault, by contrast, tend not to be targeted at a particular victim: the victim is 'chosen' almost at random because the crime is likely to be a manifestation of despair, anxiety, boredom, violence or anger within the assailant. The outlet chosen is violence, but it is rarely violence which is focussed on the identity of the victim.

The rising rate of violent crime in Australia is doubly significant: it is both a cause and a symptom of our anxiety.

While law-abiding Australians' anxieties are fuelled by concern about violent crime, they acknowledge that the crime itself may be a direct response to feelings of instability and insecurity in Australia. 'Street kids', for example, are frequently cited as the ultimate symbol of what we fear most about the changes taking place in Australian society: street kids are regarded both as a menacing group in society because their despair leads them into crime, but they are also regarded as a reproach to a society whose values have eroded to the point where the phenomenon of street kids can emerge on a large scale.

Whether we turn to official statistics or simply listen to ordinary Australians describing their feelings of insecurity, the picture which emerges is remarkably consistent. But labels like 'The Age of Anxiety' don't really tell us much. Although it is necessary to understand the various manifestations of The Big Angst, it is much more important to investigate where it came from. Why, as we move into the middle of the 1990s, should Australia be in the grip of an epidemic of anxiety? Why *now*? Why did stress rise to such high levels through a period of such enormous economic prosperity in the 1980s, through a time when increasing emphasis was being given to personal freedom, through a time of such dramatic social improvements—particularly in the position of women and in the care of the disadvantaged, and a time when technology was becoming so sophisticated that many of the most demanding and demeaning tasks which we have traditionally had to perform ourselves are now being done for us by machines?

In 1991–92, it was tempting to suggest that Australia's epidemic of anxiety was a direct result of the recession and of the bleak prospect of long-term unemployment for more than one million Australians. Obviously, the recession has had a major impact on the mood of the Australian community, but it kicked us when we were already down: the signs of stress and anxiety were apparent years before the recession. The Age of Anxiety did not begin in 1991; its origins go back much further than that. In fact, to understand the mood of Australia in the 1990s, it is necessary to look back over a period of 20 years or more. The seeds of our present malaise were sown at least as long ago as that.

One of the things we know about human beings is that, in general, they are resistant to change. Even when there are small interruptions to the rhythm and pattern of daily life, most people experience mild tension or irritation. When our lives are disrupted by changes which involve some *redefinition* of who we are or how we are going to live, the tension is correspondingly greater.

From time to time, various medical authorities publish information about the impact of unexpected or radical change on our mental and physical health. Sometimes there's a checklist: tick off which of the following things have happened to you within the last year or two. Then follows a list which typically comprises such items as these: marriage, divorce, a birth or a bereavement, a change of job, moving house, international travel, borrowing a significant sum of money. Generally speaking, such a list will be accompanied by the advice that if, during the specified period, you have experienced more than three or four of these significant changes in your life, then you should waste no time in checking yourself into an intensive care ward because something nasty is about to happen to you.

Of course, that's an exaggeration. But the principle holds

true: when we experience changes in our lives which amount to a redefinition of who we are or how we are going to live, those changes will almost always provoke some degree of anxiety, *even where the change may be both sought and welcomed.*

The birth of a child is a classic case in point. Even the most wanted and most loved baby triggers the difficult process in its parents of redefining their identities, roles and responsibilities. The birth of a baby not only changes the routines of the household, but it also changes the nature of relationships between the other members of the family and their sense of who they are. Husbands and wives become mothers and fathers; sons and daughters become brothers and sisters; parents become grandparents. Similarly, settling into a new job is a process of redefining who you are, and what you want out of life—to say nothing of the often awkward process of being integrated into the organisational and social environment of the new job.

For individuals, then, there is no mystery about the primary source of stress and anxiety: it is the result of having to adapt to changes in our lives which are so significant that we are required to re-think who we are.

For Australian society at large, the last 20 years have been just like that. The so-called Age of Anxiety is in reality nothing more than a *symptom* of the fact that what we are really living in is the Age of Redefinition. Since the early 1970s, there is hardly an institution or a convention of Australian life which has not been subject either to serious challenge or to radical change. The social, cultural, political and economic landmarks which we have traditionally used as reference points for defining the Australian way of life have either vanished, been eroded or shifted.

The story of Australia between the early Seventies and

the early Nineties is the story of a society which has been trying to cope with too much change, too quickly, and on too many fronts. Not that there was any alternative: almost all of the most significant changes have been either actively sought, or have been the inevitable consequence of other changes which we thought were desirable. It is ironic that most of the changes which have wrought such havoc in people's lives are, of themselves, positively desirable. Each change, taken separately, may be seen as enriching, enhancing or in other ways improving the lives of individual Australians. On its own, any one of the major socio-cultural changes of the period might not have created undue stress.

We *wanted* new divorce laws; women *wanted* to re-enter the workforce; we *wanted* the convenience of instant credit; we *wanted* to expand our population through migration; we *wanted* the rapid rise in our material standard of living which the Sixties promised us.

But, taken together, the scope and scale of the changes in the last quarter of the twentieth century have been too difficult for most of us to take in our stride. After all, these have not been years of trivial or incidental change; nor has this been a period in which Australians have had time to understand, absorb and adapt to one change before they moved on to confront the next. Rather, it has been a period in which Australians have been swept along on the tide of relentless change; when we have had to get used to the idea of discontinuity; when we have been forced to reinvent the Australian way of life *on the run*.

Of course, there have been many other periods in Australian history when major—even cataclysmic—change had to be confronted and absorbed. The 1890s was such a period. So too, were the two World Wars and the Great Depression of the 1930s. But although each of those periods of upheaval involved some redefinition of the Australian identity and the Australian way of life, none of them was comparable to the present era in terms of the relentlessness of change on such a broad front. Nor were any of those previous episodes as confusing or as destabilising as the present.

Living through World War II, for example, was an intensely painful and stressful experience for Australia but it was also a unifying and often inspiring experience. It created a stronger sense of Australian cultural identity, and it bound the community together with a sense of common purpose.

By contrast, the present era seems fraught with the peculiar stresses created by a confused and diffused sense of identity, the lack of a consistent or coherent sense of purpose, and a growing feeling of isolation and even alienation among Australians—especially young Australians.

The common cry now being heard around Australia is, 'Why does everything have to change so fast?' The common complaint is that individual Australians feel as if they have lost control of their own lives and their own destinies. Australians are increasingly feeling victimised by the rate and character of the changes which are having such an enormous emotional, cultural and financial impact on their lives.

The Australian way of life is now being challenged and redefined to such an extent that growing numbers of Australians feel as if their personal identities are under threat as well. 'Who are we?' soon leads to the question, 'Who am I?'

The anxieties and insecurities associated with living in the Age of Redefinition might be easy to understand but that doesn't make them healthy and it certainly doesn't make living with them any easier to take. Very few people enjoy the Last Straw syndrome. Very few people enjoy the sense that they are living on a short fuse. Very few people enjoy feeling as if the society in which they live is being redefined. The story of the 1990s will be the story of Australians' attempts to learn how to live more comfortably in the Age of Redefinition. It will be the story of how we chose to avoid the ravages of anxiety and how we managed to get our stress levels back under control.

The Big Angst may feel like a fear of the future, but it is actually a consequence of the past: it may sometimes emerge as anxiety about specific events, but it is really an underlying anxiety generated by instability. Thirty or forty years ago, fear of the future could be explained on rational grounds because of the horrors which the future seemed capable of visiting on us during the years of the Cold War. Today's fear of the future is not so much based on what the future holds as on our inability to chart a confident course through it.

The Big Angst is no fun, but at least it is no mystery either: we have simply lost our bearings.

# 2

# THE AGE OF
# REDEFINITION

It's easy to make vague generalisations about the impact of change on Australians' lives. But we need to be more specific. What, precisely, are these changes which have so radically redefined the Australian way of life, and produced such widespread feelings of anxiety and insecurity in our community? What are these conventions and institutions which have undergone such changes that they are no longer reliable as reference points for defining Australian society?

This section of the book discusses seven changes which, among many others, have raised big questions about our sense of personal identity and our sense of being a community:

The redefinition of gender roles, in the wake of the Women's Movement, has left Australian women with a radically new view of their role and status in society, and Australian men with a sense of uncertainty about how to respond to the revolution;

The institution of marriage is being redefined by the rising divorce rate and by the increasingly diverse groupings which now qualify for definition as 'families';

Rising levels of unemployment, and a changing pattern of employment opportunities, are causing a retreat from the traditional work ethic, and a re-think about the importance we attach to work;

The invention of invisible money and credit has revolutionised our financial transactions, and the new retail environment has changed the way we shop;

Rapid redistribution of household income is creating a big 'new rich' class and a big 'new poor' class; the traditional Australian middle class is shrinking, and the long-term dream of egalitarianism is under threat;

In the name of multiculturalism, Australians are redefining their cultural identity, but experiencing some pain and anxiety in the process;

A significant shift in the character of Australian politics has left voters confused and cynical, and inclined to ask searching questions about 'the system'.

# 2.1

# NEW WOMEN & OLD MEN

There is no doubt about which of the redefinitions of the past 20 years has had most impact on the Australian way of life: it is the redefinition of gender roles which has taken place in the minds of roughly half the population—the female half.

It is sobering to remind ourselves that we only have to go back as far as the mid-1970s to realise that a revolution of breathtaking speed has taken place in Australian women's view of themselves—and, by implication, in their view of men. Just 20 years ago, it was safe to say that Australian women were second-class citizens: the legal system said it, the financial services market said it, and the cultural context certainly said it. For most of the twentieth century, Australian women were conditioned to accept that they were living in a society dominated and controlled by men and that, in most cases, they would acquire a kind of second-hand identity from the men they would marry. They may have resented it; they may have been deeply frustrated by it; but they generally accepted that this was their lot.

Today, that kind of proposition sounds absurd. Today, anyone who seriously suggested that women should settle for second-class status or for a second-hand identity would be run out of town. Of course, there are still plenty of women who will cheerfully settle for a secondhand identity, but mainstream attitudes have radically changed in the past 20 years.

When the latest wave of feminism hit Australia in the early to mid-1970s, Australian women experienced what felt like an astonishing awakening: they discovered that a woman was a person. That's all. That was the heart of the entire revolution: 'I am a person, entitled to the same sense of identity and the same status in our society as any other person.' Not a very radical proposition, on reflection, but it was one which has led to some of the most revolutionary changes in the Australian way of life this century.

Once women begin to redefine the role and status of women in our society, this changes everything: it changes their view of the role and status of men, of romance, of sex, of marriage, of parenting, of family life, of work, of household management, of politics . . . hardly an aspect of the Australian way of life has remained untouched by the revolutionary change in the way Australian women have come to see themselves over the past 20 years.

The key group of women—the women who formed the pioneering generation—were those aged roughly between 18 and 35 years when the Women's Lib movement found its voice in Australian society in the mid-1970s. Those were the women who immediately sensed that the role models of their mothers and grandmothers were going to be either inappropriate or unacceptable. Those were the women whose latent resentment of second-class status was activated by the rallying cry of the feminists (Germaine Greer in particular). Those were the women who saw a wonderful prospect of liberation before them: the prospect of leading more fulfilling lives, and of being more active and complete participants in adult society.

Of course, other women held back from the revolution and found themselves rather frightened by the strident messages of the radical feminists. They feared for the safety of traditional values associated with mothering and with family life; they wondered why so many women were rushing headlong into a redefinition of gender roles when they themselves were finding such intense satisfaction in traditional wife-and-mother roles; they wondered what would become of the children of a generation of women who seemed so determined to combine family life with paid employment, and who seemed so anxious to blur the traditional distinctions between men and women.

But such dissenting voices were largely drowned out in the enthusiasm for redefining gender roles which so captivated an entire generation of Australian women in the late Seventies and throughout the Eighties.

Very quickly, it became obvious that the new values inspired by feminism would have to be expressed in some symbolic way. This is the nature of revolutionary change, after all. Most changes in attitudes and values are the result of changed circumstances but, when a revolution is taking place, attitudes often change first (because of an underlying sense of dissatisfaction which has not previously found an outlet), and new patterns of behaviour subsequently emerge.

The symbolic behaviour which women chose as an expression of their new-found definition of gender was work: full-time or part-time paid employment outside the home became a central aspiration for this pioneering generation of women. Whereas their mothers and grand-mothers had assumed that a career (or even 'a job') would be abandoned in favour of the role of wife and mother, the pioneers of the Seventies and Eighties saw work outside the home as the most potent symbol of their liberation.

This has always seemed rather strange to men, who might have seen retirement from work as a more appropriate symbol of liberation. But for women who, by cultural convention and social pressure, had been virtually forced out of the workforce when they became mothers, the chance to combine motherhood with a place in the paid workforce was a heady prospect indeed. As a symbol, it had everything: it represented a passport to a new, more tangible sense of identity; it created the possibility of at least partial financial independence; it relieved women from the humiliation of having to describe themselves as being 'just a housewife'.

Of course, the enthusiasm to stay in the workforce—or to re-join the workforce—after the birth of children had more than symbolic attraction. At a time when Australia was entering one of its most explicit phases of material-ism—a period in which the Me Generation's obsession with self-indulgence was coming into full flower—the prospect of being able to earn money while still having a family had economic as well as emotional attractions.

And so, in the period from the mid-Seventies to the early Nineties, Australian labour market statistics were rewrit-ten. In 1970, 32 per cent of married women were in the workforce; by 1990, that figure had risen to 53 per cent of all married women and 60 per cent of all mothers with dependent children.

But women who had embraced the new values of Women's Lib had not abandoned the traditional home-and-family, wife-and-mother values which they had inherited from their mothers and grandmothers. So although they were busily constructing a new framework for their lives, they were continuing to operate within an existing frame-work as well. Needless to say, this created enormous complications and difficulties for the women involved.

In many ways, it was easier for the radicals than for the

moderates. The radicals were more easily able to replace one set of values with another. But for the moderates (who represented the vast majority of the generation of women caught up in this redefinition), a very troubled future lay ahead. For these women, the challenge was not simply to live out the new values; rather, the challenge was to find a way of incorporating the new values into an existing set of values.

The solution which most of them settled for was to lead a double life: to express traditional home-and-family values at home, and to express feminist/liberationist values at work. For many women, this created the emotional hazard of having to leap a kind of symbolic barrier on the way to work each morning, and then to leap back over it on the way home at night.

Many women have suffered from a high degree of personal stress as a direct result of having to make this daily adjustment. They have not yet found a way to reconcile the two sets of values which so often seem to be in conflict, and so they have compartmentalised their lives and paid a very high emotional price for doing so.

But the idea of full-time or even part-time work outside the home as a symbol of the New Woman was so seductive that the difficulties it created for mothers were accepted as part of the price to be paid for being a revolutionary. Even those women who felt themselves to be most ground down or misunderstood as a result of trying to combine the two roles felt that to retreat from the workforce would be to admit defeat and to run the risk of being seen as a traitor to the revolution. Those mothers who elected to stay home and look after their families on a full-time basis reported during the 1980s that the strongest sense of disapproval which they felt came not from husbands (who might have appreciated the extra income or the extra stimulation associated with a working wife), but from other women. It became a common complaint among stay-at-home mothers of the 1980s that they were often treated by working women as if they were somehow letting down the revolution.

The social and cultural pressure on married women to use work outside the home as a means of acquiring a clearer and more independent sense of identity was almost irresistible. And so was born one of the most significant socio-cultural changes of the last 50 years: the emergence of the working mother as a mainstream phenomenon. Between 1945 and 1975, mothers who worked were generally regarded as being the victims of economic necessity or, in rare cases, being such stars in their fields (particularly professional and artistic fields) that it was understood that they would place work ahead of the normal family-related goals of the majority of Australian women. Since 1975, however, the working mother has become the norm: when almost two-thirds of women with dependent children work outside the home, those women who choose *not* to work find themselves having to explain their decision to stay at home.

## THE WORKING MOTHER

To understand the real impact of the redefinition of women's role in Australian society at the end of the twentieth century, therefore, we have to devote our primary attention to the phenomenon of the working mother. What is it like to be a woman who has decided to combine a job which her mother thought was a full-time job with another job outside the home?

## THE PROBLEM OF FATIGUE

First, they report having to deal with the problem of daily exhaustion. They see their lives as being a constant battle against fatigue. They go to work and get tired and then they come home only to face what is now often described as 'the second shift'. In other words, they do a day's work at work and then brace themselves to tackle a second day's work at home (including such major tasks as cooking, cleaning, washing, ironing, supervising homework, plus the myriad planning and management tasks which are involved in continuous housekeeping and parenting).

The long-term effects of this kind of sustained fatigue are easy to imagine. Women who feel as if they are constantly over-tired are almost bound to find themselves constantly on the edge of crankiness and irritability; their sense of humour is likely to be diminished; their resentment of their partner's failure to participate more actively in parenting and housekeeping is likely to be exacerbated by the sense of helplessness and despair which often accompanies sustained fatigue. Such women may also become more accident prone and, when really stressed by tiredness, may begin to entertain doubts about whether the whole process is worthwhile, and to lose sight of the very principles which led to the creation of this 'double life' in the first place.

This is by no means a universal picture, of course. Many working mothers have managed to reorganise their domestic routines so that they can cope very well. Some have decided to lower their housekeeping standards in order to be able to relax and enjoy other aspects of their lives. Others regard the stimulation and satisfaction associated with the role of a working mother as being so precious to them that they accept fatigue as a small price to pay.

But it *is* a price and it does take its toll. It is no wonder that working mothers are increasingly attracted to the idea of a part-time job which can be more easily integrated into the other roles and responsibilities which they find them-selves unable to relinquish—or even to modify to any significant extent.

So far, the most common response of working mothers to the problem of fatigue has been to grin and bear it. They recognise that, from the point of view of working women without children, or house-bound mothers of young chil-dren, they may well be regarded as a privileged group: they are seen as having come closest to the ideal of 'having it all'. They are the envy of those women who feel that they have had to choose a career to the exclusion of children, and also of those stay-at-home mothers who continue to hanker after the idea that even a part-time job would relieve the drudgery of much of their lives, would offer the stimulation of more adult companionship, would provide some useful extra income, and would help to establish a more independent sense of identity.

It is probably true to suggest, however, that the women in both of those other categories do not fully appreciate the emotional and physical burden which is carried by the working mother. As she sinks into bed at the end of another day, she dimly recalls that she used to go to bed for reasons other than restorative sleep. The sex lives of working mothers generally suffer from the effects of fatigue: the proposition that 'you can't be a work-horse all day and a show-pony at night' is one which is strongly endorsed by working mothers all around Australia.

## THE BURDEN OF GUILT

The second recurring theme in working mothers' own accounts of their lives is that they are guilty about the quality of their own mothering. It is a common source of anxiety among working mothers to reflect on the possibility that their own mothers did a better job of mothering them than they are doing with their own children. Feelings of guilt are kept secret: they may be discussed with other women in the same situation, but they are rarely admitted to spouses or other family members—and hardly ever to the children themselves.

The stereotype of a mother who is always available to her children and who is, most particularly, already at home when they arrive home from school is still very popular in Australian culture. Stay-at-home mothers who sometimes wistfully wonder whether it would be fun to take a job console themselves with the reassuring thought that, whatever else they may be missing out on, at least they are permanently available to their children.

By contrast, working mothers whose jobs extend beyond school hours may berate themselves with the thought that they are letting their children down. They also complain that they miss out on many of the most precious moments of communication between mother and child—those moments of spontaneous news-telling when the child first arrives home from school.

Working mothers therefore have to create some kind of compensatory argument in order to deal with the underlying sense of guilt which so many of them continue to feel. One popular argument is to suggest that children benefit from having a working mother, partly because she is a more stimulating and interesting person, and partly because the children are encouraged to be more independent from a younger age simply because their mothers are not available to an extent which would allow them to remain dependent for long. (An interesting challenge to this argument emerges from the recent publication by the Office of the Status of Women, *Juggling Time* [1991], which suggests that when the mothers of teenage children enter the part-time workforce, the participation of those teenagers in housework is actually likely to decline!).

In fact, there is evidence to suggest that some working mothers may actually be over-compensating for their absence from home by retarding their children's progress towards independence, in an attempt to demonstrate that their children are not suffering from having a mother who works. The link thus forged between guilt and fatigue is potentially damaging not only to the working mothers themselves but also to the quality of their relationships with their children.

Recognising the shortage of time available to spend with their children, working mothers sometimes take refuge in the concept of *quality time*. This concept encourages them to believe that, when they do have time to spend with their children, it will be time well spent: serious attention will be paid to communication , to cuddling, to social interaction, to shared activity. The argument for 'quality time' is based on the idea that the *use* of available time, rather than the mere availability of time, will determine the quality of a parent-child relationship.

But 'quality time' is a hazardous concept. It is not uncommon for working mothers to complain that some time which they set aside to spend with their children falls far short of the 'quality' ideal simply because the children turn out to be pre-occupied with some other activity, or because the intensity of the emotional spotlight falling on the children actually results in heightened tension or explosive argument. Quality time, it turns out, can be very elusive and difficult to schedule.

Other compensations for the guilt of working mothers take more material forms: expensive gifts and other indulgences may be offered to children to compensate for what the mother herself sees as her own shortcomings as a parent (even though these may not be identified in the minds of her children). Eating out, taking expensive holidays, or the purchase of elaborate in-home entertainment and recreation equipment may all be symptoms of a working mother's guilt.

Children are not slow to perceive the benefits which may flow to them from their mothers' desire to compensate for their own feelings of guilt. And yet it is difficult to find children who have much complaint about the fact that their mothers have full-time or part-time work outside the home: Mum is still Mum, whatever the shape and structure of family life might be.

## 'ISN'T THERE A BETTER WAY?'

The third significant factor in working mothers' analysis of their lives concerns an ever-present sense of confusion and dissatisfaction. Having been promised so much by the goals and values of the Women's Movement, the working mother is now perplexed to find that 'liberation' too often feels like enslavement. She constantly worries about whether some Utopia of ultimate gratification lies beyond her reach, and she is concerned by the possibility that she has actually mismanaged the strategies which were intended to let her 'have it all'.

The balancing act involved in trying to express two competing and sometimes contradictory sets of values is a very demanding act. Working mothers typically feel that they have not yet cracked the formula, and that there must be a better way of managing the complexities of their double lives.

Many of them worked out, long ago, what that 'better way' might be. It occurred to them that, since their families benefit both from the money and the emotional enrichment which they obtain through work, it would be appropriate for other family members—especially partners—to take a more active role in housekeeping. But, although many working mothers have been mentioning this elegant and obvious solution to their spouses several times a day for many years, the light of recognition and acceptance of the force of this argument has yet to dawn.

## THE SLOW, SLOW MALE RESPONSE

The widespread failure of Australian men to adapt their behaviour to match the redefinition of gender roles which has taken place in the minds of women, represents another major source of anxiety for the working mother. The problems of fatigue, guilt and confusion create enough stress: the added problem of a generally uncooperative and unsympathetic husband often turns out to be the last straw.

Although Australian men are beginning to adapt to the emerging realities of the New Woman, it is still fair to characterise the typical Australian male response as being a dim awareness that something has gone wrong with his life. Recognising that his wife leads a different kind of life from the one that she led 10 or 15 years ago (and a very different kind of life from the one his mother led), he clings to the hope that he might be able to maintain his existing pattern of living until the storm passes. He recognises that part of his wife's new definition of gender roles involves him in being a more active participant in the relationship and in the life of the family, but this has often been the source of unwelcome pressure.

The hope that things might return to their previous levels of comfort, when men were not being so actively challenged by women, is refuelled every time he visits his own mother. His mother is likely to believe that her daughter-in-law is not being a sufficiently supportive and attentive wife and so she is likely to try to compensate for this when her son and daughter-in-law visit her. She says to her son, 'Would you like a cup of tea, darling?', ignoring his wife and, perhaps deliberately, cutting right across the wife's sustained campaign to encourage her husband to make himself a cup of tea if he feels the need for one.

All this will change of course, partly because the rising generation of mothers-in-law will themselves have been working mothers, and partly because men will begin to adapt.

The early signs of that process of adaptation are now emerging. It is certainly too early to suggest that the New Man is here in large numbers, although there are plenty of relationships in which the concept of shared responsibility has never been questioned. But the early attempts of most Australian men to modify their behaviour in the light of the Women's Movement are often tentative, stumbling and unsuccessful.

A typical middle-class husband might say to his wife, 'I can see that you are tired . . . let me help with the washing up'. In his mind, this is a major capitulation to the Women's

Movement. Imagine his surprise, therefore, when his offer is greeted by a torrent of angry words: 'Just listen to what you said! You said that you would *help* with the washing-up. Well, isn't that a funny thing! I've been washing up for the last 20 years and I never thought I was helping anyone. I thought I was doing the washing-up because the dishes were dirty and had to be washed. You live in this house. You know that the dirty dishes need to be washed up. Just wash them up. Don't *help* with the washing-up, just *do* the washing-up. That's the trouble with you . . . you think that if you do anything around the house it is such a big deal.' In the face of this onslaught, the husband is likely to retreat from the kitchen regretting that he had made the offer and making a mental note of the fact that he must delete the word 'help' from his vocabulary.

That is a correct decision. His wife is enraged by the suggestion that when he begins to participate more actively in housekeeping, this is on the basis of mere help. From her point of view, he should be cooking, washing, ironing, washing-up or cleaning because these tasks need to be done and because he has some available time and energy to do them.

Gradually, men are learning the new rules. But even when they acknowledge that they should simply participate in household tasks without offering to 'help', they are still inclined to hang around after completing these tasks, drawing their wives' attention to the fact that the job has been done and waiting for lavish praise and recognition.

He says, 'I've pegged out the clothes', expecting a pat on the head or a round of applause. She says, 'That's very good. Well done! I didn't realise it was an art form. I have been pegging the clothes out for a long time and I don't remember anyone ever commenting on it. How come it is such a big deal when *you* peg out the clothes? In any case, why haven't you pegged the socks in pairs?'

Of course, they are both right. From her point of view, pegging out the clothes is no big deal because she has, indeed, been doing it for 20 years. But, from his point of view, it is a novel experience and one which he believes should be recognised and encouraged . . . and if, as she implies, there are logical grounds for suggesting that socks should be pegged in pairs, then he will need to have them explained to him.

Some women are deciding that the best way to secure male participation in housework is to offer constant praise, recognition and encouragement. Others have begun to realise that men actually do not know how to perform many household tasks which women regard as routine, and so some women are now taking a step back from their strident demands for more male participation and are beginning a training program which will make it easier for their husbands to participate more actively in household management.

Such training programs also help to minimise the risk of husbands resorting to some of the classic, time-worn strategies for avoiding participation in housework. These strategies typically involve either appearing helpless and needing to seek constant information and guidance, going slow or behaving incompetently in the hope of not being asked again, suggesting that it would be good for the children if *they* learned how to do this, or performing the task in such bad grace as to create an emotional black cloud over the domestic scene.

The justification provided by men for the use of such tactics as these is often that 'Women want it both ways', and that men had never originally agreed to the concept of sharing domestic chores. Nevertheless, recognising that the tide is running against them, many men try to appear supportive while still managing to erode the value of their support by their own lack of enthusiasm for it.

It is very difficult to generalise about the way in which Australian men and women are adjusting to the redefinition of gender roles which has been imposed on men by women. Almost every case is unique, and the degrees of adaptation vary enormously from marriage to marriage, from relationship to relationship, and from household to household.

## The Male Backlash: mock sensitivity

Nevertheless, there are some ugly signs of a male backlash emerging. The tensions created by people trying to live together with quite different views of gender roles are often intolerable and demand to be dealt with. It is not surprising that the divorce rate continues to rise, nor that the majority of divorces in Australia are now initiated by women.

Perhaps the male backlash against feminism is one of the signs that the revolution is actually well advanced and that male resistance is simply a rear-guard action. In its most extreme form, the male backlash amounts almost to a form of 'class hatred' in which men feel an underlying sense of resentment and hostility towards women in general (even though, in some cases, they may well have worked out a satisfactory relationship with one particular woman). Men are still capable of becoming suddenly and disproportionately angry in response to what they see as the unreasonable demands being placed upon them by women, and in response to their own feeling of being inhibited in the expression of their true reactions to Women's Lib.

'Class hatred' directed at women appears to be due to

a combination of two factors: on the one hand, men do sometimes feel as if they have been emasculated or, at least, made irrelevant or superfluous by the new-found independence of their female partners; on the other hand, they feel that women have sought new forms of power and independence without fully understanding the responsibilities and consequences that go with it. To such men, the most unattractive version of the New Woman is a woman who strongly attacks any sign of male chauvinism and asserts her own independence, but has no hesitation in reverting to stereotypical feminine behaviour (often characterised as blatant flirtatiousness, tears, or the resort to glamour) in order to achieve what she wants.

As time goes by, most of the men who harbour these dark feelings of resentment manage to keep them hidden and appear to go along with the new order. Occasionally, though, such feelings will break out into explicit conflict, as in the case of a husband who put his wife's university assignments into the rubbish bin instead of posting them, or the men who deliberately withhold their participation in domestic chores even when they recognise their wives' need of it and when they have the time and energy to give it.

The male backlash has been further fuelled by the behaviour of one sub-group of Australian women who have managed to enrage both the male chauvinists and the feminists. These are the fully supported stay-at-home wives of reasonably affluent men, whose children are off their hands during the day, and who have decided to elevate their leisure to the status of work. After a day of tennis, golf, bridge or an extended lunch party, they return to an unkempt house with no particular plans in mind for the evening meal. Then, mouthing the messages of the

Women's Movement, they try to recruit their husbands' support in meal preparation, housework and other domestic and parenting tasks which they know are the focus of working mothers' attention. At first, their husbands are confused: wanting to appear sensitive to the concept of the New Woman and not wanting to be written off as chauvinists, they may be inclined to feel that, like so many other men, they should perhaps be pulling more weight at home. Then it begins to dawn on them that they are being conned; that their non-working wives are cashing in on the propaganda of the Women's Movement without having personally moved an inch in the direction of feminism. Such women actually undermine the legitimate messages of the Women's Movement because, in the process of rejecting the spurious demands to be more helpful at home, their husbands are inevitably retreating from a position of *general* sympathy with feminist thinking and are having their pre-feminist prejudices reinforced.

While there is a great deal of tension within women about their attempts to express a new definition of gender roles, there is a corresponding tension within men: even among those who positively want to respond to the new messages of the Women's Movement, there is often some conflict between the desire to be sensitive and understanding and the desire to avoid being written off as a wimp.

Male sensitivity often turns out to be mock sensitivity. Men are adapting to the redefinition of gender roles by women in many different ways; in some cases, they have simply recognised that creating the *appearance* of sensitivity is a minimum condition for sustaining relationships with women. But confusion abounds: even though many men believe that they must play the sensitivity game in order to maintain sexual relationships, they still wonder whether the very sensitivity which women claim to want may actually turn out to be less attractive than something closer to traditional masculinity and they doubt whether, in the minds of women, New Men have replaced Real Men as the most desirable sexual partners.

For the time being, many Australian men are explicitly encouraging their female partners to 'have it all' while secretly resenting women's expectations that such a strategy could work satisfactorily. Men see women paying a big price (in exhaustion, in guilt, in confused values) for the gains they have supposedly made and, while wishing to appear supportive, men are still trying to decide how much of that price they are prepared to share. Indeed, the OSW report, *Juggling Time*, points out that the level of husbands' participation in housework seems to be largely unaffected by the question of whether or not their wives have paid work outside the home. Some men do a lot of housework; some do very little: those who are most active at home don't necessarily have wives who work outside the home, and those who are least involved in housework are not necessarily married to stay-at-home wives. In other words, men's degree of participation around the home is still generally unrelated to the amount of paid work being done by their wives.

Even the way in which men talk about their reactions to their wives' return to the workforce betrays some of the 'mock sensitivity' which is part of the male backlash of the early 1990s. While often expressing great enthusiasm for the idea of their wives' jobs, the typical male response to the contemporary phenomenon of the working wife is to remark on the fact that 'it's nice to have a more interesting and stimulating partner'. In other words, women's revolutionary leap into the workforce is not being assessed in terms of enrichment which this may provide for the women involved, but as a calculation of the emotional enrichment which men themselves may enjoy as a side effect. Even when men complain about the negative effect on family life of a working mother, this complaint almost always focuses on the difficulties created for *other* members of the family, with little acknowledgement of the great difficulties being faced by working mothers themselves.

If this all sounds like guerilla warfare, then that is probably not far from the truth. Perhaps men and women have always been locked in some kind of power struggle. In order to have their biological, psychological and social needs met, men and women have always had to involve themselves in complex and delicate bargaining; to negotiate workable compromises; to adopt complementary roles. Whatever the historical and cultural antecedents, however, the present situation is fraught with a new dimension of conflict, simply because it is women who are initiating the redefinition of gender roles and men who are adapting. That is a reversal of the traditional Australian cultural roles for men and women, and the resulting hostility—on both sides of the relationship—is aggravated by the fact that women are both messenger and message.

Women's redefinition of gender roles is essentially about power. Women no longer wish to live in a society in which men are seen as manipulating all the most obvious levers of power: the traditional view of women captured in such folklore as 'the hand that rocks the cradle rules the world' is no longer enough. Being 'the power behind the throne' has struck women as being less attractive than having equal access to the power of the throne itself. Rather than being the woman positioned behind 'every succesful man', women see no reason why the limelight should not be equally available to successful persons of either gender.

And so power games continue to be played. Language is one playing field, as men try to come to terms with women's determination to use words like 'chairperson' as a pro-active instrument of the revolution rather than waiting for language to evolve—as it usually does—in response to cultural change. Work is another playing field for gender power games: even after 20 years of revolutionary struggle, women still find themselves confronted at work by men who are looking for evidence of pre-menstrual tension or who believe that, when the chips are down, it is still men who *should* be the breadwinners.

Although paid work outside the home has been the pre-eminent symbol of redefinition of gender roles for Australian women, an emerging second wave of the revolution acknowledges that the most powerful position for women is to be free to choose whether they will try to combine home-and-family responsibilities with paid employment, or not. There is growing acceptance of the idea that those women who choose to stay at home to devote themselves entirely to the care of their families should be as highly valued for that choice as those who have chosen either to pursue a career to the exclusion of family, or to combine family and job. For stay-at-home mothers, this recognition has been a long time coming and, even now, they complain that men have not yet learned to attach appropriate value to the housewife role.

Twenty years on, the self-description 'housewife' still feels, when it is said, as though it implies '*just* a housewife', and the very men who claim to resent the redefinition of gender roles often turn out to be the ones who are most patronising in their attitudes towards full-time mothers.

## THE BATTLE OF THE BEDROOM

Work may be the most potent symbol of women's liberation; domestic duties might be the battlefield on which many power-struggles are fought; but it is in bed where both men and women feel that an underlying sense of conflict between the sexes is most likely to be expressed. It is becoming quite a common theme in men's discussion of the Women's Movement that 'women are getting more out of sex', or that women are becoming more assertive in their sexual encounters with men. Men who had previously thought that perfunctory sex was enough to satisfy their partners are finding that their performance is being explicitly criticised by women who now feel sufficiently liberated to take sexual initiatives and to impose sexual standards on their relationships.

Similarly, men who thought that they could get away with relationships (whether in or out of marriage) which were primarily sexual are now finding that women are demanding more sensitivity and more equality in the *total* relationship, and that sexual activity is now being placed in a broader context.

Now that sexual activity is also being used as a symbol of the redefinition of gender roles, there is predictable uneasiness on both sides. Women who are becoming more assertive often sense that men actually find women more appealing when they appear to be submissive and lacking in power. Some women have even reported that the quality of their sex lives has varied dramatically according to whether they were working or not: 'As soon as I gave up work and came home to be a full-time mother, he was much more interested in me sexually.'

Other women have had the opposite experience, finding

that their husbands had found them more attractive, stimulating and interesting companions as a direct result of their experience of working outside the home.

The uneasiness of men is less complex: it has to do with the simple question of a threat to male dominance in an area where Australian males have traditionally assumed dominance. Some men have turned away from sexual relationships with New Women simply because they find it too threatening to play by the new rules; others have assumed that sexual intercourse was one last bargaining chip in their bid to resist the new feminism, only to be disappointed by the discovery that their wives did not appear to care much, either way; others have quite explicitly retreated from heterosexuality as a defence against women whom they find too assertive and too demanding.

In sex, as in all other areas of life where the redefinition of gender roles has an impact, it all comes down to the men and women concerned being open and explicit about what a redefinition of gender roles actually means and how it is going to be accommodated within their lives. Those couples who talk easily about everything have been best positioned to talk about this most fundamental redefinition. Those who find the intimacy of communication even trickier than the intimacy of sex have been bruised and confused by processes which they have never really analysed and have therefore never really understood.

## TAKING STOCK

If better communication is going to be the key to men and women making a satisfactory adjustment to the emerging redefinition of gender roles in Australia, there is not much evidence that it is yet happening on a large scale. Certainly, women discuss the redefinition of gender roles, animatedly and endlessly, with other like-minded women. Similarly, men are interminably debating the changing role of women with other men. But direct, open, frank and well-intentioned discussion about the subject between men and women still appears to be a relatively rare event.

Insecurity is the enemy of communication. When women are themselves feeling insecure about their own pioneering attempts to redefine their roles, they are less able to communicate calmly and confidently about their goals and their needs. And when men are feeling insecure as a result of not fully comprehending what is going on (and, it must be added, as a direct result of being so relentlessly attacked by women who find male attitudes and behaviour unsatisfactory), they are much less likely to be receptive to open communication.

If no other redefinition had affected Australia's socio-cultural evolution over the past 20 years, the redefinition of gender roles would have been almost enough to account for present levels of anxiety and instability. It's not just that this redefinition permeates so many aspects of Australian life; the destabilising effect of this redefinition is exacerbated because the process of redefinition itself remains so unresolved. Many Australian women are still trying to figure out what they actually mean by 'equality', having decided that androgyny is not the most attractive option. Others are still trying to decide whether paid employment is, in the end, the best symbol of liberation. Working mothers, in particular, are often perplexed to find that their own daughters are determined not to follow in their mother's footsteps, seeing the lot of a working mother as the next best thing to slavery.

Indeed, the pioneering generation of working mothers

are relucantly being forced to the conclusion that they will probably have to wait to see how their grandchildren turn out before they really know whether the revolution has fulfilled its early promise.

Meanwhile, men continue to be uneasy about the implications for their lives of women's redefinition of gender roles. Even the most committed and enthusiastic men find that a great deal of trail-blazing remains to be done before the role of partner to a New Woman is clarified. At a time when simple courtesies may be interpreted as insults, or flirting regarded as evidence of the capacity to rape, men have learned to tread carefully and not to say too much.

To confuse the issue still further, women are beginning to reconsider the idea that feminism and femininity are not necessarily incompatible and they are now wondering whether in the early rush to assert their independence from men, too many women made the mistake of trying to *be* like men. Tailored suits, it turned out, were not necessarily the best way to symbolise independence; nor were hairy armpits. Today, the more radical messages of the pioneers of Women's Lib are being revised in the light of tensions which have resulted from trying to live out the new values.

In amongst all this confusion, the women who seem to have most clarity of understanding about their own roles, and most clarity of purpose, are those who have elected not to have children in favour of pursuing a career (with or without a male partner); those who have elected to devote themselves to their young children, and to postpone re-entry to the workforce; and those who are pregnant, and who are singly-mindedly preoccupied with the prospect of imminent motherhood. Indeed, pregnant women report some relief from the struggle to define their own identity: they welcome the simplistic definition of their

own femininity, and they respond warmly to rather traditional male attitudes towards pregnant women. But, for
many women, the euphoric experience of late pregnancy
soon yields to a return to the conflicts over which role will
be dominant: mother, wife, career woman, person-in-my-
own right, and so on.

What appears to be most significant about this complex
quest for the new female identity is that women find it easier
to define themselves in relation to a job, or in relation to
children, than in relation to a man. Men are the compli-
cating factor which confuses the issue, saps the self-
confidence, and creates the need to explain the inexplicable.

Women who embraced the new feminism of the 1970s
expected that things would turn out better than they have:
in many cases, they have swapped one set of frustrations
for another. At the same time, hardly any of the pioneering
generation of Women's Libbers would wish to give up any
of the gains they have won in terms of their personal sense
of independence and integrity, their gradual impact on
men's attitudes towards parenting and domestic management, or their successful invasion of the workplace. But
much of their satisfaction appears grim: there is a widespread sense that the tastiest fruits of the revolution are
yet to be savoured.

So the battle is far from over. Relationships between
the sexes are more demanding and more unstable than
they were a generation ago, and those demands create
new tensions, new conflicts, and new definitions of what
it means to be a man and what it means to be a woman.
The revolution began in the *minds* of women, but it is
in their *relationships* that the redefinition is still being
worked out.

## THE STORY OF CAROL

☐ I was 35 when I decided to go back to work. I had been
a physiotherapist but I gave up work when my first baby
was due. Three years later I had my second child and,
with two young children to care for, I often felt as if I
was actually going mad. I missed work and I lost touch
with a lot of my women friends. I often felt as if I didn't
have much in common with the other mothers I met at
the pre-school or at playgroup, and although I was trying
to model myself on my own mother, I felt that our lives
had actually been very different. My husband was very
committed to the idea that I would give up work
permanently when we had a family, and he was very
opposed to my suggestion that I might return to work
on a part-time basis. But I insisted, and so I got myself
on to the classic treadmill of the working mother. I often
felt guilty about having to farm the kids out, although
it was better when they finally were both at school. But
I was strongly supported by the women I met when I
went back to work. Many of them were in the same sort
of situation, and we all felt that we were too well educated
and too intelligent just to sink into domesticity.

I was earning good money and I was enoying myself,
and I thought my husband would change his mind about
the idea of me working. He went along with it, but I
could see that he was not really convinced. He never
really tried to pull his weight at home, because he
reckoned that the whole thing was my idea and that it
was up to me to manage it. I could hardly believe his
attitude.

Gradually, I persuaded him that he ought to be a bit
more active as a father, and he did start to find that he

was enjoying being more involved with the children. It gave me a bit of a break, and I thought it was better for them as well to see more of their father.

But getting him involved in domestic chores has been very difficult. A few weeks ago, I thought I had had a real breakthrough. We were expecting some guests for dinner, and my husband could see that I was flat out getting the children organised and the dinner prepared before our guests arrived. To my amazement, he went and got the vacuum cleaner and ran over the carpet in the hall and loungeroom. Usually, he makes a fuss about this kind of thing, but he didn't say a word. I was really proud of myself for having finally trained him to do something that he could see needed doing, without me having to point it out to him or pat him on the head and tell him he was a good boy. Then, when the guests arrived, he drew their attention to the clean state of the carpet and skited to the other husband about how he had done the vacuuming!

It's the same with cooking. I've finally got him to the stage where he will sometimes prepare a meal for the family, but it is always such a big deal. He won't do it my way; he has to do it his way. He can't just prepare a routine meal; it always has to be a major production, and we all have to compliment him on the result. And then he refuses to clean up afterwards. He's invented a new rule: 'The person who cooks the meal doesn't have to clean up.' But when I cook the meal, the rule seems to apply to the kids, not him . . . which means that I have to supervise.

In some ways, holidays are the worst. We rent a little cottage when we go away, and, for me, it is just like being at home. He goes off fishing and has a wonderful time, then he comes home and asks me what's for dinner. I've been with the kids all day and cleaning up the house and getting the lunch . . . the same old thing. By the time he gets back, I feel like hanging myself from a tree. Even if I go fishing with him, he still wants to know what's for dinner as soon as we get back. I say to him, 'How do I know what's for dinner? I've been out with you fishing all day.'

But we keep going back to the same place . . . he loves it, and so do the kids, and I guess I put up with it.

When I first went back to work, our sex life was terrible. I was tired all the time, and he was really sulky. When I finally got things better organised, he seemed to have lost interest. I used to hear him making jokes to his friends about the fact that he had this dynamic wife who rushed around all day and was always too tired at night . . . things are gradually getting better, but I can see that he feels a bit threatened by the fact that I am more confident that I used to be, and I am more independent.

My own mother is not at all happy with the way my life is turning out. She thinks that I should have been a more traditional mother, and you can tell she loves having the kids stay with her because she thinks that she is treating them properly. I once reminded her that she was the one who was so keen on my getting qualified and having a career, but she doesn't want to discuss it.

I often wonder whether I am handling things as well as I should. I look at some of my friends who have time to play tennis and are always home when their children get home from school, and I envy them. But then I feel a bit disloyal to the whole business of Women's Lib.

When the children were younger, I sometimes used to

almost pretend that I didn't have them. Sometimes at work I would almost forget that I was a mother, and then I would feel dreadfully guilty. If people asked me what I did I always said I was a physiotherapist . . . especially if men asked me. I always felt reluctant, somehow, to say that I was a mother as well.

But as the kids have got older, I am really quite proud of being a mother. I know some of my friends really regret the fact that they never had children of their own, and the old biological clock is ticking away for them. I regret that I haven't had more time with my own children, and I am hoping that it will be a while yet before they decide to leave home.

I have really tried to bring them up to understand the idea of equality between the sexes, but of course my son is not nearly as keen on the idea as my daughter. He still has the example of his father to follow and that is often completely different from what I say should happen. I keep meaning to teach my son to iron his own shirts, but there are times when I am quite pleased that I am still doing it for him . . . at least I feel like a real mother!

My daughter reckons that she is going to give up work when she has children, and stay at home until they have left school. We'll see! In any case, I won't be available to look after her children as my mother was to look after mine, because I am going to be a working grandmother. I was determined not to be a slave to my own kids, and so I am certainly not going to be a slave to my grandchildren.

If I could wave a magic wand, the main thing I would change would be my husband's attitude. I wish that he had been more supportive from the beginning, so that we wouldn't have had all this conflict, and I wouldn't have felt so worn out. He reckons that I still don't know what I really want, and sometimes I think he is right. But you can't turn the clock back, and I don't think women would want to go back to being as subservient as my mother was to my father.

On the other hand, I wonder why Germaine Greer never had any children . . . □

## 2.2

# In-laws & Out-laws

It's not possible for a society (or even half a society) to redefine its gender roles without having a big impact on the institutions and conventions which have traditionally either shaped gender roles or been shaped by them. If it is true that, while the process of redefining gender roles works itself out, women are finding it easier to define their identities in relation to work or children than in relation to men, this is obviously going to have some implications for the institutions of marriage and the family. But the ripple effect will not stop there. By redefining gender roles, we not only start to redefine marriage, the family and the household, but we also begin to redefine our attitudes towards politics, the place of work in our lives, our patterns of eating, shopping, mass media consumption, and, ultimately, our demand for domestic housing. Even the long-standing Australian tradition of home ownership is bound to be affected by such volcanic instability in the view of marriage and the family which emerges as a direct consequence of our struggle to come to terms with new definitions of gender roles.

The traditional family unit, on which many of our most cherished notions about the Australian way of life depend, is in disarray. A family consisting of a breadwinning father, a stay-at-home mother and a couple of dependent children is now a small minority, accounting for less than one quarter of all families. This is partly because 60 per cent of all mothers of dependent children now have paid employment outside the home, but it is also because the cosy image of stable family life in Australia has been shattered by the image of our new patterns of marriage and divorce.

We are rapidly becoming both the most divorced *and* the most married generation in Australian history because of our growing acceptance of serial monogamy. In the early 1970s, almost 90 per cent of Australian marriages were first marriages. By the early 1990s, that figure was drifting down towards 60 per cent. It is now confidently predicted by most analysts of marriage statistics that roughly one-third of contemporary Australian marriages will end in divorce, and—also for the first time in our history—the majority of divorces are now initiated by women.

At the same time, the Australian Institute of Family Studies predicts that, by the end of the Nineties, 22 per cent of Australian women will not have married by the age of 35—a level higher than at any other time in Australian history. Gordon Carmichael of the Austalian National University (*With This Ring*, AIFS, 1988) estimates that up to 25 per cent of Australians born in the 1960s will never marry. Of course, many of the rising generation of Australians will become involved in long-term *de facto* marriage relationships—the AIFS estimates that almost 50 per cent of Australians now cohabit before marriage—but higher proportions than ever before will choose to avoid the legal institution of marriage altogether.

In the December 1991 issue of *Family Matters*, AIFS Deputy Director, Peter McDonald, points out that 'in 1972, at the peak of the era of early marriages, 33 per cent of Australian women had married before their 20th birthday and 83 per cent by their 25th birthday. By the beginning of 1991, only five per cent had married as teenagers and 47 per cent before reaching 25.'

Nineteen seventy-four was a crucial year in the development of this new trend. That was not only the time when the Women's Liberation movement was gathering momentum in Australia, but it was also the year in which the Family Law Act was passed, redefining the grounds for the dissolution of marriage. The massive increase in our divorce rate in the ensuing 20 years is undoubtedly the result of the confluence of those two factors: new divorce laws *and* a radical redefinition of gender roles.

If present trends in marriage and divorce were to continue, we would ultimately find that Australians who marry once and stay married would be in the minority: they would be outnumbered by those who never marry or who marry two or more times. Of course, present trends may *not* continue and, in any case, we will gradually come to accept—as the legal system has already accepted—that *de facto* marriage is equivalent in many respects to legal marriage. Nevertheless, the institution of marriage has been irrevocably changed by the redefinitions which engulfed it in the Seventies and Eighties.

In *With This Ring*, Carmichael puts the current revolution in an interesting historical perspective:

> There seems no basis for anticipating another marriage boom. Economic conditions might improve, but the ideological trends of the 1970s were so profound that the most plausible scenario is that considerably later marriage and a much higher level of permanent failure to marry will prevail for the foreseeable future. In many respects Australia appears to be witnessing a return to marriage patterns of earlier this century, although the forces responsible for those patterns are quite different

now from what they were then. To future demographic historians even more than to those of the present day it is the very early, almost universal marriage to which the marriage boom gave rise in the 1950s, 60s and early 70s that is likely to seem atypical. At present the recency of this pattern gives it an aura of historical normality, but ultimately it probably will be seen as a phase which marked the demise of one ideology concerning marriage preparatory to its replacement by a new one.

In other words, we are recovering from the 'marriage madness' of the Fifties and Sixties and reverting to a marriage pattern more typical of the twentieth century. But the return to an earlier marriage pattern itself masks profound changes in attitudes towards marriage and towards family formation.

Australians may still think of marriage in the same way as they did 20 years ago, and they may approach a wedding with roughly the same sense of commitment and roughly the same romantic ideal in mind as they did 20 years ago. Indeed the vast majority of young Australians—whether cohabiting or otherwise—still confidently predict that they will get married at some time, but a cultural change is underway which will dent that confidence.

To put it bluntly, the way we think and talk about weddings is quite different from the way in which we now treat the institution of marriage. We still talk as if it is normal to get married and normal to stay married, but our definition of 'normal' is slow to catch up with the demographic reality. It is true, of course, that most contemporary marriages *won't* end in divorce, but so many Australian families are now being affected directly or indirectly by divorce and by the redefinition of marriage, that we will eventually have to find new ways of adapting to the increasing diversity of family styles and structures.

None of this is very surprising: the redefinition of gender roles, marriage and the family are all inextricably linked to each other. But it does mean that the emotional resources of contemporary Australians are being further drained by the effort involved not only in pioneering the redefinition of gender roles, but also in pioneering strategies for managing the increasingly widespread phenomena of broken families, blended families, single-parent families and step-families.

## APPROVAL OF EASIER DIVORCE

Considering the pace of the change, Australian society has already become remarkably tolerant of its new patterns of marriage and divorce. Part of the reason for this is the widespread belief that easier divorce has reduced the level of unhappiness associated with unsatisfactory marriages. Adults who recall tensions in their own childhood associated with the unhappy marriage of their parents readily admit that they would have preferred to have seen their parents divorce rather than have to put up with such sustained tension and hostility within the home.

Similarly, those families who had to live with the 'secret' of an unhappy marriage, or with the 'disgrace' of a divorce in the family, report that more liberal attitudes towards divorce have had a liberating effect on family life.

Certainly, it is a widely-held belief in the Australian community that easier divorce has produced a more realistic approach to marriage which may be less romantic but which might, in the end, ensure that when young people do decide to enter formally into the institution of marriage, they may be rather more serious about it. Conversely, there is some fear that easier divorce might actually reduce the sense of seriousness about marriage, and The Mackay Report on *The Family '90s Style* (1991) quoted a number of cases where young people had quite explicitly claimed that, on the threshold of marriage, they were prepared to concede that divorce was a real possibility, or that 'we are not going to knock ourselves out trying to make it work if it doesn't feel good.'

Whilst it is generally accepted that the new divorce laws are a step in the right direction, Australians are conscious of the high emotional price which families—especially children—have to pay for the relative instability of marriage in the 1990s. Instability of marriage means, of course, the instability of the family: even those people who are most approving of easier divorce find it hard to bring themselves to the point of approving of the instability of family life, and there is widespread concern in the community about the long-term effect on the children of this most-divorced generation in Australian history. The assumed effects on children of unstable family life range from a sense of confused values to the problem of divided loyalties.

It is not only the emotional consequences of divorce which are regarded as so potentially damaging to children: the financial consequences are also thought to disadvantage those children of a divorce who find themselves living in a household which is making do with half the resources available to the pre-divorce family.

## THE IDEAL OF 'FAMILY LIFE' PERSISTS

Did we know that when, by the passage of the Family Law Act, we redefined divorce, we would also be redefining marriage, and reinventing the family? Probably not, but that is certainly what has happened. And yet, while acknowledging that it is much harder to define what a family actually is than it used to be, Australians seem just as keen on the *idea* of the family as ever. As the reality of family life becomes less stable, the ideal seems to become even more attractive. This is not to suggest that Australians believe that family life is necessarily wonderful or that life outside the structure of a conventional family may not be at least as fulfilling for some individuals as life within a family is for others. It is closer to the truth to suggest that Australians simply accept the centrality of the family to their whole notion of human life and society, even though they acknowledge that they will have to re-think what 'the family' actually means.

Whatever social and emotional benefits family life may be thought to bestow on those who participate in it, the most fundamental point which Australians consistently make when they talk about the family is that it is the natural outcome of the human reproductive urge. Families are seen as being a symptom of 'the biological imperative', and Australians can't easily separate the idea of reproduction from the idea of a family structure whose purpose is to protect and nurture children—regardless of whether a marriage is involved or not.

Even while conceding that many families are desperately unhappy, and even while reflecting wistfully on some of the emotional ravages of their own childhoods, Australians continue to be generally convinced that family life offers opportunities for emotional security and fulfilment which do not otherwise occur easily in our society.

Families are still seen as having the potential to provide the emotional security of permanent relationships, as well as a strong sense of identity arising from those relationships. Even when we are not sure about aspects of gender roles, traditional labels like 'mother', 'brother', 'daughter' (and especially 'grandma' and 'grandpa') are very reassuring and comforting. Family life is thought to teach us important lessons about loyalty, responsibility and compromise, and many Australians believe that the quality of family life is an important index of the quality of life in the wider society. It is often taken for granted that a 'good' family life will produce 'good' citizens and that this pattern will repeat itself from one generation to the next. Even those who do not aspire to be part of a family themselves are still inclined to admire those who can make family life work, and may envy the benefits which so obviously derive from having the security of a stable family. Families are not necessarily expected to be happy, but they are still seen as one of society's most precious resources.

Given this exalted view of family life in the Australian community, it is hardly surprising that one of the most significant sources of anxiety for contemporary Australians concerns the widespread breakdown of family life. If families are seen as providing an ultimate source of emotional security and personal identity, then it is not hard to imagine what Australians fear: they fear that massive dislocation of families will involve equivalent erosion of the sense of security and identity which families are expected to provide.

The growing problem of street kids in our major cities is widely regarded as being attributable to the increasing breakdown of family life under the direct influence of a redefinition of marriage and an exploding divorce rate. Australians are beginning to realise what it means to say that the rising generation are the offspring of the most divorced generation in our history, and we are gradually recognising that this generation will have to rise to challenges which their parents did not have to face on a large scale: the challenge of working out an identity in the context of a fractured family, and the challenge of replacing emotional resources depleted by the loss of a secure and stable family structure.

For kids caught in the crossfire of a divorce specifically precipitated by gender role conflict, the going has been particularly tough. Such kids are not only trying to piece together the sense of an identity which, for previous generations, could have been constructed from a stable and easily-observed set of values within the family, but they are simultaneously trying to work out gender roles from the confused and often contradictory set of verbal messages and behavioural examples offered by their parents. No wonder such kids are more likely than ever to seek the emotional comfort, security and identity which the peer group offers; no wonder such kids may either rush headlong into early marriage in the hope of creating a new stable family structure for themselves or, alternatively, avoid the institution of marriage entirely; no wonder such kids will often pay more attention to the values and example of their grandparents than of their parents (and, in the process, take refuge in gender role definitions which pre-dated their parents' experimentation with new roles).

But even people who are living in reasonably stable family settings report that the family is being redefined. A recurring theme in Australians' discussion of family life is that, at a time when society itself seems to be undergoing so much radical change, it is harder to hold the family together, and harder to maintain a stable set of family values.

When Australians begin talking about some of the most

significant changes in the nature of family life, a number of themes emerge:

The working mother is often described as the villain of the piece (even by working mothers themselves), because her absence from the home and her unwilling-ness and inability to devote herself exclusively to mothering are thought to have radically changed the dynamics of the family;

Marital tension arising from the painful process of redefining gender roles often leads to a chilly atmos-phere, and to a tendency to seek more stimulation and gratification outside the family than in it;

Today's children are thought to be under more pressure at school, more pressure at play and more pressure from a media, marketing and social environ-ment more stimulating and seductive than the environment in which their parents grew up;

Parents are becoming more conscious of the responsi-bilities and skills involved in being a parent, and there is a growing sense that parenting is a more public occupation than it used to be, subject to more scrutiny and harsher judgments than was the case in previous generations;

The increasing complexity of family structures is making it more difficult to keep members of the extended family in touch with each other;

The suburban neighbourhood is no longer regarded

as a safe haven for the development of family life.

The underlying attitude seems to be that the ideal of family life is harder to achieve in the 1990s because there are so many things competing for the attention of family members. Whereas the traditional focus of family life was inside the home, the increasing complexity of roles and relationships in contemporary society has blurred this focus: home often feels like a place to which people retreat for rest and recreation rather than a place which symbolises the bosom of the family.

Men find it very easy to identify 'Women's Lib' as a major factor in destabilising the nature of the family: even among husbands who are quite supportive of their wives' activities outside the home, there tends to be a sneaking suspicion that life would be easier, happier and perhaps more satisfying for all concerned (but especially for men themselves) if more mothers stayed at home to manage the household and nurture the children. Even among working mothers, there lurks a suspicion that family life has been irrevocably changed—mainly for the worse—by their decision to take a job outside the home.

## THE IMPACT OF WOMEN'S MULTIPLE ROLES

It is probably true that much of the present instability in Australian family life springs from changes in the role and status of women, but not in the simplistic way often assumed by those who try to forge a direct causal link between the working mother and the unstable family. The real connection is far more subtle than that: it has to do with the fact that women's roles have become much less easy to define and, as a result, the transition from being

a girl to becoming a mother appears to be a more
demanding, more confusing, more complex and more
painful transition than it was for previous generations of
women.

Older women describe how they left school at 14 or 15
years of age (since it was assumed that there was no
particular need for their further education) and were then
expected to go to work for the years before their marriage.
When they married, this was the fulfilment of a single-
minded ambition which coincided precisely with the
demands and expectations of the culture. Such women felt
that, with marriage as a central goal, they grew up very
quickly during adolescence and when, in time, they did
marry, this sealed their future. They knew that they were
married for keeps. They knew that, even if the marriage
turned out to be unsatisfactory, they would be expected
to stick to it: a return to the parental home would have
been unthinkable and somewhat disgraceful.

When older Australians describe that approach to
marriage, they quickly add that they did not expect life
to be easy; they expected to have to compromise with
their husbands; they accepted that marriage would be a
mixture of good and bad. Above all, they intended to have
children early in marriage, and they were ready to accept
absolute responsibility for those children. They expected
to raise children who 'knew right from wrong', and they
anticipated the sense of contentment which would arise
from knowing that the child-rearing and housekeeping roles
had been satisfactorily performed. When the turbulent
years of raising a family had passed, those women expected
to settle into a contented retirement with a reliable
companion.

Of course, that is a somewhat idealised, middle-class

picture: the pattern was not so tranquil for many women, but the expectation of leading a life according to that kind of pattern was so strongly created among today's grand-mothers when they were young that most of them conformed to the pattern without giving the alternatives much thought.

When the daughters and grand-daughters of those women reflect on that kind of adulthood, they express respect and admiration for the toughness and perseverance of the older generation, but they report no desire to return to what seems to them to be a uni-dimensional approach to being a woman. At the same time, younger women acknowledge that, for previous generations, marriage was a particularly abrupt rite of passage which probably made the transition from child to parent easier: it was a matter of 'sink or swim'.

Today, the story is very different. Marriage no longer appears as a crucial rite of passage: as the statistics so graphically reveal, marriage is increasingly being regarded as an option rather than an expectation. But today's situation is confused still further by the fact that, particularly for women, *multiple roles* tend to diminish the relative significance of each one of those roles: a working mother, for example, cannot have the same sense of exclusive commitment to the mother role as a non-working mother might have. Similarly, better-educated women assert the need to keep parenthood in perspective as they pursue the careers which have flowed directly from levels of education much higher than those of their mothers or grandmothers.

One of the outcomes of this increased complexity of goals and roles is that young mothers may find some difficulty in coming to terms with the reality of motherhood. They are so used to making choices—and to the idea of staying flexible—that the inflexible and irrevocable reality of parenthood comes as something of a shock.

After all, the present generation of mothers have made a long series of decisions which their own mothers and grandmothers did not have to make: decisions about the level of education to pursue; about when to take a job and what kind of job to take; about whether or not and when to leave home; about whether or not to live with a boyfriend before marriage; about whether or not to marry at all; about whether or not to have children at all (and, if so, when); about whether or not to stop work in favour of having children and then, after the birth of children, whether or not to return to work.

Against the background of such complexity and flexibility, it is hardly surprising that today's mothers are much more ambivalent about mothering and flexible about the nature of family life than their own mothers were. The single-mindedness traditionally associated with being 'a good mother' comes more slowly and painfully—if it comes at all—than it used to.

The concept of independence is central to this process of redefining parenting and family life. Whereas older Austalians recall that, for them, marriage itself was the symbol of an independence which implied the acceptance of responsibility, younger Australians appear to have quite a different view: for them, independence is more likely to imply 'doing your own thing' or 'hanging loose' than accepting a new set of irrevocable responsibilities.

The redefinition of families, therefore, is inseparably tied not only to the process of redefining gender roles, but also to the process of sorting out a new set of values in response to new social and cultural realities. (See Chapter 4.2, 'Finding Our Bearings'.)

## NEW RULES, NEW MANNERS

Since family structures are changing so rapidly and the acceptance of *de facto* marriages, blended families, step-families and single-parent families is now so widespread, Australians are inevitably experiencing some uncertainty about what constitutes a family and about how to behave within some of the new family structures.

Although the ideal of a family continues to be the nuclear family, new demographic realities have forced people to accept that more or less any social context created for the nurturing of children within a reasonably small household structure would qualify for description as a 'family'.

Most Australians are still a long way from approving of some of the looser or more unconventional family group-ings—such as homosexual couples adopting children—but there is growing acceptance of the idea that almost any groupings which involve children have to be accepted as a family (even if not an ideal one).

The theoretical acceptance of a wide range of different family structures is one thing; actually absorbing them into the values and etiquette of existing family contexts is another. As more and more Australians are caught up in the backwash from divorce, and cohabitation becomes accepted as a prelude or an alternative to marriage, some very specific questions arise in their minds about appropriate forms of behaviour:

What should children call their step-parents (and is it acceptable to call two people 'Dad'?)

Where do you go for Christmas to minimise the tensions created by divorce and re-marriage, and how do you balance the children's wishes against the wishes of the divorced parents?

What do you do with the 'leftover' parent (such as the ex-husband of a re-married woman) at family events such as weddings and other celebrations?

How do you maintain contact between grandchildren and their grandparents when there is bitterness between divorced parents and, quite possibly, a desire to minimise relationships with the family of an ex-spouse?

How do you cope with the adjustment from being the mother-in-law of one husband to being the mother-in-law of the next . . . and what should be your attitude to the ex-spouse of your son or daughter?

How do you introduce your *de facto* spouse? Friend? Companion? Lover? Significant Other? (Or even 'de facto'?)

Such questions are never trivial because they symbolise the painful process of redefining the nature of the family, and they remind us that we are having to adapt to significant cultural change in our society.

Manners, after all, express and symbolise our cultural heritage: when we sense that established etiquette feels wrong, we are acknowledging that a cultural shift is occurring.

The adjustments involved in new relationships—

especially those which follow divorce or which contravene long-term conventions within a family—are always difficult for those directly involved in them, but they also produce unintended impacts on established family structures which can provoke, in turn, a great deal of social awkwardness. All of the adjustments to family relationships which typically have to be made following any marriage are compounded when a re-marriage is involved or when a new *de facto* relationship becomes known to a family.

For the married parents of daughters or sons who are entering into *de facto* marriage relationships, a good deal of anguish is often experienced. As people realise that easier divorce and more transient and flexible family relationships are becoming the norm, they try hard to appear 'modern' to their children: they want to show signs of acceptance, but they often find the process of adapting to such arrangements emotionally stressful—and sometimes disappointing, as well. It is still hard to find parents whose offspring are living in *de facto* marriage relationships who would not secretly wish that their children would get legally married, or who would not describe some feelings of relief when a marriage finally occurs.

In some families, a light-hearted approach is the best way of coping with the redefinition of family structures, roles and values: some families have now adopted the term 'out-law' to cater for relationships which involve *de facto* in-laws. Other families have decided that the complexity of titles like 'uncle' or 'aunt' (to say nothing of 'mother' and 'father') can best be dealt with by dispensing with such titles altogether. In many families, the decision has been made that children should call all related or quasi-related adults by their first names . . . often with rather grudging support from grandparents who may never quite adjust to the idea of being called by their first names by children who are not even their own grandchildren, but happen to have been drawn into the extended family circle through some step-relationship or *de facto* marriage relationship to which one partner has brought the children of a previous relationship.

## THE JOYS OF FATHERHOOD

Although most of the discussion about the redefinition of families tends to focus on the changing role of women, one of the most significant outcomes of the redefined family is that today's fathers report that they are becoming much more involved in family life. When today's generation of fathers compare their role in the family with the role played by their own fathers, they are amazed at the difference: they typically report that their own fathers were an absolutely reliable and steady presence in the family, but that they played a very small role in parenting; that they had very little contact with their children's education; that they tended to remain aloof from the routines of domesticity. By contrast, today's fathers, while stopping short of full-scale participation in housekeeping, frequently report that they are much more actively involved in the lives of their children than their fathers had been. Sometimes this involves little more than endless chauffeuring to children's activities after school and on weekends; sometimes it involves the reading of bedtime stories or the supervision of homework; but sometimes it also involves more direct caring and nurturing behaviour (including feeding, bathing, dressing, putting to bed) as well as participation in hobbies and recreation, and shared TV viewing.

For some fathers, there is still an underlying sense of resentment, because they believe that they have been forced into this more active paternal role by the prolonged absence of their wives from home. But even where some resentment might be present, fathers who become more active parents generally seem to enjoy it and to appreciate the closer contact which they have with their children: involuntary fathering tends to become voluntary after a while.

Yet those fathers who are becoming more involved in the life of the family note a curious paradox: at the very time when their focus is shifting more inside the family (particularly when compared with the more external focus of their own fathers), the other members of the family seem to be becoming correspondingly more involved outside the home. Some men become rather wistful in giving their account of this phenomenon. They enjoy their own sense of being more deeply involved at home (and being, in general, more 'sensitive') but they regret that their working wives are often too busy to join them in parenting activities. Their children, also, seem to be so pre-occupied with activities outside the home that the father's more active role sometimes seems to be simply taken for granted (a feeling already very familiar to many mothers).

Of course, there are still plenty of 'traditional' fathers about (who would not dream of changing a nappy or reading a story), but a significant change is certainly taking place. In the same way as today's mothers are tending not to follow the role models of their own mothers, so today's fathers are departing in significant ways from the role models supplied to them. The change for fathers may be more gradual and less dramatic than the change for mothers, but it is a significant change nonetheless.

Easier divorce and the rising incidence of step-relationships has played a part here, as well. When a man re-marries and faces the undoubtedly daunting challenge of forging new relationships with step-children, he may well feel that an extra effort is involved in trying to make a newly-blended family function in as normal a way as possible. Many step-fathers report that, as part of the process of trying to avoid the failures of their first marriages, they are committed to becoming more heavily involved in the raising of children.

The increasing involvement of fathers in family life—whether in conventional or unconventional settings—can probably best be understood as a *response* to the changing role of women, to the phenomenon of the working mother, and to the rising divorce rate. Whatever the reason, though, many fathers are discovering the emotional gratification which can be obtained from closer contact with their own children. (In some cases, of course, relationships with children provide a much-needed sense of stability and security which is missing from relationships between spouses.)

## REINVENTING CHILDHOOD

The idea of childhood as a free, innocent and self-contained stage of life is pretty much a twentieth-century invention. Before then, children tended to be regarded as junior adults who were waiting in the wings to assume the mantle of adulthood. Certainly, the idea that 'teenagers' might still be indulged like children is a very modern concept.

In the 1990s, we seem to be moving towards yet another redefinition of childhood, under the direct influence of the redefinition of gender roles, marriage and the family. In family structures which are more transient than ever before and which are, increasingly, able to rely on only one parent as a stable reference point for children, the nature of childhood itself is bound to be affected.

In some families, children are now more indulged, cosseted and protected because of the insecurity in the breast of a divorced parent. In other families, children are left much more to their own devices because of the pre-occupation of parents with activities outside the home and because of the increasing complexity of the logistics of contemporary urban life.

The increased incidence of working mothers has meant that greater emphasis must be placed on finding activities for children which involve built-in supervision: playtime is often replaced by more formal, organised activities. Even the concept of play itself is challenged: when time which would previously have been spent in the freedom of play has to be spent in a more supervised activity, 'play' becomes 'skills development', and a certain innocence is lost.

Australian parents typically regard their own childhood as having been marked by a freedom and innocence which is not present to the same extent in the childhood of their children. For a start, the *significance* of children in the family appears to have increased. When both men and women are experiencing so much uncertainty about their emerging roles, there is some comfort to be drawn from the fact that the role of 'parent' is unequivocally defined. This is potentially hazardous: it sometimes means that children are being used by one or both parents as a kind of emotional crutch to compensate for the breakdown of intimacy between spouses. But even where parents are not specifically using their children in this way, there is a growing sense that children are becoming much more assertive and much more anxious to define their own roles—and their own rights—within the family.

This is partly a reaction by children to the lack of

definition which they observe in roles which are still being worked out between their parents; it is partly a reaction to the reality or threat of family breakdown, as children struggle to ensure their own position within the family; it is partly due to children's exposure to adult mass media and to a classroom environment in which independence of thought and assertive behaviour is increasingly encouraged. But it is also partly due to the amount of time and energy which has to be devoted to the organisation of child care, management and supervision—especially in single-parent households, in families where both parents work and in families where visits from or to children from a previous relationship have to be scheduled and organised.

Parents frequently remark that the level of vigorous debate within their families about children's rights takes them by surprise and causes them to question whether life wasn't simpler when children had more acquiescent attitudes towards their parents. And yet, the present rise of children's levels of assertiveness is both predictable and understandable: children are much less likely to accept the word of parents who are in disagreement with each other about everything from gender roles to personal values, and they are much less likely to follow meekly the example of a parent who is having difficulties defining his or her own identity—in or out of marriage.

Perhaps every generation has complained about the lack of discipline and respect shown towards it by the following generation but, today, that situation does seem to be exaggerated by the sense that, as the family itself is being redefined, patterns of childhood behaviour are changing. Particularly under the influence of widespread family breakdown, many children are simply being forced to become more assertive at an earlier age. Parents may express a certain nostalgia about their own childhood; they may hanker after what they now see as the simple pleasures of an earlier age; they may fleetingly wish that their children could enjoy the same freedoms and the same innocence as they did. But present realities seem harsh: parents cannot easily see a way back to such a simple concept of childhood. The other redefinitions in their lives have been so significant—and so permanent—that they have left a redefinition of childhood in their wake.

## SHRINKING HOUSEHOLDS

As families fracture and re-group, it is inevitable that household structures will also be redefined. Almost 50 per cent of Australian households now contain only one or two people. In our two major cities, roughly one household in three contains just one adult—either a person living alone or a single parent—with no other adult to talk to at home. Many of these single-adult households are the result of temporary arrangements, but the fact that so many Australians are now living apart from other adults is bound to have a significant effect on levels of loneliness in our community and, in turn, on the stress levels associated with living alone. If those people feel a bit isolated, a bit 'cut off' or even a bit alienated, who can blame them?

Many of them have chosen to be alone and enjoy being alone. Others, though, feel quite anxious about their aloneness: even the most committed singles sometimes complain about 'that awful moment when you come home to an empty house', and reflect wistfully on the advantages of built-in companionship which family life offers.

Some of them are playing a waiting game: they are ex-spouses left over from a divorce, looking in from the outside on the remnants of their former home. Generally, such people fully intend to rejoin a household group as soon as they can find a suitable new partner.

Among the elderly (particularly women), many singles are not only unhappy about their solitary state but are still grieving over the loss of a life-long companion. There's nothing new about that segment of the population, but their ranks have been swelled by those who are grieving over the loss of a marriage partner through divorce, a suddenly distant relationship with their own children, or the fracturing of a sexual relationship which they had expected to be permanent. The redefinition of the household has been the result of fragmentation of what we had come to regard as our natural 'herd' groupings, and we seem to be paying a high emotional price for this restructuring. One of the inevitable social trends of the Nineties and into the 21st century will be our attempts to regroup.

Our growing problem of social isolation is due not only to changes in our household composition; it is also due to the difficulty (particularly in our largest cities) which extended family members have in keeping in touch with each other. Increasing mobility of the population and the tricky logistics of urban travel have led many family members to lose touch with each other or to rely more on the telephone than on personal contact. The Mackay Report on *Australians at Home* (1986) found that suburban Australians believe they are visiting each other less often than they used to, and that the key factor in this perceived decline is their failure to maintain contact with the extended family. Quite apart from the difficulties experienced as a result of the breakdown of the nuclear family, the loss of cohesion within the extended family fuels the sense of loneliness and, in turn, heightens our anxiety.

We are, after all, herd animals, and when the herd instinct is thwarted, emotional difficulties often result. Even among people who actively wish to live alone, the herd instinct remains strong and tends to be satisfied in other, non-familial contexts. For people who live alone, the workplace may take on a new significance as a social environment; educational, social and recreational groups of all kinds may become attractive as a compensation for the problems of loneliness; medium-density housing begins to have in-creased psychological appeal as a means of providing the comfort which flows from feeling as if we are part of a human community. (See Chapter 4.3, 'Back to the Tribe'.)

Fractured families and shrinking households have affected the way we consume the mass media. Radio has re-emerged as the most popular medium among Australian adults, and this trend coincides with the rising divorce rate and the increase in the number of people living outside the intimacy of traditional family groupings. Committed radio listeners talk about the role of that medium as a surrogate com-panion, creating the illusion of intimacy for people who lack sufficient intimacy in their own personal lives. A radio is 'a voice around the house'; a radio is a companion in an otherwise empty car; a radio personality is a familiar and reliable voice for people who suffer from the lack of familiar and reliable voices within their own living spaces.

The redefinition of the family and the household also affects the way we shop and the way we eat: traditional family mealtimes and traditional weekly shopping trips are declining along with traditional families. We are moving towards 'grazing' and snacking as informal substitutes for the formal meal. We have been attracted to take-away food, part-prepared food, frozen food or home-delivered food partly because it scarcely seems worthwhile to bother to cook a complete meal for just one or two people.

Even within relatively conventional family groupings, formal mealtimes are threatened by the increasing number of activities which compete for the attention of family members. It is now quite common for mothers to aim to have the family sitting down together for a meal at least once a week (having long since abandoned the goal of achieving this once a day). For some working mothers, the desire to maintain *some* pattern of formal mealtimes is often linked to the desire to prove that the family is not suffering from having a working mother: an occasional traditional (or, at least, traditional-looking) meal is a symbol of her continued care.

As usual, technology has played its part in facilitating and even accelerating the processes of social change: the three most popular new domestic appliances of the Eighties (the VCR, the microwave oven, the dishwasher) have all facilitated the breaking down of family activities; they have all made it easier for individuals to act individually. The VCR reduces the need for the household to co-ordinate its viewing of particular TV programs; the microwave oven accelerates the erosion of the formal family mealtime by encouraging 'relays' of diners to use the freezer/microwave combination to prepare meals when they want them, rather than when the meals are ready. The dishwasher removes one potentially valuable episode of family communi-cation—the sharing of the washing-up. Similarly, the rise in two- and three-car households and the exploding popu-larity of personal, portable audio-tape and CD players (with headphones), home computers and video games have encouraged us to act alone. As the household has frag-mented, we have been increasingly attracted to private and individual technology; the technology, in turn, encourages the further fragmentation of the household.

And so the ripples of redefinition spread. Once the structure of the family begins to be redefined, every aspect of family life will be affected. Much of the present yearning for a return to 'family values' is really a yearning for stability: under the influence of new definitions of gender roles and new patterns of marriage and divorce, the family will never again be what it was in 1950, 1960 or 1970. But, gradually and experimentally, we will learn how to construct a framework for living with the new ideology of the family.

## THE STORY OF GWEN AND BILL

☐ There has never been any divorce in our family, and so we were pretty shocked when our second daughter came to us a few years back and told us that she and her husband were separating.

 They had been married for quite a while before they had any children, and they had two lovely little kids— our only grandchildren—and everything seemed to be going pretty well for them.

 Our daughter had gone back to work and she often seemed to be very tired and cranky, and we used to go over there as much as we could to help out with the kids. Occasionally, we would persuade her to let our grandchildren come and stay overnight with us, but she was always very keen to take them back home early the next morning . . . I don't think she really approved of the way we looked after them.

 Well, to be frank, we didn't really approve of the

way she was going about being a mother. We advised her against going back to work because we thought the kids were still too young. When she said that she and her husband were going to get a divorce, the first thing we worried about was the kids. But she reckoned that she was going to put them into after-school care.

That didn't really work out, and so they ended up coming to us three afternoons a week. Now, don't get me wrong . . . we love the children very much and they are a very important part of our lives. But we didn't expect that we would have to go back to being active parents at this stage of the game. We get tired—we are not as young as we used to be—and there are times when we feel as if this is all a bit unreasonable. We never really got to the bottom of the divorce business. Our daughter wouldn't tell us what was going on, and we have practically lost touch with our son-in-law. We regret that, because we liked him and we think that he is a very good father to the children. Now, he only sees them every second weekend and for special occasions like birthdays, and we can see that it is very hard on them. They still love him, and they still can't understand why they can't see him whenever they want to.

The trickiest part is that our daughter has had a couple of serious boyfriends since the split. One of them moved in with her for a while, and that really upset the kids. They confided in us that they couldn't stand him, and they hated the idea of him sleeping in their mother's bed. Anyway, that fizzled out after a few months and now there's this new bloke who she's been seeing for the last year or so.

He has been married before, and he has a couple of kids of his own who are older than our grandchildren.

Last Christmas, our daughter insisted that he should come around for Christmas dinner, bringing his kids with him, and it was all pretty tense. We do our best to keep in touch with what is going on, but this is not how we imagined life would turn out. He introduced his kids to us by our first names, and that's what they called us: Bill and Gwen. That was a bit of a shock— his kids were only about 13 or 14.

You could see that our daughter was trying too hard. She was trying to make it into a proper family occasion, but it was pretty bloody obvious we were not a proper family at all.

Our older daughter was there, too. She is not married, although she has a long-term relationship. She brought her man with her, of course, and that is always a bit tricky, because you are never quite sure what their relationship is . . . she just calls him her friend, which seems a bit weak.

I don't know if they will ever marry. Now that this has happened to our other daughter, I think the older one might be even more cautious. She is very committed to her career, in any case.

It will probably turn out alright in the end. Only having two daughters, we were looking forward to having sons-in-law in the family. The only son-in-law we really have is basically out of the picture, and the other two blokes are a bit indeterminate. Still, the grandchildren are a joy, and we feel that it is just as well we do have the time to give to them, because they would be pretty confused otherwise.

We are not alone in all this. Lots of our friends have kids who have been divorced or are living in *de facto* arrangements. Everything seems to have changed so

much. None of us would have imagined that this kind
of thing would go on in our own families. I blame the
Sixties for a lot of it . . . not that either of our girls
were ever into drugs, I'm pretty sure, but it was a period
when kids seemed to get the idea that all they had to
do was please themselves. Doing your own thing. I don't
think it was a good basis for marriage or for establishing
a family. We tried to give our girls the same values
that we had grown up with, but the world did seem
to have changed so much that we often felt as if we
were not on the same wave-length.

I suppose, deep down, we hope that both the girls
will ultimately get married and settle down with one
partner for the rest of their lives. We never say that
to them, of course.

The world has changed, we realise that. There's not
as much innocence in the kids, and there's not as much
stability among the parents. They have to work it out
for themselves, and I'm sure they will.

But, sometimes, we feel as if we are part of the last
generation of true Australians. We are very relieved that
we don't have to go through all the things that our
daughters' generation seems to be going through. Life
is much more complicated for them than it was for us
. . . their values just seem to be so different from ours.

Anyway, we hope that things might settle down
reasonably soon. We have been planning an overseas
trip for years, but we have had to keep putting it off
because of all these little crises in the family. There's
no way we can go away while the grandchildren are still
so dependent on us—even though they are growing up
quickly, they still need a lot of looking after.

One thing's for sure: you never stop being a parent.□

# Whither the Work Ethic?

The best way to think about work is to regard it as 'occupational therapy'. Of course, it is also a source of income, but the benefits of regular and satisfying work are far greater than the simple reward of the paypacket. People with a job are able to define their own identity in terms of their work; the rituals and routines of work create a structure which is a welcome contrast from the unpredictability of other departments of life; people with work are generally able to develop a sense of purpose and direction which gives meaning to their lives.

Employment is therefore one of the most effective therapies for people who are suffering from the stress and anxiety which has resulted from the Age of Redefinition. It is no accident that so many women whose emotional lives are in turmoil as a result of their redefinition of gender roles have sought refuge in a job and then found that it is the job which preserves their sanity.

One of the most therapeutic aspects of work has always been that the work-group supplies an important source of stimulation and social contact. During a period of such instability in Australian family life, the appeal of the workplace as a social environment has increased dramatically: the herd intinct is more easily satisfied at work than at home for thousands of Australians. In some cases, the work-group actually becomes the social group after work; in other cases, personal relationships at work supply emotional enrichment and support which is simply missing from life away from the office, shop or factory.

As we move through the Age of Redefinition, Australians become more likely to discuss their jobs in terms of the people they work with, and the *social* satisfactions of work, rather than simply discussing the content of the work itself. The workplace has become a source of stability, security, identity and satisfaction for people who might previously have expected to obtain all those gratifications in their private lives—specifically in the context of their families.

When stay-at-home mothers first return to the work-force, it is a common experience for them to discover that going to work is actually easier than staying at home—in spite of the fact that they experience greater physical fatigue. To some extent, they are reporting the therapeutic effect of a working environment which is more structured than the domestic environment; to some extent, they are reporting the additional emotional gratification they obtain from stimulating interactions with other adults; to some extent, they are reporting relief from the pressure of having to *manage* the domestic environment and of having to make constant decisions about what to do next. The standard joke (among both men and women) that, after a holiday with the family, 'you go back to work for a break' reveals a core of truth: absence from work often implies an absence from the comfort and reassurance of a familiar ritual, a familiar structure, and a welcome sense of mastery over the work that has to be done.

But although work has seemed to so many Australians

to be a refuge from the Age of Redefinition, it is now becoming clear that work itself is being redefined, simply because there is not enough of it to go around.

Once unemployment exceeded 10 per cent of the labour force in 1991–92 (with the unofficial figure even higher than that) and there was no serious prospect of it falling below seven per cent or eight per cent for the foreseeable future, it became clear that the long-mooted idea of 'structural unemployment' might have to be taken seriously. In other words, Australians might have to face the fact that, on a long-term basis, our society would be able to create fewer jobs than the number of people wanting to work. Structural unemployment would mean that, no matter how motivated people may be to get a job or create work for themselves on a self-employed basis, the supply of available work simply cannot grow to meet the demand.

Once we adjust to the idea that, at one time or another, most Australian families will be affected by the threat or the reality of unemployment, we are forced to re-think the whole idea of work, and the place of work in our society. There is simply no point in saying to an unemployed young adult who has never had a job that, once he or she finds work, life will take on a new meaning and purpose. There is simply no point in suggesting to an unemployed person that work is the best way of defining one's personal identity. There is simply no point in saying to a man in his early fifties who, through retrenchment, has been pitchforked into early retirement that work is the best way of structuring the day.

All such suggestions are simply offensive and depressing. They serve only to reinforce what is already painfully obvious to the unemployed person: that the occupational therapy provided by work is not available to them; that the refuge from the Age of Redefinition provided by work is inaccessible to them; that the absence of work can add immeasurably to the other stresses of life in the Age of Redefinition.

There is no doubt that unemployment can exact a heavy emotional toll. Growing numbers of Australian families are beginning to understand how stressful it is for a young person to face the bleak prospect of long-term unemployment. Every day stretches before that person as a vacuum to be filled with whatever activity can be invented. 'Will we go writing or lifting?' says one unemployed Sydney youngster to another—meaning, 'Will we go graffiti-writing or shop-lifting?' When the day is empty, *some* structure must be found to replace the structure otherwise provided by work.

It is the common complaint of their parents that unemployed young people are sleeping in until 10, 11 or 12 noon, simply because no work awaits them and there is no motivation to get up. The cocoon of the bed is its own therapy, when the therapy of work is unavailable. And so, of course, are the cocoons of alcohol, drugs, endless videos, the insulating effect of anti-social behaviour, loud music, surliness, violence or casual sex.

There is plenty of documented evidence to suggest that the loss of a job—let alone long-term unemployment—can produce physical and psychological illness. For a start, self-esteem takes a battering and, as Professor Stephen Leeder of the Department of Community Medicine at Westmead Hospital in Sydney has noted, people with low self-esteem and low morale are less likely to take proper care of themselves. That tendency is highly hazardous to health. Research conducted by the Australian Institute of Health (reported in *The Australian* of 1 June 1992) has revealed that the mortality rate for unemployed males is 17 per cent higher than for employed males; that their blood pressure is 57 per cent higher; that their rate of smoking is 50 per cent higher. Unemployed men visit a doctor twice as often as working men. While comparable figures were not available for women, the study did show that unemployed women have an 80 per cent higher rate of visits to outpatient wards than working women, and a 35 per cent higher rate of admission to hospital. Responding to all this, the national vice-president of the AMA, Dr Brendan Nelson, was quoted as saying: 'With Australian unemployment expected to be around 10 per cent for another two years, we have a health crisis on our hands.'

The removal of occupational therapy from a person's life almost always signals the need for some other kind of therapeutic support to be provided in its place. Conversely, for unemployed young people whose self-confidence has taken a battering and who are struggling to define some meaning and purpose for their lives, the therapy of finding work can produce spectacular results: 'I couldn't believe the difference when my son finally got a job—he was like a completely new person after the first couple of weeks,' says a typical mother.

The problem is that such spectacular therapy is simply not available to more than a million Australians—both young and old—who want it. It is all very well for health professionals who study the social, emotional and physical problems of the unemployed to conclude that a job would solve most of those problems: when there is no prospect of a job, other solutions to the problem must be found.

It's not as if the problem of structural unemployment has suddenly emerged: the Industrial Revolution demonstrated what technology can do to a labour market, and the more recent revolution in information technology has demonstrated the point all over again. As a society, we have known for 20 or 30 years that, sooner or later, we would have a shortage of jobs for our population, and we have speculated vaguely about the dawning of the Golden Age of Leisure.

But when you talk to an unemployed person in the 1990s about the Golden Age of Leisure, it doesn't ring true. We have simply failed to prepare ourselves for the concept of structural unemployment. As a society, we have not yet worked out what to do with those pockets of our communities where youth unemployment runs as high as 50 per cent or more.

Those young Australians are not revelling in the Golden Age of Leisure: they are facing the daily challenge of trying to figure out what to do. Leisure is time off, but you only have time off by contrast with time on: if you don't have work, you don't have leisure. Unless we come up with a radical redefinition of the role of work in our society, unemployed Australians will continue to find that they have neither work nor leisure.

The harsh possibility of structural unemployment is potentially as destabilising for Australian society as the redefinition of gender roles. It means that the traditional source of identity, dignity, structure and purpose for many people's lives has been taken away from them. It means that *other* sources of identity, dignity, structure and purpose will have to be supplied. It means that, in addition to the growing emphasis on vocational education, a parallel emphasis will have to be placed on education for a life of unemployment, part-time employment or occasional employment. It means that Australians will have to adjust to the prospect of having several careers rather than one (including the possibility of having a couple of part-time careers, simultaneously). It means that Australians will have to be taught how to structure and enrich lives which would otherwise be structured and enriched through work. It means that Australians will have to be taught strategies for providing themselves with alternative therapies to the therapy of work.

One possible strategy, of course, is for unemployed Australians to be organised to participate more actively in voluntary community work of all kinds. Another possibility is for a much larger number of those with creative potential to be given guidance and support in the creative arts without any expectation that their creative output should become commercially viable.

Another—more likely—strategy for coping with the excess of labour supply over demand would be to re-think the place of part-time work in our society. If we are not able to create sufficient work for those who want it, nor to develop strategies which will supply alternative forms of 'occupational therapy', then we may elect simply to redeploy some of the available work on a part-time basis rather than redefine the role which work is going to play in future Australian society.

None of these alternatives would be necessary if there were to be a sustained upswing in employment. Perhaps Australia will embrace the idea of a reinvigorated manufacturing industry; perhaps tourism will emerge as a genuine alternative to fading primary and secondary industries; perhaps a radical new wave of cottage industries will emerge to soak up the unemployed.

## THE RETURN OF 'SERVANTS'

One of the probable sources of new jobs in the 1990s—
indeed, of a whole new industry—is the area of domestic
cleaning and maintenance services. The trend is already
underway, but the emerging home services industry is still
largely *ad hoc*, and has barely scratched the surface of its
potential.

As the vast majority of mothers continue to work and
two-income households maintain high levels of affluence,
it will dawn on everyone that it is neither practical nor
desirable for a mother (even with the help of a cooperative
partner) to continue to do all of the unpaid domestic work
which used to comprise her full-time job. In the same way
as she is beginning to realise that paying for meals prepared
by someone else allows her to buy time (and energy), so
she will come to realise that it would also make sense for
her to employ someone else to do a great deal of the
domestic work which she no longer has the time or energy
to do.

As this industry develops, everyone wins: instead of
people in two-income households feeling as though they
must also do the domestic work on an unpaid basis, their
level of affluence could allow them to pay for that work
to be done, and thus to generate significant employment
opportunities for others and leisure opportunities for
themselves. This would provide one channel, at least, for
a partial redistribution of wealth without recourse to a
heavier burden of personal income tax: it suggests one
possibility for a work-based alternative to the burgeoning
welfare industry.

And so a 'servant' class will be reborn. But, given our
contemporary attitudes towards social class, we will

certainly not give it a label like that. We will speak of the 'domestic services industry', in the same way as we now speak of the 'hospitality' and 'tourism' industries. Domestic services will include basic house cleaning, gardening, window washing, car washing, pet care and, ultimately, will expand to include the cooking (and perhaps serving) of evening meals for the family and the provision of in-home child care (perhaps beginning as a kind of part-time nanny service).

One of the problems about the development of the domestic services industry is, of course, the question of status. In the short term, parents are hardly likely to hold their breath as their children approach the end of secondary school, hoping against hope that they will decide to go into 'domestic services'. But that is only a short-term issue: the tourist industry suffered the same kind of status prejudice until quite recently, but it has now come to be regarded by the Australian community as a fully legitimate industry offering comprehensive training and long-term career paths in a range of disciplines.

In time, the domestic services industry will acquire similar status to the tourist industry and will be increasingly organised along commercial lines. At present domestic services tend to be provided by individuals who are informally engaged by householders on a more or less casual basis. Because of the egalitarian ideal embraced by so many contemporary Australians (see Chapter 2.5), great care has been taken to maintain relationships with people involved in domestic help which make it clear that this is not a master-servant relationship: the egalitarians of the Seventies and Eighties felt it necessary to clean the house ready for the arrival of the cleaner, or to engage in detailed discussion with the ironing lady about her own domestic problems, in order to emphasise the equality in the relationship.

As the domestic services industry expands, it is unlikely that this egalitarian spirit will survive: arrangements will be more formal and commercial, and even if lines of status are not clearly drawn, a more competitive domestic services marketplace will mean that cleaning staff, working in highly-organised teams with tight schedules, will be too busy to stop and talk.

The widely respected economic commentator, Philip Ruthven of the Ibis Group, believes that the domestic services industry will become a major supplier of new jobs and will make a significant contribution to what he predicts will be a new Golden Age of full employment before the end of this decade. While acknowledging that many more Australians will settle for part-time work, Ruthven believes that, by the end of the Nineties, most Australians who want work will be able to find it—and the explosion of the domestic services industry will be a big part of that story.

No doubt other new industries will also emerge: even so, the signs do not suggest a rapid return to full employment, and many economists favour the more pessimistic view that structural unemployment is likely to become a more or less permanent reality. If unemployment does not fall dramatically within the next few years then, as a society, we will find ourselves engaged in the painful process of redefining work (or, alternatively, radically restructuring the labour market) and we must begin to face the implications which flow from that.

Of course, it is all too easy to glamorise work itself. Plenty of people who have work—even if they are obtaining some degree of occupational therapy from it—do not necessarily enjoy what they actually do on the job. There is such a thing as unsatisfying work; there are plenty of jobs which are themselves a major source of stress. Indeed, people will generally judge their work to be a negative experience for them if it involves tasks which are unsuitable to their temperament or aptitudes; if they can find no basis for taking pride in what they do; if the work itself is boring and unsatisfying; if the workplace is torn by personal conflicts, faction fights, or an 'us and them' mentality; if the boss is not worthy of respect; if effort is not acknowledged and appreciated; if the organisation appears insensitive.

But The Mackay Report on *Australians at Work* (1989) found that such complaints are relatively rare, and that it is much more common for Australians with a job to acknowledge that work *is* a therapeutic experience for them—if not because of the content of the job or the culture of the organisation, then because of the relationships which develop with colleagues and associates.

## FEMINISING THE WORKPLACE

If Australians are slow to recognise that the place of work in our society may need to be redefined, they can hardly avoid noticing that the workplace itself is changing in quite dramatic ways.

For a start, it is a far more female environment than it has been at any time since World War II. Even in the 10 years from 1980 to 1990, the proportion of females who worked rose from 50 per cent to 67 per cent (and, as we have already seen, the working mother became a major phenomenon of the Australian labour market).

The presence of vastly increased numbers of women at

work not only alters the character of relationships at work and the emotional climate of many workplaces, but it also means that men's traditional attitudes to work have been affected by the strong symbolic significance which so many women attach to their new-found employment. The *Australians at Work* study found evidence of some underlying resentment among men at the extent to which their traditional territory at work has been invaded. It suggested that, in response to women's enthusiasm for work as a symbol of their independence, men are developing two forms of defence.

The first defence is simply to play it down. Among the husbands of working wives, for instance, it is common to encounter little discussion of the *content* of their wives' work: wives' jobs are most likely to be discussed in terms of the impact of a working mother on the life of the family. Typically, Australian men still prefer to discuss the effect of their wives' work on *them* rather than on the women concerned: 'She takes more care with her appearance'; 'she's got more to talk about'; 'the extra income is useful'; 'she's always too tired and cranky'; 'she's off my back more than she used to be'.

Whereas women will cheerfully speak in detail about their husbands' work, men will often not even mention the fact that their wives work unless they are directly questioned about it: it is tempting for Australian men to create the impression that they are the sole breadwinners for their families. (One of the things that has infuriated some husbands is that, in the first flush of a non-working wife's return to work, she may want to regard the money she earns as being her own, whereas the husband's earnings are treated as common property.)

The defence of ignoring women's symbolic commitment

to work also shows up in the workplace itself where many men are still having great difficulty coming to terms with the fact that women should be treated as having equal access to work, equal opportunities for advancement and equal status to men. Affirmative Action is still strongly resisted by many men (and, indeed, by many women as well), but whether or not the workplace is formally committed to Affirmative Action, older and more senior men can still find it difficult to take the claims of working women entirely seriously.

As recently as 1991, a senior marketing executive at a Sydney management conference, faced with an audience comprising almost equal proportions of men and women, asked the question, 'What are all these women doing here? Do they have real jobs?'

A more aggressive response to the arrival of large numbers of women in the work force—and one of the most savage forms of the male backlash—is the assertion by some men that the working wife is the primary cause of unemployment. Such men argue that, if women had not chosen to use work as the symbol of their liberation, young Australians would not be squeezed out of the job market. Men who hold this view, of course, deeply resent the presence of married women at work and find it difficult to take them seriously as work colleagues. Such an attitude is relatively rare; more typically, men have enough trouble coping with women's impact on the workplace without even raising the larger question of their impact on the labour market itself.

Among both husbands and managers, women at work still suffer from the male prejudice that it is 'nice' for women to have a job as a kind of 'interest'; that part-time work is the most appropriate option for women because of the demands of their domestic responsibilities; that, when the crunch comes, it is really men who are the breadwinners.

The second defence among men who feel that the workplace has been invaded by women is to down-grade the importance of work itself. Men who have not been accustomed to working with women as equals appear reluctant to enter into a competitive relationship with women at work: the 'threat' posed by an ambitious and successful woman may well be met with the comment that 'No job should really be *that* important'.

As women celebrate their freedom to work, some men react by complaining about the burden of work. As women revel in the sense of independence which work offers them, less secure men are likely to rail against the extent to which they have to depend on employment for survival. At a time when many women are looking forward to improving their position at work, men who are threatened by such ambition are inclined to look towards retirement as a means of escaping from a workplace whose character has been transformed by the female invasion. At home, similarly, some husbands have retreated from their previous single-minded commitment to work in response to having a working wife. In such cases, being one of two breadwinners has eased the burden of responsibility and correspondingly reduced the husband's sense of *having* to work.

As the effects of the 1991–92 recession deepened, the relationship between gender roles and attitudes to work became more complex. In two-income households where a husband was retrenched and his wife wasn't, new tensions emerged as both partners struggled to come to terms with the sudden redefinition of the significance of work in each of their lives. (See 'The story of Joanna' at the end of this chapter).

It would be wrong to suggest that the majority of men are defensive about women's increasing participation at work, but resentment of the success of working women is one factor in the current backlash against the Women's Movement which is evident among many Australian males.

Of course, all this will change as the rising generation of Australians enter the workplace with the idea of gender equality more firmly established in their minds. For the present, however, adjustment to women at work is an important part of the redefinition of work itself. 'Talking shop' used to be the almost exclusive province of men: today, women are just as likely to want to talk about their work as men are and, indeed, many working women are much *more* enthusiastic about discussing work than men are. 'Women's talk' is taking on a whole new meaning.

## THE RISE OF PART-TIME WORK

One of the implications of the growing numbers of married women (especially working mothers) in the Australian work force is that part-time work is more popular than ever. Twenty-five per cent of the Australian work force already have part-time work, and the increasing gap between employment supply and demand suggests that the part-time worker will become an increasingly common phenomenon.

People who have satifying part-time work claim that they have managed to get the best of both worlds: they have the therapy (and the income) associated with regular employment, but they also have access to much more spare time—for leisure, for study, for attending to domestic responsibilities. Part-time workers tend to enthuse about the structure of their lives in ways which suggest that many more people would settle for part-time work if they understood the benefits of it. One of the most significant of those benefits is that a person with a part-time job feels the full effect of leisure. The long-promised Golden Age of Leisure is closer for the person with part-time work than for most other members of the Australian community, because the part-time worker has the necessary time and energy to devote to the enjoyment of recreation and relaxation, as well as work.

But because the Australian labour market is not yet fully responsive to the over-supply of labour, we have not really come to terms with the potential benefits offered by large-scale adoption of part-time work. People who have part-time work typically regard their jobs as being in every way as serious and significant as the jobs of those who work full-time (except that, of course, they earn less money). They sometimes claim to have higher levels of enthusiasm and commitment than full-time employees because—particularly in the case of working mothers—the concept of part-time work is so precious to them and because their balanced lives bring them to work with a fresher, more relaxed approach. (Although employers are discovering the virtues of part-time work, part-time workers nevertheless feel as if they are sometimes treated as second-class employees— as if the fact that they have chosen part-time work is regarded by employers as a sign of *reduced* commitment.)

The need to develop a more enlightened attitude to part-time work is only part of a larger question: how is the workplace going to be restructured to accommodate the competing demands of work and family—not only for the army of working mothers but also, increasingly, for the fathers who are beginning to take seriously the sharing of domestic responsibilities? Talk of establishing child-minding facilities in the workplace is one symptom of the need for change, but that may not turn out to be the best or most practical strategy: the more fundamental requirement is for employers to acknowledge that employees also have family responsibilities which should be regarded as complementary to—not competitive with—responsibilities at work. Sooner or later, working parents (mothers *or* fathers) who need to stay at home to care for a sick child will have to be able to say so—rather than pretending it is they who are sick in order to secure the sympathy or understanding of the boss.

## THE 'UNEMPLOYMENT MENTALITY'

At a time when unemployment is running at such a high level, it would be tempting to think that people who have a job would value that job more highly than at other times. And yet, a clear impression to emerge from the workplace of the mid-nineties is that, since there is such widespread anxiety about security of employment, the general level of motivation and commitment to work may actually be declining. Insecurity is always a demotivating experience: when Australians feel as though their employment prospects are uncertain and that retrenchment or early retirement might be offered to them at any time, the sense of involvement in the job is understandably destabilised. Insecurity erodes commitment and, as high levels of unemployment are sustained, even the majority of Australians who do have work begin to suffer from the debilitating anxiety which—as in so many other departments of their lives—flows from the sense that they are being involved in the process of reshaping our society.

The restructuring of Australian industry; doubts about the best direction for Australia's long-term economic recovery; the constant threat of new forms of automation which may replace human labour . . . all such factors raise questions in Australians' minds about their long-term employment prospects, and about prospects for the rising generation of young Australians.

Younger Australians adjust more quickly to the idea that there may be interruptions to their working lives or that they may have to make signficant changes in career direction in order to maintain employment. But older Australians find such concepts difficult to absorb, because they grew up and entered the work force with the idea that work was available to anyone who wanted it and that, generally speaking, you could choose the kind of job you wanted.

And so, a curious new attitude emerges in relation to work: rather than seeing the shrinking job market as a reason to feel more committed to a particular job, a kind of 'unemployment mentality' is beginning to spread even to those who have work. This mentality is based on the proposition that the welfare net will support those who cannot find work; that work may be something you *choose* to do rather than having to do; that work should offer some specific emotional benefits in order to be worth doing. 'What's in it for me?' is a question increasingly being asked as the unemployment mentality spreads.

This rather surprising implication of a tightening job market shows up at both ends of the age spectrum. Young people who remain unemployed for prolonged periods may never discover—or may simply forget—that work does have therapeutic benefits beyond wages. The reactions of young Australians to various proposals for a youth wage below adult award levels reveal the corrosive effects of the unemployment mentality: at a conference to discuss youth unemployment organised by the Liberal Party in Perth during 1992, one young speaker claimed that the Liberals' youth wage proposal did not offer a sufficient margin above the dole and, in his view, it would not be worth getting out of bed to go to work.

Once work becomes less reliably available, there is an inexorable change in attitude to it. Even among those who have work (but who face the possibility of periods of unemployment, periods of part-time work, or a series of career changes through their working lives), there is a tendency to look for meaning outside their jobs—in the family, in recreation, in hobbies or in other voluntary pursuits. Leisure takes on a new significance as the context for the search for a new sense of purpose which is unrelated to work. In this climate, early retirement becomes increasingly appealing: people who have revised their traditional view of the centrality of work will perceive the prospect of early retirement as an advance to new meanings, rather than a retreat from old meanings.

The unemployment mentality (work as an option, rather than a necessity) is the enemy of the so-called 'Protestant work ethic'. That traditional work ethic appears to be on the wane in Australia as a direct consequence of the bitter lessons being learned by people who can no longer rely on the availability of work. The work ethic thrives when the supply of work equals or exceeds the demand for it. When demand exceeds supply, some other ethic must be created.

A society which lives with massive unemployment for long enough eventually has to face some fundamental questions about the structure of its labour market, and about the place of work in its overall socio-cultural and economic system. For instance:

Is it going to be possible to create the one million or more jobs which are currently missing from the Australian labour market? If so, where do we seriously believe they will come from, and what are we doing to encourage their creation?

Are we committed to the idea that everyone who wants to work should have a job? If not, what alternative to 'occupational therapy' do we propose in order to protect the mental and physical health of those Australians who have no job now, and no prospect of a job in the future?

Have we over-emphasised technology in the workplace? Has the combination of investment allowances on capital equipment and payroll tax loaded the dice against employment? Are there industries where we could have deliberately decided *not* to replace people with machines without adversely affecting the bottom line?

Are we prepared to face the possibility that available work could be distributed in a different way, so that part-time employment becomes even more commonplace than it is now? What would that mean for our standard of living?

Should we consider a tax reform involving income-splitting between spouses in order to create a financial incentive for one partner to undertake unpaid domestic work while the other has paid work outside the home? Would that relieve some of the pressure on the labour market? Would it be an appropriate acknowl- edgement of the value of unpaid domestic work? Or would it lock one partner into being too dependent on the other and limit that person's access to the labour market at some future time?

Is there to a be a Golden Age of Leisure and, if so, how will it be funded? If we reject a redistribution of available work and fail to generate sufficient new jobs, will we accept that, in order to sustain a reasonable way of life for unemployed Australians, personal income tax rates must go higher, rather than lower?

Perhaps new industries (particularly in the service area) will evolve quickly enough to solve the present unemployment crisis. Perhaps the expectation that automation and elec- tronic information technology would permanently shrink the labour market was based on false assumptions. Perhaps work is always going to be found, ultimately, for those who want it and the only real challenge is to overcome stereo- typed perceptions of the status which we attach to various jobs (such as domestic services).

Whether or not we have to adjust to the idea of 'structural unemployment', we certainly have to adjust to the idea of a sustained period of unemployment which is socially, culturally and politically dangerous for us. If we can't soak up the pool of unemployed within a few years, then we shall have to come back to the difficult question of trying to decide whether we believe that work should remain central to the identity, dignity and sense of purpose among Australian men and women. If, as a society, we make that decision, then we would have to fundamentally re-think the present structure of our labour market—certainly offering much more part-time work, and perhaps deciding that paying able-bodied people *not* to work makes little sense if there is useful work which could be done in return for that payment. On the other hand, if we decide that we do not expect everybody to work, then we will need to make much more serious and imaginative efforts to find alternative sources of satisfaction for those who don't.

For those Australians who have lost their jobs, the lack of any serious debate about the future of work in our society is particularly distressing. Few things are more disheartening than the feeling that we are the mere casualties of an economic accident.

## THE STORY OF JOANNA

☐ My husband has a totally different attitude to his work from his attitude to mine. He wants me to take more sickies. I think he may even be a bit jealous of my work, because I do feel it is important and I feel obligated to go to work. And I enjoy it. He just doesn't understand my approach.

I think Peter tries to understand, but he still resents it. He often says that I am working too hard—which means that I am working too hard for *his* liking.

My job has to fit in with the family. His job doesn't. We all have to fit in with him. If I have had a bad day, I am not allowed to take it out on my husband and kids, or they all think they are suffering because of my job. But if he has a bad day at work, look out . . .

Peter is a bit better trained now, but it has been a struggle. He does help out with the kids, but he still does virtually no housework.

The worst thing is this assumption that his career should take precedence over mine. I still have to fight for my rights.

When it's all boiled down, I'm sure that he really thinks that I should be at home with the kids, full time. I'm sure he really thinks that *all* mothers should be at home with their kids. Even when he pretends to be understanding, I don't think he really understands. He is getting more tolerant, but that is about as far as it goes.

At least we don't have the problem one of my friends has. She went back to work and she was really involved and happy in her job, but then her husband was retrenched. It has really knocked the stuffing out of both of them. She never intended to be the breadwinner, and she now realises that she has to work, come what may . . . she really has to hang on to that job because the family depend on it.

At the same time, her husband is shattered, and he hasn't really come to terms with the fact that he might be at home for quite a while. She jokes with some of us that she has a 'house husband', but she has threatened us with violence if we ever say anything like that to him. All he will say is that he is looking for another job.

It is hard for her to get him to adjust to taking on proper responsibility for running the house, even though she is now the only one with a full-time job. She reckons that, practically every morning, he says things like 'Do you want me to cook the dinner tonight?' as though he doesn't want her to think of it as an established routine.

So there's a case where you could have a total role-reversal, but they haven't adjusted to it at all. Not yet, anyway. I'm glad it hasn't happened to us. My husband would be hopeless and, to be truthful, I don't think I would like to be the sole breadwinner myself.☐

## THE STORY OF LEO

☐ I can't decide whether or not work is a big part of my life. Obviously, it pays for everything else I do, but I don't know whether it has the same importance for me that it used to have. I go there and I do it, but I don't think I really like it as much as I used to . . . it is a less vital part of my life.

I find it is becoming more stressful. It's partly because so many people have been laid off that you are never sure where it is going to end. We seem to be constantly reorganising and there are definitely fewer people than there used to be to do the same amount of work. I have seen a lot of my mates go, and it breaks your heart. Some of them have been replaced by machines, and you can see what they are thinking . . . it is just as if all those years counted for nothing because it turns out that a machine could do what they used to do.

In some ways, I suppose I hope that I might be offered a redundancy package . . . it would force the decision to take early retirement. But I don't know for sure. What if I take the package and then find it hard to make ends meet? Or what if I turn the package down and then find that I am going to be given the heave in any case, a few months later?

My wife has never worked. She goes to the hospital once or twice a week and serves tea and does voluntary work. If you are both involved in something, you don't get on each other's nerves as much as you could. But there was never any need for her to have a paid job. Anyway, I don't know if I really like the idea of your wife having to work . . .

It is a completely different thing with my daughter. She is in her late twenties, and she is as keen as mustard. She lives on her own and her job seems to mean everything to her. Apparently she gives some of the blokes at work a run for their money, and it is quite funny when she tells us how they react. She reckons she has got nothing to lose, so she is going to go as far as she can. She has no thought of getting married . . . even if she did, I'm sure the job would still come first.

My son is not so lucky. So far, he hasn't been able to find a decent job and he has had to make do with a few casual bits and pieces. Theoretically, he is living in a flat with a few of his mates, but when he runs out of money he has to come home. That is a depressing business. He lies in bed till all hours of the day and just sort of drifts around. It really depresses my wife . . . she is quite glad to get out of the house when he is moping around like that. It's hard to know what advice to give him.

He thought he would go for a trade, but he missed out on TAFE again this year, and anyway the building trade is not what it used to be.

You realise how much work gives you when you see someone who hasn't got any. A bloke at the plant who is on the same basic style of wage as me worked out that if he stopped work and got all the benefits you get if you are not working, he would only be getting $43 less each fortnight than what he is now. He owns his house and his car . . . yet he is still coming to work. He can see the value in it. He reckons he would go off his rocker if he just sat at home all day. But some of the young people seem to think that if they can organise the dole and the other bits and pieces they seem to be entitled to, they don't have to bother going to work. It's a different mentality. I can see it starting to creep into my son's thinking. He has resisted going on the dole, but I think he will probably have to if nothing better turns up.

The thing that really gets to me is that I feel as if I am more conscientious than most of the other people at work . . . there seems to be a lot of apathy. People don't seem to be as serious about it as they used to be. You would think that they would try extra hard when they know that there is so much unemployment around, but it seems to have no effect on them. In fact, I am amazed at how little work some people can get away with.

Sometimes my wife reckons that I take my job too seriously. But it has been my life, and I suppose that I am lucky that I have always had work. But, to tell you the truth, I never really thought about it. Everyone had work, really. It's only lately that you hear people talking about what they would do if they didn't have a job. Things are certainly changing. The more I think about it, the more I hope I don't have to face that decision about the retrenchment package. I would rather stay where I am.□

## 2.4

# MANAGING INVISIBLE MONEY

If attitudes to work are going to change (under the influence of sustained high levels of unemployment and growing evidence of an 'unemployment mentality'), then attitudes towards money will inevitably change. Whereas older and more affluent Australians are still inclined to regard work as the ultimate virtue and money as being the just reward for those who work hard, younger and less affluent members of the community—especially those who are experiencing long-term unemployment—are beginning to revise this ethic. If it turns out that work will not be available to all those who want it, then attitudes towards the symbolism of money will be radically redefined—both by the haves and the have-nots.

At a time when vast numbers of Australians are relying on unemployment and other social security benefits, the traditional connection between money and work has begun to break down. Among people who regard work as either an unlikely or optional source of income, the centrality of money as a symbol of worth is bound to be challenged.

It would be premature to suggest that traditional, work-related attitudes to money have already changed, or that Australians have retreated significantly from money-based materialism. However, there are certainly signs of an erosion in traditional attitudes to money which corresponds to the erosion in traditional attitudes to work.

It is probably inevitable that, as distribution of household income becomes increasingly unequal (see Chapter 2.5), people who are slipping towards the bottom of the financial heap are going to have to revise the value they place on money, simply as part of the process of retaining their own self-esteem. The highly visible financial disasters of the 1980s have provided comfort to many under-privileged Australians, and to those who are struggling to make ends meet: such people reflect on the fact that 'money does not bring happiness' and are inclined to mock the obsession with money which they believe characterises people who are able to earn large quantities of it. For people who do not have access to a regular income (apart from pension payments), it is easy to take refuge in the proposition that 'money is the root of all evil' (without even going so far as to acknowledge that it is the *love* of money which was proverbially regarded as being the root of all evil).

In other words, the rapidly widening gap between the rich and poor in Australia—largely under the influence of unemployment—means that a dichotomy is opening up in Australians' attitudes towards money: for those with no prospect of becoming affluent, affluence is almost bound to be sneered at, and money will come to be associated with survival rather than comfort.

But Australians' attitudes towards money are changing more rapidly and in more radical ways than can be explained simply in terms of the impact of unemployment and the resulting changes in attitudes towards work.

## THE CREDIT CARD REVOLUTION

In fact, money is being redefined in Australia primarily under the influence of the new technology of money. In the past 15 years or so, Australians have had to adjust to the switch from thinking of money in terms of cash and cheques to the present reality in which money is increasingly invisible and intangible. Today's money increasingly consists of electronic impulses accessed by pieces of plastic.

Since Bankcard was launched in 1974, credit card and other plastic card usage has exploded to the point where about four-fifths of Australians now hold one or more credit or debit cards. (Australians, by the way, are among the world's most enthusiastic plastic-toters. According to *The Economist* of 27 June 1992, credit cards are held by only one per cent of adults in Italy, Germany and Holland, only four per cent in Switzerland and 33 per cent in Britain. Japan [63 per cent] and the USA [60 per cent] are more our style.)

The effect of Australia's large-scale participation in the credit card revolution has been a virtual redefinition of the nature of financial transactions. Managing money is actually harder than it used to be. When money is invisible and intangible, the very concept of money changes and, except for the more sophisticated users of the system who rapidly adapt to it, the sense of *control* over money recedes.

There is no doubt that many of those Australians who felt that they had been sucked into a kind of credit whirlpool during the 1980s were victims of the new technology of money. As the use of invisible money became more widespread, so the distinction between money and credit began to blur: the fact that so many plastic cards were multi-purpose cards (offering not only the convenience of

cashless transactions but also access to instant credit and
to the use of automatic telling machines) compounded the
confusion.

Australians who were slow to comprehend the redefinition of money under the influence of the new technology
easily found themselves caught in accidental debt. 'The
bank told me that I had $2000 to spend on my Bankcard,
so I spent that . . . now they are saying that I have to pay
a big interest bill' sounds like an extraordinarily naive
response to the new credit-based system of invisible money,
and yet responses like that were heard from disgruntled
users of the new invisible money/credit systems who had
clearly not been adequately educated about how to manage
a system which offered invisible money and instant credit.

Even among more sophisticated users of the new technology of money, however, there has been some resentment
of the implied pressure created by credit card usage to live
in a state of permanent indebtedness to the banks and other
credit card providers. When credit card statements arrive
in the mail, carrying the seductive suggestion that only a
small proportion of the bill needs to be paid, consumers
who are experiencing financial difficulty at that time may
easily find themselves taking what seems, at that moment,
like the easy way out. Even if the actual interest rate on
the available credit is understood, the idea that 'it's only
for a month or so' often serves to lower the credit
consumer's resistance still further. And so the credit trap
is sprung and the consumer finds it difficult to wriggle free.

The difficulties of managing invisible money and instant
credit are, of course, quite separate. But since the two
challenges arrived at precisely the same moment (with the
launch of Bankcard in 1974), they have really become two
facets of the same process of redefining the nature of

financial transactions. Those people who now report that they find it difficult to keep track of how much money they have in their bank account are often the same people who report that they had no idea of the extent of their debts until they began to confront a growing interest bill.

The proposition that the banks intended the marketing of credit cards to encourage people to increase their debts is supported partly by the nature of the launch of Bankcard, and partly by the more recent determination of the banks to change the basis of charging for credit card usage so that quick payers are no longer able to use the system free of charge.

The launch of Bankcard was one of the most dramatically successful new product launches in Australian marketing history, but it must be remembered that this was not a conventional new product launch. Consumers were not obliged to take any action in order to obtain a Bankcard: the cards were simply sent to bank customers in a large-scale distribution program which gave the vast majority of bank customers immediate access to the new card-based system of financial transactions. This meant that the system changed before its users were really prepared for the change. It meant that consumer behaviour changed much more rapidly than consumer attitudes. It meant that people were responding directly to the new technology of money without having expressed any particular interest in it or desire for it. In effect, the Bankcard launch was an exercise in mass manipulation of the Australian market—at least in those cities where the launch was based on unsolicited distribution of cards.

Regardless of any ethical issues which may arise from the Bankcard launch strategy, it is certainly the case that consumers were overtaken by events. They did not fully understand the nature of the system when they began to use it, and many of them stumbled in their attempts to develop strategies for mastering it. Instant credit, combined with invisible money, created the new hazard of accidental debt.

Inevitably, therefore, Australians' attitudes towards saving began to change. The Mackay Report on *Money* (1984) reported that, by the early 1980s, Australians were expressing widespread uncertainty about how to come to terms with 'easy credit', and how to cope with what seemed to be emerging as an inexorable shift away from a savings-oriented approach to money towards a credit-orientation. At that time, Australians were already aware of some conflict between the traditional view that saving was a virtue and the more aggressive, more reckless concept of 'using other people's money, and worrying about it later'. The dramatic increase in the use of credit, the growth of financial services, the depersonalisation of banks and the approaching dawn of the cashless society were, at that time, leading consumers to have a reduced sense of control over their own money.

Since then, of course, the trend has accelerated. The feeling that the financial system has become far more complex and less easy to understand has made some people feel insecure about electronic financial transactions, and has made others feel all too ready to behave irresponsibly as a reaction to a system which they cannot really comprehend.

One of the implications of growing uneasiness about the redefinition of financial transactions is the changing image of credit cards. Whereas plastic cards became, during the 1980s, a kind of status symbol, they are now more mundanely regarded as mere instruments of the banking system with something approaching commodity status. Whereas once the challenge was to obtain a plastic card— with the implication that one had 'qualified' for it—today's challenge is to manage the card (or, increasingly, the collection of cards) so that it does not overwhelm, enslave or trap its owner by its seductive power.

The sense of magic associated with plastic cards is receding in the Australian community as the cards themselves come to be assessed in the light of the harsh reality of instant credit. Whereas once it looked as though plastic cards were a genuine service which banks provided for their customers' benefit, they are today being reassessed as a marketing device which was designed to train bank customers to live in debt. Perhaps it is no coincidence that Australia's fastest-growing retail bank, Bank of Melbourne, has never issued credit cards. It confines its plastic to debit cards which provide all the convenience of credit cards but only allow the customer to spend money which has previously been deposited in an account with the Bank.

## REDEFINING THE BANKS

Since it was the banks who introduced Australians to the new technology of money and credit, it is not surprising that the banks themselves have now been subject to quite harsh redefinition in the minds of Australians.

In precisely the same way as Australians are now raising questions about the nature of our political institutions because of the redefinition of politics wrought by the major parties themselves, so the community is expressing sustained hostility towards the banking system as a direct result of the radical redefinition of the nature of financial transactions brought about by the banks themselves.

The Marketscan report on *The Banking Market* (Mackay Research, 1992) revealed that as a direct result of deregulation of the banking system, Australians have come to the conclusion that banks are aggressive, commercial marketing organisations who are out to maximise their own profits. Whereas that might seem in the 1990s to be a perfectly reasonable view of the business of a bank, it represents a sharp contrast with the community view which survived through the mid-1980s. That view was that banks were virtually social institutions: they were perceived as prudent, responsible, conservative organisations who carefully rationed credit and, as a result, encouraged the population to recognise the virtue of saving. Banks, pre-regulation, were almost regarded as 'temples of money', with a quasi-religious role in helping to regulate and restrain the recklessness and irresponsibility of ordinary mortals. At that time, branch managers were highly esteemed in their local communities: along with the clergy and the medical practitioners, the bank manager was seen as one of the pillars of the local establishment.

Although many Australians would like to return to a time when banks had that kind of status in the community, the more general view seems to be that the redefinition of banks is a *fait accompli* and that there is no turning back of this particular clock. Banks are now regarded as operating in a rougher, tougher marketplace in which customers often feel exploited, relationships seem to be of decreasing importance, loyalty is a thing of the past, and customers are penalised for having too little money in their accounts.

Banks have undergone a fundamental shift from being perceived as prudent, to being perceived as powerful. During the second half of the Eighties, Australians observed with growing anxiety the close connection between the so-called 'corporate cowboys' and the banks who made such corporate philandering possible. That connection, supported by the perception that banks were aggressively marketing 'too-easy credit' to their customers, led to a rapid revision in community opinion about the morality and probity of banks.

Even in the relatively conservative pre-deregulation era, of course, banks copped their share of criticism. The very fact that they were so strict in their rationing of credit was regarded as an outrage by many customers (particularly those who had experienced financial services marketing in other countries—notably the USA): the proposition that 'banks are bastards' has had long currency in the Australian community, but the basis for the assertion has shifted quite markedly.

In the contemporary banking market, customers feel that, although they are able to operate the system themselves through the use of plastic cards and ATMs, the system is increasingly complex and mysterious. There is a growing sense that distinctions between banks are becoming less significant as the instruments of banking become more and more interchangeable between different institutions. Customers are coming to perceive the banking system as being linked into one vast, electronic network in which customers are little more than numbers—or, perhaps, electronic impulses like new-style money itself.

In spite of customers' resentment and hostility, the process of adaptation to new systems of financial transactions and to new banking products and services is well advanced. Indeed, part of the explanation of the current hostility towards the major banks is simply that, as customers do adapt to the new system, their attitudes must change and they experience the short-term problems of anxiety which inevitably accompany any attitude-change as radical as the redefinition of money and banking.

Looking to the future, the customers of Australian banks identify a number of probabilities (most of them unwelcome):

They anticipate that there will be fewer big banks and that they will become even more centralised, even more automated, and even less accessible to customers who are looking for the sense of a personal relationship.

At the same time, it is assumed that small and medium-sized banks will continue to develop, drawing support from customers who want to retain some semblance of a personal relationship with their bank and whose demands for personal service cannot be met by the major banks.

It is generally expected that routine transactions will increasingly be conducted through ATMs or bank branches which are effectively no more than cash shops. Although the majority of bank customers still resist the use of ATMs (and even their most enthusiastic supporters will often baulk at actually *depositing* money through an ATM), it is assumed that there will be an inevitable drift towards the increasing automation of transactions. Correspondingly, it is assumed that it will become harder and harder to establish personal contact with authoritative people in a bank: it is assumed that regional offices will become more common and that the local branch will have little real significance or authority.

It is anticipated that the range and diversity of bank products and services will increase—including moves by banks into insurance and superannuation.

All of these anticipated trends, of course, merely emphasise the extent to which perceptions of banks are *changing*.

Negative attitudes towards banks have been aggravated by the perception that, at the very time when personal service is thought to be declining, bank charges are increasing. Further, the customer's sense that the banking system is 'beyond me' in sophistication is often compounded by a sinking feeling that it is also beyond the comprehension of bank staff at the branch level.

## THE NEW WAY TO SHOP

The radical change brought about by the new technology of money and credit has contributed to yet another redefinition which has destabilised Australians in the past 20 years: the redefinition of the retail marketplace.

Twenty-five years ago, shopping was an essentially local and personal experience. Supermarkets had begun to arrive on the Australian scene, but they tended to appear as part of neighbourhood strip shopping centres, and they were a logical progression from the 'cash and carry' grocery stores of the late Forties and Fifties.

In the space of just 20 years, however, the fundamental character of retail shopping in Australia has changed. Self-service has become the norm everywhere from the largest department store to the smallest pharmacy. A few retailers—notably butchers and some clothing boutiques—continue to offer personal service to individual customers, but the trend is against them.

Today, shopping is increasingly being done in regional shopping centres, and it increasingly involves an interaction with a system, rather than with a shopkeeper.

Self-service has brought many benefits to the shopper: it provides a much greater feeling of freedom and autonomy in the retail environment, and it reduces the sense of pressure on indecisive or ruminative shoppers. Self-service arrangements also save time, because the shopper can go straight to the merchandise rather than having to go through a sales assistant, although the goal of instant satisfaction is often thwarted by the length of queues at the checkout.

But self-service is not all joy for the customer. For a customer to feel comfortable in a self-service environment, it is necessary to be well-informed about the products being purchased, and to feel confident about the quite complex value-for-money decisions which have to be made. For self-service to work, from the customer's point of view, the retail environment must be generally supportive, friendly and informative—and it is fundamental that personal assistance should be available when it is required.

In reality, the swing towards bigger supermarkets (even evolving into hypermarkets) and towards the placing of self-service retail stores within vast regional shopping centres has exerted new pressures on the customer. The alleged convenience of the supermarket is often offset by an environment which shoppers regard as unhelpful and unsupportive—if not actually hostile. Shoppers suspect that self-service retail arrangements often involve quite subtle 'tricks of the trade' on the part of the retailer, reducing the customer's feeling of comfort and trust and increasing the sense that the customer had better become more alert.

For example, are items which are on 'special' this week really cheaper than they were last week? And, if so, is their quality comparable? What is the 'real' price of products which seem to be almost permanently on special? (Indeed, how do we know the 'real' price of anything?) Why are packs which are sold singly apparently more expensive than packs which are banded together in multiple offers? Why is it sometimes more economical to buy the smaller pack than the larger pack? Why is it so hard to buy *single* items of hardware (such as nuts and bolts or picture hooks)?

Such questions indicate the extent to which the shopper feels a sense of powerlessness in the face of increasingly sophisticated retail techniques. Indeed, to hear housewives describing their experiences in regional shopping centres suggests that the contemporary redefinition of shopping is not all good news for the customer.

You park your car in the middle of acres of asphalt, gazing around in the hope of finding a landmark which will help you to find your car again. Then you go to an enormous supermarket which seems to be on a larger-than-human scale. You wrestle with a trolley that seems to have a mind of its own, and you find yourself being put on the defensive by the various tricks which the retailer might be playing on you—everything from pricing to display techniques, lighting, music, re-arrangement of the store to create deliberate confusion . . . and so on. Finally, you move with your loaded trolley to the check-out, where the operator hardly acknowledges your existence as a human being. You submit yourself to EFTPOS, which is a mystery, and you hope that you will end up paying only for the contents of your own trolley, but that requires a leap of faith, since the transaction is invisible. Then you push your loaded trolley back to the carpark, wandering round and round in the hope of stumbling accidentally upon your car. Eventually you do, and you load the goods into your boot. Then you wrestle with your conscience about what to do with the trolley, deciding that you had better take it back to the collection point. Then you drive home and lug the plastic bags full of products into the kitchen and pack things into your cupboards and fridge. Although it is supposed to be very modern and convenient, it often feels rather as if we have become pack-horses, and as if shopping has actually become less convenient.

In spite of such feelings of resentment, however, the regional shopping centre continues to attract growing numbers of customers. After all, it is convenient to have a wide range of shops collected in one place, to be able to park the car once rather than several times, and to be able to complete a shopping expedition under one roof. And yet, customers' reaction to regional shopping centres contains some surprisingly hostile elements: they believe they are often designed to 'trap' the customer; that the layout is deliberately confusing; that customers are forced to go out of their way (for example, when moving from the top of one escalator to the bottom of the next) in an attempt to encourage impulse buying.

The proposition that 'the shops are getting nicer but shopping itself isn't' captures the popular mood. Although shoppers are impressed by the architecture, the glamour, the technology and the increasing richness in the diversity of goods on offer, there is a growing feeling of defensiveness and disappointment that shopping has become so deper-sonalised and that so much of the contemporary retail system seems to have been designed for the benefit of the retailers and the banks, rather than the customer.

In spite of these criticisms, customers believe that retail stores are becoming visually more attractive and that, in any case, there is the attraction of potentially lower prices associated with large outlets and high turnovers. In some supermarkets, at least, store re-design programs are now responding to customers' dissatisfaction with the monolithic warehouse style of architecture: long aisles are being broken up into different-shaped spaces; specialty shops-within-a-shop create more manageable and accessible areas; some staff are designated to offer guidance and advice to customers who seek it.

It is easy to see why many commentators on the future of retailing are predicting a return to more shopping from home. Older customers can recall the convenience of a time when someone from the local grocery store collected a list in the morning and returned with the goods in the afternoon. The idea that we might develop some modern equivalent of such customised convenience is an idea with growing appeal: the use of the telephone and the home computer will undoubtedly increase as retailers begin to understand that customers (especially working mothers) may no longer be able to find the time to do battle with the supermarket on a regular basis. As computer-driven technology improves and it becomes possible for shoppers to scan available merchandise, make assessments about relative values, and even 'try on' different styles and colours of clothing using a computer-generated image of themselves on the screen, a swing away from the three-dimensional retail marketplace seems inevitable.

At the same time, there will be many occasions when consumers will still prefer to visit a shopping centre rather than shop from home. There is a clear distinction in most shoppers' minds between 'doing the shopping' (which is a relatively mundane, routine and repetitive procedure) and 'going shopping' (which is a more creative, potentially self-indulgent and pleasurable excursion). Whereas technology will make it possible for routine shopping to be done most easily from home (supported by much more efficient home-delivery systems and much more ambitious home-storage facilities), the pleasure of browsing and ruminating about less routine purchases will continue to drive shoppers to go to actual shops. But those shops are themselves bound to change: when we reach the point where going out to shop is a more special and less routine event in our lives, the shops will need to reflect that. So we will undoubtedly see the further development of the shopping emporium as an entertainment centre and as a stimulating experience for the shopper. 'Going shopping' will finally become as enjoyable as going to a theatre, a cinema or even a theme park. By then, the regional shopping centre will have metamorphosed into something which is a genuine response to customer demands, rather than a system which seems to have been imposed on the customer.

For the present, however, retail store customers often have to cope with feelings of powerlessness and even intimidation. As the shopping experience has moved away from the idea of a personal relationship between customer and shopkeeper towards an interaction between shopper and retail system, customers have begun to recognise their own need for more information, more guidance, more support and more reassurance in the task of coping with a retail environment which offers few of these things.

The explosion of self-service retailing has coincided with a proliferation of new products and new brands which make purchase decisions more complex than ever. In other words, at the very time when customers were being thrown back on their own resources to make purchase decisions, those purchase decisions became more complex than ever. How does one decide between the competing claims of seven or eight brands of VCR? How, for that matter, does one distinguish the best buy among all the competing value, ingredient and health claims in the margarine market? As debate about the relationship between fats in food and cholesterol in the body becomes more complex, how does one balance the competing claims of manufacturers for their breakfast cereals, their biscuits, their snack foods? In any product category, what do the experts regard as the best buy? What is 'the inside story'? Whereas it was once possible to talk over such matters with the grocer, the greengrocer, the pharmacist, the butcher or the draper, the contemporary retail environment has separated the customer from the expert. This is why shoppers prize any personal relationships which they may happen to establish with particular sales assistants in a department store, for example. It also accounts for the continuing success of *Choice* magazine or the ABC's high rating TV program, *The Investigators*. And it explains why, in the Nineties, consumers are starting to pay more attention to advertising, and to demand that advertising should be more informative and less vacuous.

Indeed changing attitudes towards advertising are a symptom of the redefinition of the retail marketplace. As consumers feel less confident about the motives of retailers, and less supported in the retail environment, so they want to be able to place more trust and confidence in the *direct* communication they receive from manufacturers, via advertising. As esteem and trust in retailers continue to decline, trust in advertising appears set to increase—especially if advertisers will respond to consumers' need for more usable information, more honesty, and less hype.

It is a paradox that, as the retail environment has become more visually attractive, the shopping experience has become steadily colder and more impersonal. Even those initiatives in product labelling which have been designed to plug the information gap created by the de-personalisation of retailing have been met with some suspicion by consumers. The fact that food products, for example, must now list ingredients on their packages seems like a welcome development, except that most consumers are unable to understand the coded form in which those ingredients are listed. 'What on earth is vegetable gum?' is a typical cry from consumers who want to know more about the purchase decisions they are making, but need their information to be presented in a form which is easy for the layperson to understand.

Bar codes have further complicated the system. Although now accepted as part of the retail scene, the bar code system adds to consumers' sense of the growing complexity of shopping, and makes price manipulation seem easier than it previously was: 'What goes on between the bar code and those magic wands they have at the checkout is a mystery known only to themselves.'

The revolution in retailing wrought by the new technology of money and credit has destabilised consumers' perceptions of price and value. Shoppers typically like to know what is 'the right price' of a particular item, so that they are able to make judgments about the appeal of special prices, and so that they can more accurately make comparisons between competing brands. But in today's retail environment, the value-for-money equation is getting harder to figure out: for all the appeal of specials and economy packs and other price manipulations, the underlying sense that there is a *right* price for any item (which reflects the cost of its manufacture and distribution, plus a fair profit for all concerned) has been challenged.

Australians have had to make some rapid adjustments to the new technology of financial transactions. Money has become invisible; credit has become a way of life; banks appear less trustworthy; shopping has become less personal. The rate of change in the character of financial transactions is likely to increase as the technology becomes more sophisticated. And so the process of adaptation goes on, and the level of anxiety goes up another notch. The stress of managing new-style money may not compare with stresses induced by the redefinition of gender roles or of the institution of marriage, but it is an ever-present small stress which has, over time, provoked its fair share of insecurity and crankiness.

## THE STORY OF MARGARET

☐ It's surprising how often you feel a bit on the defensive when you go shopping, these days. It's not just that you get intimidated by the staff being rude or taking no notice of you—we've had plenty of that in the past, although I think it is actually getting a bit better. What I really mean is the way the whole system seems to be sort of stacked against the customer.

   Going to one of those big regional shopping centres is a good example. Unless you really know your way around, you can easily get confused. Although it's all very beautiful and attractive, it is disorientating, somehow.

You feel as if you are in a space ship—a lot of those places are kind of unreal. At first I thought I must be a bit thick, but then I found a lot of other people get lost and confused as well, so I began to wonder whether it was all deliberate. Perhaps they design those places to encourage you to wander round and round in the hope that you will buy things on impulse that you hadn't intended to buy.

I'm sure retailers have quite a lot of tricks up their sleeves that we don't really understand. Even in the supermarket, they switch things around unexpectedly . . . it's all designed to trap the unwary, I suppose.

I've never really understood how those bar codes work. I suppose that's another example of the system which the customer doesn't really understand any more.

It is all supposed to be more efficient and convenient, but I can remember when my mother used to give a list to the grocer when he called to the house, and he would return the stuff in a cardboard box later in the day. That seems pretty convenient, I must say!

The bank is another example of what I mean. Those hole-in-the-wall machines are wonderful and it is convenient to get money out when the bank is shut, but if you ever have a problem, you just know it is going to be a real hassle. They always act as if the system couldn't possibly be wrong and the customer must be a mug. Half the time I think the staff don't really understand these systems either, so they are probably a bit on the defensive themselves. Once when the machine said I was overdrawn and I knew I couldn't be, I took the little bit of paper into the enquiry counter in the bank and told them my story. You could see they were inclined to believe the computer rather than me. It makes you feel very small.

I know it is expensive to employ staff, and I know that there are a lot of good things about self-service, but I just wish that some of these places could have a few more people around to help you when you need help.

I can see there is a lot of good in all this, but sometimes I feel as if the world is ruled by computers and all these systems haven't necessarily been thought out from the customer's point of view.

One thing that is really easy is spending money . . . credit cards have made it easier than ever, but that's been a bit of a trap for a lot of people, too. Come to think of it, the whole thing is a bit of a trap. The more we go into self-service and credit card type of things, the more you realise you have to be on the alert. I suppose our kids will be better at all this, because they have grown up with all the new systems. But I wonder if they'll ever really learn the value of money . . . as far as I'm concerned, you can't beat having the money in a purse. If you haven't got it, you can't spend it.□

# 2.5

# Divided by the Dollar

Social class may be a state of mind, but economic class is a stark reality. When sociologists and market researchers talk about 'socio-economic status', they acknowledge that the concepts of class and wealth are linked and that when economic class distinctions emerge, social class distinctions are bound to follow. Whatever else may constitute 'class', wealth is always, one way or another, at its heart.

Nevertheless, in the years following World War II, Australians have tried to separate social and economic class, and have focussed their interest almost exclusively on economic status rather than social status. We have tended to think of social class as implying a much clearer and more rigid stratification of society than has been present in post-war Australia, and we have thought that Australia lacked the kind of cultural heritage which would feed a class system. We have been pleased to think of Australia as being an essentially middle-class society.

Indeed, for most of this century, Australia has portrayed itself as the embodiment of the egalitarian dream: a relatively classless society in which power and influence—and wealth—were available to any who, through a combination of education, hard work and luck, may be able to achieve them. While our history has incorporated an approximation of a 'landed aristocracy', contemporary Australians have not attached much importance to that, nor have they generally felt particularly deferential to those who might have been thought to inhabit the closest thing that Australia had to an upper class: professional people (notably lawyers and doctors), established business families and established pastoral families.

Even when it came to questions of wealth which might have implied class, Australians have tended to think of the rich as being not unlike the rest of us: because Australia's *general* (and anticipated) level of economic prosperity had become so high, the sense of envy of the rich was not particularly strong. Living in a society which strove for almost universal home ownership and car ownership, and which seemed to have achieved a widespread sense of being 'comfortably off', Australians living in the second half of the 20th century generally lost interest in the question of social class.

As Manning Clark wrote in the Epilogue to Volume VI of *A History of Australia* (1987): 'In the second half of the 20th century Australians lived in a country where neither the historians, the prophets, the poets nor the priests had drawn the maps . . . Australians no longer apologised for the way they talked, the way they walked, or the way they behaved . . . The domination of class over class . . . was challenged. In an age of doubt about everything, even the past lost its authority.'

As the middle class grew more prosperous and numerous, earlier acceptance of class distinctions gave way to the feeling that we were actually becoming a classless society. The rich and poor no longer seemed to count as reference points for defining a structure of social class in Australia, and so the egalitarian ideal flourished. Australians were inclined to mock the British sense of class, and they prided themselves on the fact that, in Australia, Jack really is as good as his master, and that we are even better at *egalité* than the French.

There is a certain cockiness which goes with the concept of egalitarianism, and post-war Australians became good at that, too. Believing that Australia was becoming a classless society, Australians were ready to thumb their noses at those who tried to act as if they were superior to the general population: they welcomed the idea of prime ministers being called by their first names, and the easy intimacy which the Australian brand of TV current affairs brought to its handling of the powerful, the rich and the famous.

The same attitude produced a general reluctance in Australians, up until the 1990s, to offer much in the way of service to customers of retail stores, of tradesmen, or even of professional people. Service providers, celebrating the egalitarian ideal, felt that they were at least as important as the customers or clients they were obliged to serve, and so 'service' remained largely foreign to the Australian culture.

## THE TALL POPPY SYNDROME

One of the most easily identifiable symptoms of the drive towards a classless society in Australia is the so-called 'Tall Poppy Syndrome'. This rather tired label has been taken to refer to a tendency for Australians to 'cut down the tall poppies': that is, to denigrate and humiliate those who achieve excellence, success, fame or honours in any field. The underlying assumption has been that Australians are so committed to the middle-class mentality that they are only comfortable with mediocrity and that they strongly object to anyone who succeeds, because this implies some distancing from the pack.

The Tall Poppy Syndrome is actually something of a myth. The Mackay Reports on *Leaders & Heroes* (1979) and *Class & Status* (1986) identify a flaw in the conventional wisdom on this subject. There is little evidence to support the proposition that Australians resent success or wish to slash tall poppies: the truth is that Australians are only irritated by those tall poppies who *act* tall and who respond to their own success by displays of arrogance. Australians are not uncomfortable with success, but the egalitarian ideal has made them very uncomfortable with the idea that success implies superiority or that success gives anyone the right to swagger. Part of the middle-class ethos of Australia is that we should be modest about our success and humble about our achievements. The tall poppies who 'cop the treatment' are those who, explicitly or implicitly, send signals to the community that they regard themselves as being a cut above the rest of us. 'They're up themselves' is one of the harshest criticism which Australians can make of each other: they don't automatically make it in the face of success, but only when they see evidence of self-satisfied smugness or arrogance associated with that success.

Australians' conversation about tall poppies reveals the extent to which they have embraced the egalitarian ideal. It is generally assumed that even people who have very high status—through wealth or achievements—would have roughly the same values as the rest of the community and, in most important respects, would lead the same sort of life. In this sense, Australians seem to have accepted the idea of a classless society—or, at least, the idea that, in Australia, the majority of the community are so materially comfortable that there are no grounds for people to act as if they have ascended to a higher plane.

During the heyday of the egalitarian dream (1950–1990),

Australians never assumed that wealth or other achievements implied a superior class: they did not object to giving appropriate credit or even adulation to their heroes, but they were very unforgiving of heroes whose attitude suggested that they were not part of the vast Australian mainstream.

For the same reason, Australians have never been tolerant of snobbery. Indeed, 'snob' is another term of significant abuse, because it suggests that a person of wealth, power or influence has lost touch with the Australian ethos or, perhaps worse, that someone who is very obviously part of the mainstream middle class has decided to adopt an air of superiority. Conversely, Australians have remained comfortable with the idea that there are rich and powerful people in the community—or even a landed aristocracy of sorts—precisely because such people have generally been regarded as sharing in a common way of life with less wealthy or less powerful fellow-Australians.

The extraordinary economic prosperity and stability of the Fifties and Sixties fuelled the fires of Australians' egalitarian zeal. During the years that followed, the vast majority of Australians would have regarded themselves— and everyone else—as essentially 'middle class' and the sprawling suburbs of Australia's capital cities symbolised the absolute dominance of a home-owning middle class. Certainly, there were white-collar and blue-collar distinctions and a pride among some sections of the community in describing oneself as 'a worker', but the culture accommodated the view that the gap between the worker and the boss was not so significant as to amount to a class distinction.

As Australia moves through the 1990s, a serious

challenge to the egalitarian dream is being mounted. It's not that Australians have gone cold on the idea; it is simply that the gap between rich and poor is opening up and is being sustained to an extent which makes it hard to believe that there will not be a merging of new economic strata with new social strata (since affluence always defines class, in the long run).

If Australians have resisted the idea of clearly-defined social classes, it is because the gaps between rich and poor never seemed significant enough to amount to 'class' or, perhaps, because neither the very rich nor the very poor were sufficiently numerous to amount to classes which could be contrasted with the broad middle class. But all that is changing under the influence of a redistribution of household income in Australia which, in the past 20 years, has laid the foundations for a revolutionary degree of renewed social stratification. As the gap between rich and poor widens and the numbers of rich and poor dramatically increase, so the sense of egalitarianism will begin to be eroded.

When a society begins to be stratified into three almost equal, readily-defined sub-groups based on wealth, that society is sowing the seeds of a new era of class distinctions. In Australia in the mid-1990s, the signs of a re-emerging class structure are becoming evident. Australians may still resist the idea of social class and may still cling to the egalitarian ideal, but the economic facts do not encourage such social idealism.

Census data and estimates by IBIS Business Information Pty Ltd show that, in just 16 years (1976–92), the proportion of Australian households with an income of more than $72,000 (based on constant 1991–92 values) rose from

15 per cent to 30 per cent. At the same time, the proportion of households with an income of less than $22,000 rose from 20 per cent to 30 per cent.

By 1992, that top 30 per cent of households controlled 55 per cent of household income while the bottom 30 per cent of households controlled a mere 10 per cent of household income.

Obviously, the group in the middle has been shrinking. If we define the economic middle class as being households with incomes between $22,000 and $72,000 in 1991–92 terms), then the middle class has shrunk from 65 per cent of households in 1976 to 40 per cent of households in 1992, and it controls about 35 per cent of household income.

There is no sign of this trend towards redistribution of household income reversing. In the early Nineties, the growth of upper-income households levelled out, although the growth in lower-income households continued apace. The trend need not be regarded as irreversible, of course, but the signs suggest that a new stratification of Australian society has occurred: the deed has been done. It remains to be seen how we will cope with the more sharply defined class distinctions which will emerge in the wake of such stark economic stratification. For an Australia which has become enchanted by the egalitarian dream, this will be a particularly painful process.

## WERE WE EVER EGALITARIAN?

The egalitarian dream was promoted by many Australian political leaders (especially Labor Party politicians) throughout the 20th century, but the conventional wisdom that we may actually have become a classless society is relatively recent.

Yet how conventional was that wisdom? While Australians collectively prided themselves on being a one-class (or, more correctly, a middle-class) society, individual Australians seemed very anxious to position themselves in some complex, unspoken socio-economic hierarchy—especially when it involved positioning other people beneath them. The Mackay Report on *Class & Status* (1986) suggested that Australians were conscious of very fine distinctions relating to social status: money was generally accepted as the index of 'class', but even among people living in a relatively homogeneous suburban street, private—and deeply satisfying—distinctions tended to be made between those who were house-proud, those who satisfactorily maintained the nature strip, those who parked 'bombs' in the front yard, those who had a microwave oven, a VCR *and* a dishwasher, those who 'spoke nicely', and so on. The evidence of that study suggested that Australians actually *wanted* a sense of social hierarchy: even within the broad mass of a self-described middle class, comfort was drawn from some unspoken sense of a pecking order.

Although Australians believed that there was a very small gap between the top and bottom of Australian society, they seemed to compensate for that by a quite astonishing sense of subtle superiorities and inferiorities within the social structure. As one respondent in the 1986 study put it: 'I suppose we do have an upper class and a lower class, but in between them you probably have about 43 variations.'

Nevertheless, by the 1970s, Australians had generally come to believe that the class structure in Australian society was much weaker than it had been and that class distinctions were much more subtle and hard to define. They explained their changing attitude to class and status in

terms of the generally higher standard of living which
Australians enjoyed in the years of post-war prosperity,
right up to the 1980s. It has been widely assumed that,
because the broad mass of Australians are able to acquire
most of the traditional trappings of status, so the idea of
social class has diminished. Even today, Australians cling
to the belief (increasingly contradicted by the facts) that,
because the general level of material status is so high, we
are less impressed by status than would have been the case
several generations ago. A typical Australian view, even up
to the end of the 1980s, would have been that, because we
are *all* so affluent, the class system that used to exist—
partly imported from the UK and partly home-grown—has
become irrelevant.

Australians identify a number of symptoms of the decline
of a sense of class: they believe that traditional authority
figures (bank managers, clergymen, professional people . . .
even the police) attract much less automatic respect than
they used to; they note the disappearance of signs on
domestic gates which said 'Tradesmen—back entrance';
graziers note that they now dine in the same restaurants
as the shearers who work on their property; women who
employ domestic help often form bonds of friendship with
the ironing lady or the cleaner—based on the idea of
equality.

Today, some of the earlier signs of class distinctions in
Australia are regarded as either laughable or offensive.
Executives of major corporations recall a time when clear
class distinctions were drawn between those who received
monthly and weekly salary and wage payments; when there
was a clear distinction between 'officers' and others in some
organisations; and when the school you attended was likely
to be a significant determinant of your employment

prospects in the upper levels of management.

Even at the height of egalitarian zeal, however, there was always one, undisputed, lower class in Australia: the Aboriginal population. However much Australians may have touted themselves as being committed to social justice and equality, lingering prejudice against Aborigines throughout the 1970s and 1980s clearly positioned them as 'the bottom of the heap' and reinforced the general view that, if there were a lower class in Australian society at that time, then it was populated by the homeless, the unemployed and the dispossessed. Aborigines were seen as the quintessential symbol of that state.

At the other extreme, Australians acknowledged that there were some extraordinarily wealthy people in the community, but the general community attitude towards them was that they were more to be pitied than envied. It is a commonly held view among Australians that extreme wealth is likely to be associated with unhappiness (and, perhaps, that such wealth would have been acquired through dishonesty or, at least, dubious business activity). Thus, although middle-class Australians from the Fifties onwards saw themselves as being on a constantly rising escalator of material prosperity, they never aspired to fabulous wealth. An important part of the egalitarian ideal of Australia was that, although individuals wanted to better their own position—and to take secret pride in their superiority over fellow inhabitants of the middle class—it was important not to get 'above yourself' or to achieve a level of prosperity which could be regarded as beyond the standard of a middle-class lifestyle. Home ownership, multiple car ownership, a house full of appliances, wall-to-wall carpets, regular holidays (increasingly incorporating interstate or overseas travel) and a serious commitment to leisure and recreation were regarded as the symbols of middle-class prosperity. The boundaries of the middle class were very elastic, but the underlying sense of egalitarianism restrained many Australians from wanting to appear flamboyant or *too* successful. (Marketing organisations testing ideas for prizes to be won in competitions generally found that a top-of-the-range Holden would be preferred to a Rolls Royce.)

So the egalitarian ideal contained many contradictions and complexities: but it certainly had a big impact on the socio-cultural evolution of post-war Australia. In essence, it allowed middle-class Australians to indulge their expectation of great material prosperity; it encouraged the middle class to 'act rich'; it gave strong materialistic underpinning to the idea of social equality and resistance to authority.

In other words, the egalitarianism of Australia in the second half of the 20th century was an egalitarianism based on the assumption of prosperity. More than simply implying that Australia would be a classless society, it really implied an Australian confidence that we would all be 'well off'. As Australia moves through the 1990s, that almost universal expectation of comfortable prosperity is breaking down into sharply contrasting alternative expectations. At the top end, prosperity is greater than could have been imagined 20 years ago; at the bottom end, the prospect of poverty is descending like a chill on those Australians who are living through the long night of unemployment.

## WILL WE HAVE AN UNDERCLASS?

The idea of an underclass has been alien to Australians who continue to embrace the egalitarian ideal. Even to those

Australians who have been striving to better themselves within the context of a broadly comfortable middle class, it has never seemed likely that significant numbers of Australians would fall off the affluence escalator and land in a poverty trap.

But that is precisely what has happened. Australians who have been able to speak airily of the underclass in American or British society will shortly have to face the fact that there is an underclass on their own doorsteps.

The Australian Council of Social Service reports that more than 600,000 children are living in a family where neither parent has employment. 'Unemployment,' says the ACOSS 1992 Budget submission, 'is the single greatest contributor to poverty in Australia.'

That theme is echoed in a 1992 study of homeless families commissioned by the Australian Institute of Family Studies and undertaken by Jean McCaughey. *The Australian* of 19 May 1992 reported Ms McCaughey's conclusion that more middle-class Australians are falling into the poverty trap as a direct result of long-term unemployment, and that middle-class families find it more difficult to cope with homelessness and poverty precisely because they have always had such confident expectations of a comfortable standard of living.

Charitable organisations report a dramatic increase in demand for their services from people who have found themselves unexpectedly confronting poverty. In Sydney, The Smith Family reported a 35 per cent increase in the number of people seeking assistance during 1991–92, and they estimated that 70 per cent of this increase came from families who had never previously had to seek charity.

A 1992 Salvation Army survey of more than 6,000 client families revealed that almost 10 per cent of those seeking assistance were home owners, and almost 15 per cent were in full-time employment.

Such data suggests that the conventional signs of membership of the Australian middle class are no longer necessarily valid: even people with a home and job may feel themselves being sucked down into poverty by the pressure of debt, or by an income level which cannot sustain a recognisably middle-class way of life.

In August 1992, *The Independent Monthly* quoted Professor Bob Gregory, economic historian and member of the Reserve Bank Board, as saying this: 'I don't think there's any doubt that if these trends continue, notions of an underclass will fit our society. The unemployed are relatively diffused in Australia at the moment, but because the disadvantaged move to—and group in—areas where rents are lowest, you will get underprivileged areas developing. There will be suburbs where you'll know not to walk at night.'

Gregory's bleak prediction is based on the emerging pattern of unemployment. In a submission to the Conference of Economics at Melbourne University in July 1992, he reported that, in the period from 1970 to 1990, one quarter of Australia's full-time male jobs had been eliminated—an attrition without precedent since the depression of the Thirties. Of full-time, non-managerial job opportunities opening up in that time, 70 per cent were taken by women. As we have already seen in Chapter 2.3, men conditioned to accept the idea of themselves as full-time breadwinners have to struggle to come to terms with any lesser view.

Gregory's point is that new jobs being created are generally less senior, less well paid and less permanent than the jobs which are disappearing. 'You can look at it in terms of a manufacturing business in Brunswick closing down, and a whole lot of full-time workers laid off,' he says. 'Then a McDonald's opens downs the road and hires a lot of young people to serve behind the counter. Next a Woolworths around the corner takes on a group of middle-aged ladies as part-time sales staff. The result, of course, is a net employment gain. But the manufacturing guys are still looking round for work, and in the end just don't get their jobs back.'

For people who have grown up in middle-class Australia and who have learned to expect that they will participate in an egalitarianism of affluence, it is a dreadful shock to find that the dream will not come true. For those who still sit comfortably in the shrinking middle class, there is no real awareness, yet, of the burgeoning lower-class beneath them: Australians who are economically secure are still inclined to sneer at people in poverty as if that is a state which they have chosen. Even as levels of unemployment rise, many older and more affluent Australians are inclined to blame young people for not getting a job; to attack unmarried mothers for having deliberately chosen a welfare-dependent way of life; to believe that the homeless are also hopeless.

As awareness of the size of the underclass grows, such complacency will presumably evaporate and a new sense of the starkness of Australia's dollar-driven social class divisions will emerge. Whether that will lead to a more compassionate sense of the needs of the total community, or a more defensive, self-protective sense of superiority among the affluent will be one of the more compelling social questions of the Nineties.

Unemployment is undoubtedly the primary cause of the rapid rise in the number of disadvantaged households in

Australia. A family which consists entirely of unemployed people is not simply facing a bleak economic prospect; it is a family which is learning to adjust to a new way of life which bears no relationship to the expectations of the Australian post-war middle class.

While Australians sometimes agonise over the apparent unfairness in a situation in which some families have two or more jobs while others have none, there is little real awareness of the poverty trap created for the unemployed children of unemployed parents. The role models, the diet, the means of passing the time, and the attitudes to money in such a household are so different from those of the middle and upper socio-economic strata that it is no longer possible to talk glibly about 'the Australian way of life'. Increasingly, it is necessary to acknowledge that there are many different 'ways of life' and that the increasingly unequal distribution of household income in Australia is opening up big cracks in the rosy picture of a comfortable, middle-class society.

Virtually all of the factors which have created The Age of Redefinition are subtly inter-connected. The redefinition of gender roles which led so directly to a redefinition of marriage and the family has also made its contribution to the widening gap between rich and poor in Australia. The phenomenon of the working wife has boosted household incomes at the top end of the economic ladder while, at the bottom end, the rising divorce rate has precipitated the downward economic spiral of many Australian households.

A divorce which does not involve some down-grading of the parties' level of prosperity is unusual. Some Australians are already speaking of divorce as 'a luxury we can't afford'. It generally involves the sub-division of a family's property into two households, both of which are less affluent than the pre-divorce household. For divorced mothers who have custody of their children, divorce can easily mean a dramatic slide down the economic heap, and an unexpected struggle to make ends meet, particularly if the children's father is unwilling, through bitterness or hostility, to accept continuing financial responsibility for children whom he may now be permitted to see only on alternate weekends.

Sole parents show up in disproportionately high numbers among those seeking assistance from welfare agencies and, even where a sole parent has employment, the shock of adjusting either to a lower income (among women who were previously relying on a higher income earned by their husbands) or a single income (among women who were previously contributing to a two-income household) can be devastating and debilitating. The sense of emotional liberation which the divorce may have been expected to achieve can be swamped all too easily by a sense of economic insecurity and oppression.

## A CHALLENGE TO COMPLACENCY

In the space of just 20 years, Australia has been through a breathtaking restructuring of the economic framework which generally determines social class. The speed of change has been so great that most Australians have not caught up with it, and the implications of having to adjust to a three-tiered society have been neither understood nor confronted.

The egalitarian myth persists. People who are now disadvantaged and may well be facing long-term poverty have not lost their sense of connection with more affluent strata of society. Vandalism, assault and other acts of violence against the affluent are telling signs that the expectation of participating in the middle-class dream remains intact. The people who forced a Sydney man to douse his new luxury car with petrol and then set fire to it explained to him that they were doing it because he was rich. If an underclass is emerging, then it is not going to go down without a struggle.

At the other extreme there are signs of dangerous social complacency among more affluent Australians. The tendency to blame the victim is alive and well; although the recession may have dampened some of the more strident and flamboyant expressions of affluence, upper-class Australians are as anxious as ever to improve and protect their financial position with little or no thought for the consequences of the rising tide of poverty around them. Wealthy Australian individuals and corporations have not increased their giving to charitable organisations to any marked degree: the ideal of Australia as an egalitarian society quickly evaporates when equality involves a sharing of scarce and diminishing resources rather than a sharing in affluence and prosperity.

The redefinition of social class which is likely to flow from the current restructuring of household incomes will lead to some ugly consequences. Urban violence is likely to increase through the 1990s, as a direct response to economic inequality. Rich Australians will become increasingly concerned with the protection of their property: luxury cars will not be casually parked in the street; compound suburbs will begin to emerge; the home security industry will boom; affluent Australians will carefully avoid 'no-go' areas in our major cities; elitism will develop.

At the lower end of the social scale, the desire for a stronger sense of social identity and cohesion may well lead to greater hostility towards the affluent as class enemies; to the organisation of more street gangs; to increasingly militant demands for better welfare provision; to a growing appetite for the instruments of escape—entertainment, drugs, violence, crime.

Australia is approaching a significant crossroads on the question of social class. Are we to accept that the redistribution of household income has some economic inevitability about it and that we will slip inexorably into a renewed recognition of social class? Are we to assume that the underclass will retire, with gentility and acquiescence, into a subservient role—perhaps leading to the re-emergence of a 'servant class'? Are we to decide that a massive increase in welfare support is required—with a correspondingly massive increase in personal taxation on the affluent? Will we decide, instead, that lower personal tax will provide an incentive for more wealth-creation and that this will provide a trickle-down benefit to the whole community? Will we make a concerted attempt to revive or create those industries which could significantly reduce unemployment and rescue the underclass from economic oblivion? Will we restructure the labour market so that available work is redeployed? The questions which arose at the end of Chapter 2.3 arise again here.

All of these questions represent a potential field day for social engineers, and for political philosophers. But unless such questions are addressed as a matter of urgency, the egalitarian dream will have evaporated and Australia will have to confront again the implications of an institutionalised class structure. Whatever the economic facts may be, and however much Australians might wish to make private judgments about their own status in relation to others, the strong underlying belief in egalitarianism persists. If that belief is to be dented or abandoned, that will represent one of our most radical redefinitions of ourselves.

## THE STORY OF FRANCES

☐ When I lived in the bush, I never turned on an electric light until I got married. We always wanted our own home and we worked towards that and finally got it. I suppose, looking back, we were quite poor, but we never thought of ourselves as lower class—not at all. In fact, thinking about it, I think we had our values straight in those days. We didn't rely on a lot of material things to bring us happiness, and I think my parents did a very good job of instilling discipline into me. We were always well dressed and well spoken . . . we knew we were not as rich as some of the graziers in our district, but that never really worried you.

At the same time, we were conscious of some really down-and-out kind of people . . . mostly Aborigines who used to come into town and get drunk and hang around in the parks. But, mostly, we thought we were pretty much the same as everyone else.

How things have changed! My kids think that they have to have everything. When my daughter got married, she expected to move into a lovely home straight away and have everything that opens and shuts. It sort of seemed as if she and her husband were trying to out-shine us, and I felt a bit sad about it.

I suppose the truth is that they are wealthier than we have ever been. They both work, and they seem to go overseas at least once a year . . . my husband and I have never done that.

At least we are better off than a lot of those snobby

type of people who get themselves into heavy debt just to keep up with each other. Boats seem to be the latest thing . . . first it was two cars, and now it is two cars and a boat. There's even a bit of that kind of thing going on around here, with dirty great boats stuck out the front of people's houses.

Basically, I think we live a pretty middle-class type of life, but I have to admit that, when you look at our street, you'd have to say that there are a lot of shades of 'middle'. Even when the kids were growing up there were some houses that you didn't want them to visit, and others where you were perfectly happy for them to go. I suppose that, in a way, it's a kind of class distinction, but it's more to do with forming little cliques of people who lead the same kind of life and share the same kind of values. It's not that you necessarily feel superior or inferior to other people, but you are conscious of being different from them. I mean, if you go down to the RSL, you are expected to be interested in football. If you are not, there's not much point in going down there—it's not a question of whether you are on the one level or another, but just what you are interested in. Although . . . I suppose we have always felt superior to *some* people, to be honest.

Australians are really quite funny about class, aren't they? We all say that we don't have an upper class or a lower class and yet we attach so much importance to money and the things that money will buy. I sometimes think it all comes back to money. I'm sure my daughter and her husband think that they have moved up a class, but it is only that they are wealthier. I am a lot wealthier than my parents were, too, but I didn't think that made me any better than they were.

I don't know where all this unemployment is going to lead us, though. If a lot of people really can't get a job, I guess that is going to change things a bit. You can't pretend you are middle class if you are on welfare, or if you have to go and get a loaf of bread from the Salvation Army handout. I think a lot of crime and violence is caused by the fact that there are more poor people in our society than there used to be and they are angry about the fact that they don't seem to be able to do anything about it.

I feel sorry for them. But, in another way, I feel even more sorry for the people who have a lot of money and think they are better than anyone else. You never used to find that in Australia, but you do find a lot of people putting on airs and graces these days, just because they live in big houses or can afford to drive Volvos and things. On the other hand, there is a bit of a shake-out going on, isn't there? In the country town where I grew up, the farmers' wives are working in shops in town now, to help make ends meet. That would have been unheard of in my day.

It's all very confusing, isn't it? It's not like England where everyone seems to know what class they are in and they just stick to it. Here, we have grown up with the idea that everyone can be prosperous and we don't have rigid class distinctions. But you still have this sneaking feeling about it . . . I know this sounds awful, but there are some very wealthy migrants around here and I would never think of them as being upper-class. So I suppose there is more to it than money. But perhaps, in another generation or two, their kids really will be in a different class from us.

People say that Australia is a classless society and I

want to believe it, but I don't really think it's true—not anymore.

The thing I notice is that some people are going up and some are going down. Previously, you used to feel that we were all pretty much on one level and that anyone who wanted to succeed could do so. I don't think it's so easy any more, and I don't like the way things are going.□

# 2.6

# ARE WE ALL NEW
# AUSTRALIANS?

Australians have entered a period of anxiety about what it means to be Australian.

The redefinition of gender roles by women has probably had more impact on the *personal* well-being of Australians than any other factor in the Age of Redefinition. The effect of unemployment has been correspondingly severe in its impact on Australians' *economic* well-being. But, underlying the personal and individual stress which Australians suffer as they adapt to life in the Age of Redefinition is a widespread sense of anxiety about our *cultural* identity.

Strong community response to the emerging push for a more independent sense of Australian nationhood (possibly evolving into republicanism) reflects anxiety in the Australian community about changes in the racial composition of the Australian population, about appropriate levels of migration, about the long-term consequences of multiculturalism and about Australia's relationship with the rest of the world—especially Asia.

Australians accept that this is a nation of immigrants and that, particularly since World War II, it has been an increasingly multiracial society. It would be hard not to accept the multiracial character of the Australian community: after all, 23 per cent of all Australian residents were born overseas and, among people born in Australia, 25 per cent have at least one parent born overseas. Fourteen per cent of Australian residents speak a language other than English at home.

In Sydney, which has always been the primary destination for immigrants, 30 per cent of residents were not born in Australia and a further 20 per cent have at least one overseas-born parent. In Sydney, almost a quarter of the population report that they speak a language other than English at home.

It's no wonder that anxiety about the racial composition of Australia, and about the whole question of Australia's cultural identity, is higher in Sydney than in the rest of the country. But it is still a widespread concern: multiracialism is something which Australians understand and accept as a demographic reality of the Australian way of life; multiculturalism, on the other hand, is something about which they are still reserving their judgment.

## MIGRANTS ARE WELCOME IF...

As a multiracial society, Australians have been remarkably hospitable towards migrants. There have always been outbreaks of racial prejudice against the latest wave—whether Greeks, Italians, Yugoslavs, Turks or Vietnamese—but the traditional Australian attitude towards migrants is that they have come here to become part of the Australian way of life and that, accordingly, they should be assimilated as quickly as possible. Long-standing Australian attitudes towards migration are easily identified:

Migrants are welcome, as long as they are prepared to embrace the Australian way of life and its values;

Migrants are welcome as long as they make the learning of the English language a top priority;

Migrants are welcome as long as they are not robbing Australians of jobs and other opportunities (including educational opportunities);

Migrants are welcome as long as they leave their own racial and cultural tensions behind, and do not import prejudices and conflict into the Australian culture;

Migrants are welcome as long as they are largely assimilated (with some tolerance for the preservation of 'quaint' ethnic customs and behaviour);

Migrants are welcome as long as the culture they import (especially their food) enriches our culture and is accessible to us;

Migrants are welcome as long as they do not lower the Australian standard of living (by imposing too much strain on our urban infrastructure, or on our welfare system).

The important underlying theme in those attitudes is that Australians have long regarded assimilation as being the key to a successful immigration program. They have assumed that migrants wanting to come to Australia have been attracted by the Australian way of life, and they have therefore taken it for granted that migrants would want to enter into that way of life as quickly as possible. The idea that migrants would want to 'stand off' from Australian society has seemed like a contradiction of their desire to come here: Australians have been particularly perplexed by any signs of ethnic enclaves which have suggested an aloofness from the rest of the Australian community.

Indeed, more racially prejudiced Australians have felt that 'if anyone is going to erect barriers, it should be us', as though it is peculiarly offensive for immigrants to establish a state of separateness from the host community.

Australians' attitudes towards immigration, even when benign, have generally been egocentric and one-sided: they have been conscious of their own difficulties in accommodating people who are racially and culturally different from themselves, but they have rarely spent much time contemplating the difficulties faced by immigrants in trying to comprehend and adapt to the Australian culture. The typical Australian view is that migrants have, by definition, committed themselves to a process of adaptation and that it is they who should be making the primary effort to adjust: there is little currency for the idea that because Australia actively sought its migrants, local communities might therefore have a responsibility to help them adapt.

In effect, the traditional Australian attitude towards migrants is that they should become as invisible as possible, as quickly as possible. Assimilation has, in effect, meant homogenisation, and the term 'New Australians' which came into vogue in the Fifties and Sixties was a term which Australians enjoyed using because it implied that the goal of immigration was assimilation and that migrants would place their new-found Australian identity ahead of the ethnic context from which they had come.

From the migrants' point of view, of course, becoming Australianised is not half as easy as Australians might think or wish. The idea of deliberately shedding a cultural heritage is neither attractive nor realistic and, even among

the majority of immigrants who take up Australian citizen-
ship, the sense of 'belonging' to the home country remains
strong. Confirming Australians' worst fears, many
migrants who settle in Australia discover that they do not
experience strong emotional attraction to the Australian
way of life and often find that they are, indeed, consciously
dissociating themselves from it. The Mackay Report on *The
Multiculture* (1985) confirmed a widespread suspicion in
Australia that migrants do sometimes feel superior to the
Australians they meet. Migrants take pride in their cultural
heritage, their close family ties, their educational qualifications, their capacity for hard work and the quality of their
parenting: on all these grounds, migrants will quite often
come to believe that they compare very favourably with
Australians.

Of course, Australians concede some of this. Those who
are coping with the stress of divorce and the restructuring
of blended or step-families may look wistfully at the families
of Greek, Italian or Asian migrants who, it is generally
believed, pay more attention to the extended family and
have a greater commitment to the stability of family life
than Australians do. (Indeed, 1986 Census data confirms
that married people of Southern European or Asian ances-
try separate and divorce to an extent well below the
Australian average.)

Similarly, Australians readily concede that migrants are
often more industrious than Australians; more ambitious
for their children's education; more committed to establishing a sound financial footing in their new country.

But such admiration will sometimes be tinged with envy
or even resentment: Australians are very quick to accuse
migrants of 'rorting the system' by tax evasion, by abuse
of welfare provisions, or by operating exclusively in the cash

economy. The parents of Australian students who are competing against Asian students at school will sometimes take refuge in the prejudice that Asian students are too single-mindedly committed to achieving good exam results, without engaging sufficiently in other facets of the social, sporting and cultural life of the school.

In one respect, Australians are very welcoming of migrants and of the multiracial influence on Australian culture: the addition of ethnic food to the Australian diet has been widely regarded as one of the most pleasant manifestations of the influence of migrants on the Australian way of life. But there is a very big difference between embracing ethnic food as a symbol of cultural diversity and actually embracing the substance of multiculturalism itself.

Multiculturalism is still a relatively new and uncomfortable concept for the Australian community. The switch from thinking that it was the host community's responsibility to encourage the assimilation of migrants to the contemporary concept of encouraging ethnicity is a very big switch indeed. Now that 'assimilation' has become a dirty word, such a switch raises deep questions about the Australian identity because it calls on Australians to redefine their long-standing concept of what an Australian is, and their long-cherished stereotypes, myths and legends about the Australian character, the Australian style and the Australian ethos. Older Australians may speak with pride of the Australian pioneer, the Australian soldier, or the Australian sports-star, but such references rarely accommodate the notion of ethnic diversity. (Of course, the cultural redefinition being experienced by Australians in the mid-90s is as nothing compared with the cultural upheavals of eastern Europe, and yet it is probably true that Australia is alone among Western societies in the boldness of its multicultural initiatives.)

There seems little doubt that one reason for Australians' current reservations about the concept of multiculturalism is their perception that the racial balance of migration is shifting markedly towards Asian migrants and away from the traditional European sources of Australia's immigrants.

The reality is that about four per cent of Australians were born in Asia. If the present trends in immigration were maintained, the proportion could rise to about seven per cent by the year 2021, according to *Australia's Population Trends and Prospects* (1990, Australian Government Printing Service). But the *perception* of the level of Asian migration is much higher than this—a perception which is possibly influenced by the visual evidence of large numbers of Asian tourists as well as Asian migrants themselves.

Australians' resistance to Asian migration is easy to understand, given their well-established pattern of attitudes towards migration. Asians are seen as being physically so different from Europeans as to make their assimilation difficult; their cultural heritage is assumed to be quite unlike that of traditional Australian racial groups; their religious beliefs are scarcely understood; their attitude towards Australians is felt to be aloof and ungiving (often on the basis of the prejudiced stereotype of 'inscrutable' Asian countenances).

It is the perception of a fast-growing Asian immigrant population that has most sorely tested Australians' willingness to embrace the idea of positively encouraging ethnic diversity. When confronted with an ethnic and cultural group which is regarded as being so obviously different from the Australian mainstream, Australians begin to wonder whether their multiculturalism can extend this far.

They revive the fear that Australia may become a number of separate cultures within one society, to an extent which will inevitably lead to tensions and conflicts.

It is by no means only Asian migrants which stimulate such concern. Religious minorities are the focus of similar doubts about the wisdom of multiculturalism: many Australians believe that the growing Muslim community represents a threat to the harmony of Australian society because its values and customs are so different from those of the host community.

The fundamental reservation which Australians have about multiculturalism is that, by encouraging the mainstream of ethnicity among migrants, Australia might also be encouraging the maintenance of socially undesirable influences which spring from ancient tensions, conflicts and even hatreds within and between ethnic communities now represented in Australia.

For example, Australians take great exception to signs of conflict between Serbs and Croats in Australia, on the grounds that, by having chosen to migrate to Australia, such ethnic groups should be prepared to bury their traditional differences in the interests of building up the unity of the Australian nation.

It is a widespread prejudice in the Australian community—apparently unsupported by crime statistics—that Turks and Vietnamese are peculiarly pre-disposed towards violent behaviour, simply because of their cultural heritage. Even when it comes to British migrants, Australians will often express the attitude that, particularly among trade union officials, British migrants have brought class prejudices with them which do not easily fit into Australian society and which create undue tension and conflict.

## NOSTALGIA: A FORM OF RACIAL PREJUDICE?
## OR AN URGE TO CLARIFY OUR ROOTS?

Resistance to multiculturalism is based on the strong residual feeling among Australians that migrants *should* be assimilated and that, when they show signs of clinging to ethnic and cultural values and behaviour which vary significantly from the Australian norm, this represents a threat to the harmony and integrity of the Australian way of life. Australians want to believe that being an Australian should imply something more than simply living here: the notion of *shared culture* seems fundamental to any concept of an identifiable society. Although Australians are now beginning to talk more easily about the idea of a multicultural society, they are still very defensive and very anxious about the idea that the Australian cultural identity is up for grabs.

In the short term, Australians are taking refuge either in racial prejudice or in a kind of cultural nostalgia. At a time when it is hard for them to define the contemporary Australian identity, and even harder to anticipate the nature of Australian culture in the next century, it is tempting to look back: the resurgence of interest in and support for Anzac Day in the early 1990s is at least partly a reflection of an Australian desire to capture the sense of a cultural identity which has for so long been missing from the Australian consciousness. Contemporary celebrations of Anzac Day have very little to do with Gallipoli: increasingly, they express a desire to recognise Australia's unique heritage and to create a vehicle for communicating that heritage to young Australians and, indeed, to newly-arrived Australians.

Growing emphasis on the idea of celebrating Australia Day springs from a similar desire to ensure that the

Australian identity will not be so diffused by multiculturalism as to lose any meaning at all.

Another manifestation of the same desire is the strong pressure building up in the Australian community to have a more open and serious debate about Australia's whole approach to migration. Under the influence of the recession of 1991–92, Australians feel they have an economic justification for raising questions about the level and composition of Australia's migrant intake, but the economic justification is partly a smokescreen: furtive debate about the whole question of migration and multiculturalism has been taking place for years. Australians recognise that it is very easy to be branded 'racist' when debating the subject of migration and multiculturalism, and they note with some horror the hostility which was directed at such public figures as Geoffrey Blainey and John Howard when they attempted to open up the migration debate in the late 1980s.

Under the influence of the recession, there is growing support for the idea that, when it comes to migration, 'enough is enough': this mood reflects an attitude that Australia has been very tolerant, very welcoming and very open to the idea of multiracialism and even multiculturalism—up to a point. Because Australians believe that the poor state of the economy does legitimately raise questions about our migrant intake, they believe that the time has come to explore other facets of the question as well.

The mid-1990s may well see a temporary backlash against multiculturalism. Australians are resentful of what they perceive as their inability to participate in an open debate about the racial and cultural composition of Australian society, and, almost regardless of what decisions might be made about the level and composition of migration, there are signs of a strong desire to return to a policy of assimilation.

To some extent, that desire is simply another expression of frustration about the pressures and instabilities of life in the Age of Redefinition. The reality is that Australia has taken enormous strides in the direction of becoming a multicultural society and that, contrary to Australians' own worst fears about themselves, the level of prejudice and racial violence in the Australian community is remarkably low by world standards. It is, after all, only a matter of 25 years since Australia officially abandoned its White Australia policy and, as Gerard Henderson pointed out in a 1992 *Time* essay, multicultural Australia is a place 'where ideological belief tends to dissipate'. Henderson also remarked that 'intermarriage statistics are perhaps the best gauge for determining the success of multiculturalism' and noted that, against that criterion, Australia has done the work of integration very well.

Nevertheless, multiculturalism stands as an important symbol of Australia's current uncertainties and insecurities. The idea of 'One Nation' seems to many Australians to be at odds with their current understanding of the concept of multiculturalism. As we move through the Nineties, there is bound to be growing tension about this question: Australians will continue to wish that ethnic minorities could attach more importance to their Australian identity, and ethnic minorities will continue to wish that Australians could be more tolerant of the idea of a diverse cultural heritage.

Clearly, both sides of the multicultural debate will have to recognise that the only real tension on the subject of multiculturalism concerns the level of commitment to the ideal of Australian nationhood. Australians want migrants to become Australians first, and to let their ethnic origins recede before that commitment; migrants, for their part, want Australians to accept not only that the emerging Australian cultural identity *is* diverse and is all the richer for that, but also that migrants want to be part of the new emerging Australian identity. The challenge, for both sides, is to isolate the common ground which will define an underlying unity in our diversity. (See Chapter 4.3, 'Back to the Tribe'.)

In his *Time* essay, Gerard Henderson quoted the Australian rules football coach, Kevin Sheedy, discussing the addition of a player of Aboriginal heritage to the existing racial and cultural mix of his team: 'We've got Irish people, we've got Catholics, we've got Germans. What matters is that the bloke can get the ball.' In fact, football is one area where Australians are quick to accept people from diverse ethnic backgrounds as long as they accept the shared values of the game, and a uniquely Australian sense of identity. After all, long-standing prejudice against Aborigines did not prevent general acceptance of Mal Meninga as Australia's Rugby League captain, and the Wallabies seem to have done rather well with a couple of blokes called Campese and Carozza. (Soccer, by contrast, has often been criticised as a sport which encourages the perpetuation of ethnic diversity at the expense of a shared Australian identity.)

As with so many other social and cultural accommodations which Australians are being asked to make in the last quarter of the twentieth century, the multicultural accommodation is being made on the run: the call to stop and reconsider our migration policy is just another symptom of the widespread desire in the Australian community to slow down the rate of change and to take time to consider what kind of Australia we really want. Unfortunately for all concerned, the luxury of being able to take time to explore such questions seems not to be available: as usual, our attitudes and values will evolve in the wake of changes in our social and cultural environment and, in the end, we will come to realise that we are *all* being assimilated into a new culture. Perhaps we are all going to be New Australians.

## THE STORY OF GEORGE

☐ I remember the first time my wife tried to fob me off with a plate of spaghetti. I couldn't believe she was serious. We always had meat and two or three vegetables for dinner, and it took me a long time to get used to it. The same thing with garlic . . .

When I was a young bloke, there were a lot of Greeks and Italians at our school. My father used to call them reffos, but I don't think anyone thought that was too dreadful. We had to call them New Australians, which sounded a bit artificial, but we went along with it.

These days, it's a totally different scene. They reckon the Aussie kids at school are called 'skips' now . . . I suppose it's after Skippy on the TV. So it's wogs and skips and slopes . . . Look at the names of some of the football players—it's getting to be like America, where half the names are Italian or some other foreign-sounding names. I suppose that's fair enough. We need to build up our population, and we had to do it through migration. And they have brought a lot of changes to the Australian way of life—food is just one of them.

But I do think you have to draw the line somewhere. Most other countries seem to be a bit fussier than we are about who they let in. I know you have to take your share of refugees and boat people and that, but I am a bit worried about some of these Turks and Yugoslavs. People from some of those countries bring an enormous amount of conflict with them—you can see it in the soccer. We shouldn't allow that kind of thing in Australia—if they come to Australia, they should learn to live like Australians. We don't want to end up like Lebanon.

No country that has tried to create a mixture of different races has ever done so without a lot of tension and strife. If we are going to Asianise Australia, there will be big trouble ahead. But we don't seem to be doing anything to stop it. You have got places like Cabramatta which are really like a Vietnamese community where Australians feel unwelcome. On the other hand, you have got these wealthy Chinese coming in from Hong Kong and places, pulling down nice Australian homes and putting up these great big mansions. The local councils don't seem to be doing anything to stop them.

Imagine if we tried to go to some of these other countries and do what they do here. You wouldn't be allowed to get away with it. That's what I mean . . . we might be too easy-going.

I realise that you can't turn the clock back, but I reckon we should be thinking much more seriously about how many more migrants we want, and where we want them to come from. Aren't we entitled to do that? Of course, if you say anything about it, you are in danger of being labelled a racist, but I think a lot of Australians feel the same way as I do.

Perhaps I'm just particularly conscious of it where I live. This used to be a typical Australian suburban street.

Now there are only three Australian families and the rest are Asian. There are about 20 of them in the house next door, and they have 13 cars and two trucks between them. It's destroyed our street, but we just let it happen.

You have to ask yourself whose country it's becoming. This has been basically a European country until now— apart from the Aborigines, of course. There's all this talk about how we are really part of Asia, but that is a pretty big leap, if you ask me. It will be a long time before we *feel* Asian, if we ever do. Can't we trade with them and everything, without feeling as if we have to become an Asian country? With all this republican business, you want to be sure that you don't start kow-towing to the Asians, just because you have stopped kow-towing to the British.

I do think they should all be made to learn to speak English and I don't think they should be allowed to put signs up on shops in a foreign language. This is our bloody country, after all, and you can't read the signs on half the shops round some parts of Melbourne.□

# POINT OF ORDER!

Australians have never been famous for the esteem in which they have held their politicians. A quick glance through some back copies of *The Bulletin* or *Smith's Weekly* reveals a long history of cynicism about the integrity, quality and vision of players on the Australian political stage.

The cynicism of the mid-1990s, however, is rather more than a simple extension of what has gone before. Today, Australians are trying to come to terms with the fact that the nature of politics itself has been redefined, and the level of cynicism in the community is now so high that the demand for some redefinition of our political institutions has become one of the factors fuelling the debate about the possibility of Australia becoming a republic.

The level of anxiety about politics in Australia seems to have risen largely because of a growing sense in the community that the two-party system has either lost its way, or, perhaps, lost its point. The story of the past 20 years has been one of blurred distinctions between the major parties; of parties' policies being stolen from each other; of political philosophy being largely replaced by pragmatism and the politics of personality.

Nineteen seventy-two was a critical year in the trans-formation of contemporary Australian politics. Following 23 years of uninterrupted Liberal/Country Party (later National Party) supremacy, Gough Whitlam swept the Australian Labor Party into Government on the basis of a widely-accepted proposition that it was time for a change. Whitlam's strategy had been to broaden the base of ALP support in the community by appealing directly to white collar employees. He effectively re-positioned the Labor Party as a party which could embrace the values and ideals of the Australian middle class (without losing its blue collar links to the trade union movement), and he also successfully appealed to an emerging sense of nationalism.

Whitlam came to power as an almost messianic figure. After a succession of make-do Liberal prime ministers following Menzies, Australia was badly in need of some new inspiration and a new sense of vision: Labor under Whitlam promised all that and more.

Three years later, following a constitutional crisis, the Whitlam Government was unceremoniously dumped. But the impact of the Whitlam strategy and the Whitlam style on Australian politics has been far greater than the specific achievements of that Labor Government might suggest. By blurring the traditional distinctions between Labor and Liberal policy, and by so successfully destabilising traditional voting patterns in the Australian electorate, Whitlam transformed the political agenda.

Before 1972, the pollsters' rule of thumb was that about five per cent of the Australian electorate were swinging voters. By the early 1990s, it was probably safer to assume that about 30 per cent of the electorate could change their vote from election to election or, at least, experience genuine uncertainty about how they might vote next time.

Before 1972, it was possible for Australians to describe quite easily the philosophies and broad policy directions of the two major parties. Since Whitlam, those traditional distinctions have been much harder to draw, and the links between the major parties and their traditional power bases have been much less stable or certain. While it is true that trade union support for Labor can be generally assumed, trade union influence is in decline. On the other side of the fence, the traditional support for the conservative parties in the business community has been significantly eroded, and the pattern of corporate donations to party funds reveals the extent to which business no longer gives automatic allegiance to the Liberal Party.

Before 1972, it was generally assumed that the party and its policies were more significant in the political process than the charisma or style of party leaders. Rather like their support for football teams, Australians tended to support political parties, regardless of who happened to be wearing the team's jersey this season, or who happened to be captain. Since Whitlam, however, that has all changed: along with the blurring of distinctions between the parties' policies has come the overwhelming emphasis on the personal style of party leaders. By the 1980s, it was possible for Labor to campaign in the NSW State election on the basis of the slogan, 'Wran's our Man'.

## THE RISE OF 'PERSONALITY POLITICS'

Like Whitlam, Bob Hawke was the classic example of a 'charismatic' politician. Unlike Whitlam, however, Hawke's rise to power was based almost exclusively on his personal style rather than policy. (Indeed, as his first election campaign as Leader of the Labor Party drew to a close, he backed further and further away from specific policy commitments, taking refuge in the idea that policies would emerge under the influence of his new consensual approach to politics.) His period as Prime Minister was marked by an apparently deliberate lack of political vision:

the politics of consensus virtually precluded the possibility of erecting any clear philosophical signposts. And yet, Bob Hawke's personal popularity with the Australian electorate rose to record levels at the very time when the general feeling of esteem for politics and the general level of faith in the political process was sinking lower and lower. Bob Hawke was the consummate politician of the 'trust me' school: his popularity depended upon the sense of a direct, personal relationship between him and the Australian people which had little, if anything, to do with political philosophy or even with political performance. Hawke became a presidential figure who finally convinced himself—and many of his colleagues—that it was his personal charm and magnetism which would ensure Labor's continuing success at the polls.

The paradox of Bob Hawke's prime ministership was exquisite: while the electorate continued to enjoy a kind of mass love affair with their Prime Minister, their anxiety about the nature and quality of Australian politics increased. One implication of this was that, when they finally began to tire of Hawke, they could see no *political* reason for him to stay on as Prime Minister: their support for him had been almost entirely *personal*.

Because support for Hawke was so uni-dimensional (being based on feelings of affection for the man, rather than respect or support for his policies), Hawke was always a vulnerable figure. The declining vote for Hawke Labor in successive elections told the story of that vulnerability, and yet Labor held office partly because of a very sophisticated campaign strategy directed at swinging voters in marginal seats. Although that strategy continued to deliver a parliamentary majority, it ran the serious risk of failing to reinforce the loyalties of the party faithful and led to the situation where, because of a failure to shore up the Labor vote in safe Labor electorates, there was a decline in overall support for Labor which was not, however, reflected in parliamentary seats.

Quite apart from the skill of the party strategists who served him, Hawke was also an extremely lucky politician because, for most of his Prime Ministership, he was faced with a divided and uncertain Opposition.

In 1987, when it appeared that John Howard would have no difficulty in replacing Hawke, Howard was seriously undermined by the Joh-for-Canberra push on behalf of the Queensland Premier, Sir Joh Bjelke-Petersen, and by bitter divisions within his own Party as the unresolved leadership rivalry between Howard and Andrew Peacock played itself out.

John Howard has been, in many ways, a politician swimming against the tide of personality politics. The widespread support for Howard—particulary in NSW—is based on the feeling that he is a man of integrity and conviction. At a time when it has been difficult for Australians to know what their political leaders actually stand for, Howard has tended to discuss issues and to develop political philosophy to an unfashionable extent. His reward has been to be elevated to the status of elder statesman in the minds of many Australians, but to have consistently missed out on the top job. And yet, for many Australians, Howard symbolises Australian politics as they would prefer it to be played: a politician whose convictions exceed his charisma, and who appears to prefer debating the issues to playing the man.

But, in 1989, John Howard was replaced as Liberal leader by Andrew Peacock; a politician who, his Party no doubt believed, had more of the personal style thought necessary to win elections in the era of post-ideological politics.

Along with personality politics, this has become the age of pragmatic politics. Political leaders themselves are rarely prepared to suggest that there are philosophies or policies which are peculiarly suited to their own parties. Indeed towards the end of the 1980s, a curious alliance developed between Labor's Bob Hawke and the then NSW Liberal Premier, Nick Greiner, based on their shared conviction that we had entered the era of 'post-ideological politics'; an era in which politics would come to be seen as having more to do with management and a reaction to unfolding events than with philosophy, vision or a sense of political conviction.

## BLURRING THE PARTY DISTINCTIONS

Against this background, it has become difficult to get Australians to describe how they think a change of government would make any significant difference to the way the country is run. It is difficult to find much conviction in the Australian electorate that party politics really mean much any more. It is hard to get young Australians excited about politics, because the lack of any clear sense of political direction in the major parties has led to a deepening cynicism in the community. That cynicism has been further fuelled by the Australian Democrats' founder, Don Chipp, and their subsequent leaders, positioning the Democrats as the party that would 'keep the bastards honest'—with the clear implication that, to those in the know, the major parties *are* bastards who *need* to be kept honest.

Even when, in 1991–92, the major parties issued comprehensive economic and political manifestos, the community remained unconvinced and its level of cynicism remained high. In the case of the Liberals' Fightback and Labor's One Nation economic statements (or 'packages' as they were frequently described), this cynicism was partly due to the complexity and inaccessibility of the documents themselves, but it was also partly due to the fact that they bore catchy brand names which seemed almost to trivialise their contents. What could 'Fightback' possibly mean, in simple policy terms? And was 'One Nation' a genuine proposal for producing a more cohesive Australia, or was it a catchphrase?

To some extent, the major parties' attempt to present comprehensive economic policy statements to the electorate in the early 1990s was a reflection of the fact that both Federal leaders at the time—Keating and Hewson—were inspiring so little confidence and trust that the parties were forced to push the policy line rather than the personality line. But by creating such complex packages, and by giving them the equivalent of brand names, the strategy seemed to backfire: far from differentiating the two parties, the Fightback/One Nation contest seemed only to blur the distinctions between them even further. Even when the voters identified the goods & services tax (GST) as an apparently distinctive feature of Liberal policy, they recalled that they had first heard about a GST from Paul Keating as a Labor Treasurer—further emphasising that policy distinctions between the parties are difficult to sustain.

## THE RETREAT FROM COMMITMENT

All of this has been watched by the electorate with a jaundiced eye. Personality politics may be fun, but there is a growing sense in the Australian community that there should be more to politics than this. Widespread anxiety about the state of politics in Australia is based on an uneasy feeling that, if the parties are not going to stand for some identifiable philosophy, and leaders are going to be chosen on the basis of their potential as television performers or even as head-kickers, then the only appropriate response is cynicism.

That cynicism is reflected in a turning-away from support for the major parties. In the 1990 Federal election, almost 20 percent of primary votes were cast in favour of candidates not representing the two major parties. Support for independent candidates continues to exceed the predictions of most political pundits, and surveys by Irving Saulwick & Associates tell the story of eroding public support for the Labor *and* Liberal parties.

In April 1992, the highly-respected Saulwick Poll reported that only 28 per cent of Australian voters were confident of Labor's ability to govern well, and only 34 per cent said they were confident of the Liberal and National Parties' ability to do so. Similar uncertainty was revealed by a Newspoll survey, published in July 1992, which showed that, when asked to nominate Keating or Hewson as preferred Prime Minister, 30 per cent of respondents felt so uncommitted as to choose neither.

An earlier Saulwick Poll mined the same vein of disillusionment when it revealed that a quarter of the electorate would prefer to vote for an independent candidate or a minor party rather than for one of the major political parties.

All of this is a clear demonstration of anxiety, instability and uncertainty which results from a redefinition of something as significant as the character of our major political parties. The swing away from policy in favour of personality has inevitably led to uncertainty in the electorate. The belief that leaders are pragmatists rather than philosophers not only fuels voters' cynicism, but also makes the distinctions between them much harder to define. The current low level of confidence in the political process is reflected in voters' lack of confidence in their ability to make sensible judgments about political parties and about politicians.

The level of cynicism about politics and political institutions in Australia is most starkly revealed in the attitudes of young Australians who are approaching the age when they will be entitled to vote. Typically, teenagers find little to interest or inspire them in the political process, and they often report that politics is the most boring subject ever discussed at home. They claim that they can't see the point in voting and that, once they are entitled to vote, they will find it hard to crank up much interest or concern.

Of course, the experience of actually voting has some impact on the political attitudes of young people: it is easier to remain aloof from the process and uninterested in it when you are not being called upon to vote. Nevertheless, the level of apathy about politics and about the obligation to be entered on the electoral roll is sufficiently disturbing for the Electoral Commission to feel the need to undertake, from time to time, advertising campaigns which are designed to 'sell' young Australians on the virtues of voting. In a country where voting is compulsory, that is a remarkable recognition of the failure of the political process to fire young imaginations.

Young Australians—like their elders—would like to feel that there is some inspiration to be found in politics, but they search for it in vain.

## WHY DID LABOR WIN IN 1993?

The 1993 Federal election was a model case of how voters
are likely to behave in the Age of Redefinition. It was a
striking example of how widespread the lack of commitment to either major party has become, and a demonstration of the fact that, in such circumstances, it is
*uncommitted* voters who, when they finally resolve their
indecision, are likely to determine the outcome of an
election by opting for the status quo.

Of course, the fact that the· Australian electorate
returned an incumbent government to office in 1993 could
be seen as nothing more than the maintenance of a long-
standing Australian electoral pattern. Since the newborn
Liberal Party, under Menzies, wrested government from
Chifley Labor in 1949, Australia has elected an opposition
to government on only two occasions: Whitlam Labor in
1972 and Hawke Labor in 1983. (The Liberal-led Coalition
of Malcolm Fraser might also have been elected to government from opposition in 1975 but, as things turned out,
it was already installed by the Governor-General *before* the
election.)

Clearly, in contemporary Australian politics, the best
way to win elections is to be the incumbent government!

In spite of that very conservative voting history, it was
widely believed in the Australian community—and widely
predicted by political commentators—that the Labor
government under its new leader, Paul Keating, was heading
for defeat in 1993. Two arguments were typically advanced
in support of that view: first, that unemployment was
so high (at over one million) that no government could
survive in the face of such damning evidence of economic

mismanagement; second, that the Coalition's policy initiatives were so comprehensive that they amounted to a blueprint for Australia's recovery.

In fact, neither argument carried sufficient weight to sway the electorate. Although it was true that unemployment had become a major issue in the minds of most Australians by 1993, neither side of politics was seen as having any credible answer to the problem and it was widely assumed that unemployment would stay high, regardless of who was elected. (Indeed, many Australians were beginning to believe that politicians' talk of 'job creation' may have been missing the point: as unemployment stayed high, the community was beginning to wonder whether, as outlined in Chapter 2.3, the real solution to unemployment was to find ways of redeploying the available work so that it could be shared more widely throughout the community.) Thus, although unemployment was regarded as a stain on the reputation of the Labor government, there was little confidence that a change of government would radically alter the situation.

When it came to the Coalition's comprehensive policy proposals (published as 'Fightback'), the community remained poorly informed about their precise content and, more particularly, confused about their likely effects (especially in relation to the goods and services tax, changes to Medicare, and reform of the labour market).

Ironically, the very fact that the Coalition had so actively marketed a complete policy platform for so long before the 1993 election may have been counter-productive. Instead of feeling that they had only to consider whether to reject the incumbent government, voters also felt that they had to consider the detailed claims of the Opposition. Instead of simply voting a government *out*, the electorate was being deliberately asked to vote an opposition *in*.

It is conventional wisdom in Australian politics that 'governments lose elections; oppositions don't win them', and there appears to be a great deal of evidence to support that view. Generally speaking, Australians need to feel that a government is 'finished' before they will reject it at the polls. In 1993, there was no strong feeling in the community that the Labor government was worn out, bereft of ideas, corrupt, divided, or had any of the other characteristics which would lead the community to acknowledge its civic duty to put the government out of its misery (as it had felt in 1972, and as the Victorian electorate felt in 1992). Given that the incumbent government was by no means 'on the nose', the Coalition had a daunting task to win in 1993.

As things turned out, the Coalition was not up to that task. Although their defeat was initially assumed to have been brought about by their proposal to introduce a new tax—the GST—subsequent research (The Mackay Report/Keynote, *Why did Labor win?*, April 1993) suggests that, in fact, the reasons for Labor's retention of office were more complex than that.

The key to understanding the result is to be found in the widespread sense of uncertainty in the electorate which had been well documented in the year—let alone the weeks—leading up to the 1993 election. The Mackay Report/Keynote, *The Keating/Hewson Factor* (April 1992) had reported that the electorate was unstable, unfocussed and uncommitted.

Long-term evidence from the quantitative polls supported that proposition. Even up to the last week of the election, some quantitative polls were suggesting that the 'undecided' vote had remained as high as 15 per cent of the electorate. Clearly, many voters were so confused about the options—and so lacking in enthusiasm for either side of the contest—that they felt genuinely uncertain about how to vote.

Such a large body of uncommitted voters added a new dimension to the 'swinging' voters in the community: whereas the number of swinging voters had been increasing steadily for twenty years, the emergence of so many uncommitted voters, remaining undecided almost up to polling day, became the single most critical factor in the 1993 election—and the factor which most confused those commentators who were attempting to predict the election outcome.

In order to understand the significance of the uncommitted voters in 1993, it is only necessary to remind ourselves of the social, cultural and economic context in which they were voting. As the foregoing chapters of this book have suggested, Australians are living through a period of relentless change and instability, and their levels of personal anxiety are correspondingly high. At a time when so many of them are complaining that their lives are out of control, any opportunity to maintain—or regain— control is welcome.

In this context, it was virtually certain that those voters who were still unsure about how they would vote up to the last week of the election campaign would *tend* to favour the maintenance of the status quo: after all, being uncommitted is an inherently conservative position. Similarly, those who felt confused about the detail of the Coalition's proposals would *tend* to resolve their confusion by rejecting those proposals.

Most fundamentally, those who felt that the election was an opportunity to maintain some sense of stability, at a time of such widespread instability, would *tend* to stick with the government.

In other words, those people who were feeling insecure, uncertain or uncommitted in the lead-up to the 1993 election were probably going to settle for the conservative option—that is, to leave things as they were. In the event, enough voters felt like that to tip the scales in Labor's favour. (It is one of the ironies of contemporary Australian politics that, in 1993, a Labor government was perceived as the conservative option: the Liberal-led Opposition were cast as the radicals who were prescribing changes which, though not widely understood, carried the threat of still greater instability.)

Given this set of attitudes, it is not surprising that, when the dust of the election had settled, many people reported feelings of relief and reassurance. Certainly, some felt that a major opportunity for 'taking strong medicine' had been bypassed; some felt that the electorate had 'squibbed it' by playing safe; some felt that the decision to stick with 'the devil you know' was a symptom of a conservatism in the Australian community so deep as to amount to a malaise.

More generally, though, the community seemed prepared to congratulate itself on having played safe. Labor had come to appear 'safer' than the Coalition for several reasons:

Labor was widely regarded as having become a middle-of-the-road party which, in spite of its continuing strong links to the trade union movement, had become much closer to the business community as well and had achieved widespread acceptance among both blue collar and white collar Australians;

Nothing being proposed by Labor seemed outlandish or revolutionary: even Paul Keating's proposal to stimulate debate about the republic struck a responsive chord in an electorate already prepared to debate questions of national identity and the political institutions which support it;

In spite of lingering signs of hostility to Paul Keating, the electorate felt that it had his measure and that, compared with John Hewson, the Prime Minister was a known quantity;

By contrast with the Coalition's perceived obsession with economics, Labor was seen as having more compassion and a greater interest in broader questions of culture and of social justice.

In the end, therefore, Labor's election victory appealed to voters as a 'business-as-usual' result. The attitude that *neither* side offered a basis for optimism, inspiration or excitement turned out to favour the incumbent.

Undoubtedly, the Coalition's proposal for a new, broadly-based consumption tax was a significant thread in the fabric of the 1993 election campaign but, as things turned out, the election seemed not to have been the simple 'referendum on the GST' that Paul Keating had promised it would be. There were too many other factors working against the Coalition—and too many other reasons for sticking with Labor—for the GST to have been the whole story, or even the main point of the story.

Rather, the election result was another sign of insecurity in the Australian community and a symptom of our lack of confidence in politicians to make much impact on some of our most pressing social, cultural and economic problems.

## IS THERE SOMETHING WRONG WITH THE SYSTEM?

That lack of confidence is also beginning to show up as doubt about the integrity of Australia's political institutions themselves. To quote Irving Saulwick again: a 1991 survey of Australians' confidence in some of our most important institutions rated the political system as being at the bottom of the heap. When asked about their level of confidence in the education system, the legal system, the media, the banks and the political system, respondents to the Saulwick survey rated the education system highest and the political system lowest. Indeed, 62 per cent of them expressed either little or no confidence in the political system.

Such a figure accurately reflects the mood of the Australian community. When Australians talk about the political system, they almost always slip into a negative tone of voice. But what, precisely, is the basis for such pessimism about politics?

One explanation has already been offered: when there has been so much radical redefinition of the nature of politics, anxiety and loss of confidence will be the inevitable result. As long as voters feel that there is nothing much to choose between the major parties on the basis of policy, their cynicism about the value of the choices they make is an inevitable consequence. Who stands for privatisation? Who stands for deregulation? Who stands for lower taxes? Who stands for the best social security provisions? Who cares most about helping us to provide for our old age? The difficulty in supplying answers to these questions emphasises the extent to which the Australian electorate is confused about which party stands for what, and about whether *any* party has a long-term commitment to *any* particular point of view.

A second factor fuelling Australians' cynicism about the political process concerns the *adversarial* nature of two-party politics. While many Australians recognise the historical origins of this approach to politics in the Westminster system, they find it hard to see how the two-party, adversarial approach to politics can continue to be appropriate when the distinctions between the two parties themselves are so hard to define. In other words, the redefinition of party politics implies the possibility of a redefinition of the whole parliamentary process itself.

It is a source of widespread astonishment in the Australian community that, at the very time when parties seem quite capable of stealing each other's policies or of invading each other's traditional philosophical territory, it is not possible for politicians from both sides of the political fence to work together in a more co-operative and harmonious spirit. The quality of parliamentary debate is regarded not only as a symptom of the adversarial nature of the institution, but also as a symptom either of the poor quality of politicians who are attracted to that system, or of the effect of the system on those who are enmeshed in it.

The common cry of parents, in particular, is that they would not let their children behave in the way that politicians typically behave in parliament. The parliamentary behaviour of Australia's politicians is no longer regarded as a joke—even though some incidents may be seen as amusing; rather, it is rapidly approaching the point where parliamentary behaviour is regarded as a national disgrace. 'Why can't they stop attacking each other and start thinking about running the country?' is one of the most oft-heard questions in the Australian community.

Adversarial politics may have made sense at a time when

the philosophical distinctions between the parties were stark and when arguments about *principle* could be justified; today, the idea that politicians would be arguing over a point of principle or philosophy is almost unthinkable. To the electors living through the Age of Redefinition, it seems that politicians are much more likely to be arguing over matters of personality, prejudice and power than over issues which affect the long-term health of the body politic. Personal abuse and gamesmanship—rather than policy issues—seem to the voters to have become the currency of national politics.

Following Labor's win in the 1993 Federal election, the community began to express the hope that, since Paul Keating was now installed as the 'legitimate' Prime Minister, he might bring new confidence—and therefore new dignity and integrity—to the conduct of parliamentary debate. Keating's long-standing reputation as something of a larrikin in Federal politics was amply confirmed during his interim term as Prime Minister, in the period between his overthrow of Hawke and his first Federal election as the incumbent Prime Minister. While many voters clearly enjoyed the more colourful aspects of Paul Keating's personality, he often served as a symbol of what was perceived as wrong with a parliamentary system in which personal invective and abuse carried more weight than serious political argument. Labor's convincing victory in 1993 was widely seen as having secured Keating's position to an extent which might enable him to adopt a more statesmanlike approach to the conduct of Federal politics: certainly, the parliamentary behaviour of key political figures sends clear signals to the community about whether the two-party system is really working.

As long as the main difference between the parties is

perceived as being the difference between the personalities and style of the leaders, then the erosion of faith in the system is likely to continue. Even if another 'charismatic' politician arose to energise and inspire voters, that would not address the underlying difficulty. But if policy differences *based on substantial philosophical differences* began to emerge (in such areas as labour market reform, trade policy, social welfare, taxation, superannuation and relations with the States) then the electorate may, once again, come to feel as if a clear choice could be made, on sustainable grounds.

Another factor may also operate in favour of the existing system. With the apparent failure of the Democrats to establish themselves as a stable and effective third force in Australian politics, voters will tend to look mainly to independent candidates as a focus for expressing their disenchantment with Labor and the Coalition. Whether the unpredictability of a parliament controlled by independents would seem preferable to the conventional two-party system is a moot point, still unresolved in voters' minds.

In any case, the community's present view is that, over the past 20 years, the major parties themselves have had a declining influence in determining voting intentions: if the parties do not soon re-emerge as expressions of genuine philosophical difference, then the call to re-examine the nature of the parliamentary process will gather momentum.

A third factor contributing to cynicism and loss of confidence in politics is simply that Australians are starting to wonder whether they are over-governed. The concern is not so much about the actual number of politicians; rather, it is that Australia may have too many houses of parliament. Conflicts between State and Federal parliaments—and between the various State parliaments themselves—are regarded as a particularly unproductive expenditure of political energy, and Australians question whether 15 houses of parliament may be too many for the efficient government of 17 million people. The sheer number of parliaments is often blamed for the problem of too many bureaucracies and too many duplications of bureaucratic and political activity between State and Federal governments.

Particularly in areas such as health and education—but even in relation to things like road rules—Australians fail to see why national policies cannot be developed. Whilst there is little love felt in the Australian community for Canberra and for the idea of more centralised government, even that is beginning to appear preferable to the inconsistencies and inefficiencies which seem doomed to arise from the large number of State and Federal bureaucracies.

Against the background of a redefinition of party politics wrought by the parties themselves, the Australian electorate is talking about the need for more far-reaching redefinitions. Although Paul Keating's 'One Nation' package was primarily designed as an economic statement, the name itself tapped into an emerging belief that Australia should be a more unified nation and that its available political and bureaucratic resources could be much more efficiently deployed if they were not so diffused.

## AND NOW ... A REPUBLIC?

The widespread support for the idea of Australia becoming a republic which emerged during 1992–93 is closely related to the underlying sense that Australia is overdue for some kind of re-examination of its political institutions. Enthusiasm for a republic was initially unfocussed, as Australians simply became caught up in the attractive idea of being a more independent and more clearly-defined nation. Part of the initial excitement arose from the yearning for a new sense of vision and a clearer sense of national identity. As debate about the republic proceeds, however, it has begun to incorporate the idea that Australia's political structures and systems might be quite significantly reformed on the way towards defining a new sense of nationhood.

Cutting our ties with the British Monarchy is seen as the easy part: the more interesting questions concern the basis for electing a head of state, the powers of the head of a republican state and the implications of a popularly-elected head of state for her/his relationship with parliament.

The evidence from early opinion research on the subject suggests that Australians would almost certainly demand the right to elect their own head of state, and that they would expect the head of a republic to have the power to force a government to call an election in circumstances such as those which arose in 1975. (After all, in spite of widespread outrage at the actions of Sir John Kerr in dismissing the Labor government in 1975 and instructing the caretaker Prime Minister, Malcolm Fraser, to call an immediate election, Sir John Kerr's judgment was given ringing endorsement by the voters at the election which followed.) In other words, the Australian community shows some sign of believing that, if the ties with the British monarchy are to be severed, *some* safeguards should be built into the system to ensure that an incumbent government does not acquire undue power.

But the matter does not end there. Given the underlying discontent with the present system of adversarial, two-party politics, Australians seem eager to seize the opportunity presented by the republic debate for engaging in a wider debate about the political process itself. While they are considering the question of a newly-defined head of state, they may well insist on considering the parallel question as to whether the present parliamentary system is the best we can do.

The process of political party redefinition which was so dramatically and successfully begun by Gough Whitlam in 1972 may yet find its logical conclusion in a more fundamental redefinition of the political system itself.

## THE STORY OF JASON

☐ It's a bit hard to know what to say about politics. None of my friends at school ever really talk about it, except when something really sleazy has happened. Everyone is pretty cynical about it.

When we were in primary school, we went on a visit to Parliament House. Even though we were only about eleven or twelve at the time, we were all pretty disgusted. They were having Question Time and it was really childish. They were acting like little kids. When one would be talking, the people on the other side would all be pretending to laugh at him, and carrying on in this really mocking way. You felt that no-one was really very serious about what was going on. It was all a kind of show. Our teacher was really embarrassed.

We had a mock Parliament at our school once, and it was more serious than what you see in Canberra. In fact, quite a lot of kids came up with really good ideas, and they all debated it properly. I was quite impressed.

Mum and Dad talk about politics quite a lot, but they

are pretty cynical too. I know they have changed their vote quite a bit over the last few elections. Dad reckons that you can't stick to one party like you used to be able to. His dad always voted Labor, but my father says that any intelligent person really has to weigh it up . . . the parties keep switching around so much that it is hard to know who stands for what. But when politics is discussed at home, I usually tune out.

I don't know what I will do when I have to vote. Some of my mates reckon they are not even going to bother registering, but I think there is a fine if you don't vote. So I will have to think about it when the time comes. It would be good if there was someone who really inspired you. One of our teachers quotes this saying about how you get the politicians you deserve, so maybe that's right. But I don't know what we are supposed to do about it.

When I vote, I mightn't even vote for the main parties. I might look at an Independent, or a Greenie, or something like that. But I'm not getting too worked up about it.□

# 2.8

# ET CETERA

Gender roles, family life, household structures, politics, work, money, social class, and our cultural identity . . . these are fairly significant re-definitions for Australians to have had to face in the space of a mere 20 years or so. But the list goes on, and will go on. There are many other areas of Australian life which have experienced—or are about to experience—continuing upheaval and redefinition.

HEALTH: Under the influence of a proliferation of health messages (many of which appear contradictory) relating to diet, fitness, unhealthy products and presumed links between diet and disease, Australians are in the process of redefining what they mean by health. A clear distinction is now emerging in people's minds between health and fitness: health no longer seems to mean 'absence of sickness'. The more positive concept of 'well-being' has entered the debate and there is a swing towards the idea that health may be the result of happiness, rather than its cause. At a time of heightened anxiety, mental and emotional health are more likely to be taken into account as key factors in promoting physical health.

TRADE UNIONS: Australians have great respect for the historical role of trade unions in Australian society.

They feel gratitude towards trade unions for their organisation of the labour market in the past, but their respect for unions has declined as they have come to feel that, having fought so hard for justice in the labour market, unions now frequently appear to be fighting for injustice: wages and conditions which are 'over the top' in the community's view. So, trade unions are also being redefined. Massive union amalgamations, falling membership and a relative lack of interest in union membership among women have eroded their traditional strength. Enterprise bargaining may pose a new threat to the traditional status of unions, but will probably result in trade unions discovering a new role for themselves in the industrial democracy—acting as consultants and advocates in individual workplace negotiations, rather than as a monolithic institution with direct influence at government level. In the trade union movement—as in so many other areas of Australian life—the message for the Nineties is likely to be 'back to basics'.

INFORMATION: As we come to terms with the growing significance of electronic information technology, we find that information moves at such high speed and in such vast quantities that it is no longer possible for us to absorb, interpret and evaluate it in the ways in which we are traditionally accustomed to processing information. We are learning how to be more ruthless, more selective and more skilful in avoiding the stress of information overload, but we are still so impressed by the technology and capacity of the information explosion that we continue to believe that information is inherently good and that the more you get of it, the

better. All this will change as we acquire the techniques for discriminating between relevant and irrelevant, useful and useless information. We no longer
seem to believe that 'no news is good news', but we
will soon have to accept that 'too much news is bad
news', and that it is neither possible nor desirable to
attend to all the information now available to us. The
mobile phone and the fax machine have further
redefined the nature of business information—speed-
ing up the flow of messages, and demanding ever more
rapid responses.

SCIENCE: At the very time when science is introducing
us to more and more modern marvels, our respect for
science seems to have declined, and young Australians
are less attracted to the study of science than was the
case a generation ago. Australians seem to be in the
process of re-evaluating their attitudes towards science: some of us are now recognising that we had used
it as a replacement for religion and, in the process,
blurred an important distinction between faith and
reason. Now that we are developing an understanding
of the fact that scientific data is itself subject to
constant reinterpretation, we are coming to terms
with the uncertainty of science. In addition, many of
the difficulties facing humankind at the end of the
second millennium are being blamed on an uncritical
acceptance of the output of science and technology.
The social analyst and science writer, Richard Eckers-
ley, in 'Youth and the Challenge to Change' (the first
essay in the Commission for the Future's *Apocalypse?
No!* series [1992]), goes so far as to argue that 'science
has been the main factor behind our predicament'

(though he hastens to add that, if used more wisely, 'science could provide the impetus for the cultural transformation necessary to secure our future'). All of this seems to have contributed to a general increase in the level of scepticism about the value of scientific endeavour, and a desire to 'keep scientists in their place'. (Economics is probably next in line for this kind of revisionist treatment.) It may be that the growing popularity of science as entertainment (or infotainment) in the mass media is a symptom of our retreat from reverence for science. Ironically, the rising standard of science journalism may be doing for science what *Jesus Christ Superstar* did for Christianity.

ENVIRONMENT: We have experienced a revolution in our understanding of our relationship with the physical environment. We've discovered the word 'ecology'. We have started to adjust to the idea that most of the Earth's resources are finite and that, if we continue at our present rate of consumption, life will become increasingly difficult for us and questions of survival of the species may even arise. Until more conclusive information is available about the state of the planet, ecology will remain one area of science where the boundary between faith and reason will remain indistinct. Nevertheless, however much Australians may be unsure of the details, they are convinced by the main line of argument, if for no other reason than that the skies in our major cities are getting browner.

UNIVERSITIES: The demise of Colleges of Advanced Education and their incorporation into a series of newly-formed, amalgamated universities means that the term 'university' is itself being redefined. It is no longer possible to make the previously safe assumption that every Australian university degree is a good degree by world standards. As in America, Australian university degrees now have to be carefully evaluated according to the strengths and weaknesses of individual departments and schools within the wide band of universities. Spoken or unspoken, we are beginning to form an impression of second-tier universities which causes us to re-think what we believe a university should be.

MANNERS: Chapters 2.1 and 2.2 have indicated how the redefinition of gender roles and of marriage and the family have loosened our grip on what constitutes acceptable social behaviour. Even common courtesies are capable of being interpreted as power plays. Paradoxically, it seems that we have now entered a period in which some people (particularly men) seem prepared to behave with deliberate discourtesy in order to avoid harsh social judgments! The question of social etiquette has been further confused by our changed eating habits: table manners are harder to sustain when a meal is being eaten in front of the TV set, and the increasing use of take-away food has made many of the customs traditionally regarded as 'good manners' rather irrelevant. (Do you set a knife and fork for the eating of a home-delivered pizza? Are the fish and chips eaten straight off the paper, or transferred to plates? Do table manners apply more, or less, when we are eating out . . . and what if we are eating at a fast-food restaurant?)

CURRENT AFFAIRS: In the mass media, the proliferation of news and current affairs material means that we are redefining what qualifies as 'current affairs'. With increasing emphasis on the visual, and with the voracious appetite of the mass media needing to be satisfied by endless hours of program material, our definition of news and current affairs is becoming looser, and the distinction between current affairs and entertainment is blurring. At the same time, newspapers are being redefined as it emerges that, in order to survive, they have to metamorphose into something more like daily magazines than traditional sources of hard news.

And so on . . .

# 3

# A KIND OF
# ADOLESCENCE

There are a couple of different ways of looking at Australians' responses to life in the Age of Redefinition. We could regard rising levels of anxiety and insecurity in the community as a perfectly appropriate response to the fact that the Australian way of life is indeed in a state of flux; that the old simplicities and certainties have gone; that the social, cultural, political and economic future appears very uncertain.

People at the frontier of geographical, scientific or creative exploration generally do experience some anxiety, and Australians in the 1990s are certainly at the frontier of socio-cultural change. There's no good reason why we should feel calm, content, confident or even happy. (Indeed, there is a British psychiatrist who believes that, given the human condition, happiness is an inappropriate and aberrant response which calls for psychiatric treatment!)

Nevertheless, viewed in the context of the geo-political upheavals of the world in the 1990s—or even in the context of Australia's own painful establishment of European civilisation in an alien land—it is fair to question whether Australians are coping as well as we might with the contemporary pressures on us. The redefinition of gender roles is a serious matter, but it is not life-threatening. The attempt to create a multicultural society is a brave experiment, but it is not as harrowing as the redefinitions of national identity which are taking place in Eastern Europe or Southern Africa. Unemployment is a debilitating and frightening experience, but it is not in the same league as famine. The redefinition of Australia's political parties has had a destabilising effect on the electorate, but we are not in the grip of a fascist dictatorship. Our artists and intellectuals may feel themselves to be under-valued in Australian society, but they are at least free to say so. For all our economic uncertainty, the average Australian is still well off in material terms, compared not only with the rest of the world, but also with previous generations of Australians.

Our situation may be serious, but it is far from being desperate or irrecoverable. Viewed from that perspective, it is tempting to suggest that Australians' current level of anxiety is something of an over-reaction to events. After all, the redefinition of Australian society is taking place in a way which is, by world standards, remarkably peaceful and in an atmosphere of astonishing tolerance and goodwill. So, is our anxiety inappropriate? Are our insecurities an exaggerated response to the instability of life in the Seventies and Eighties?

Those questions lead to an alternative interpretation of the mood of Australia in the Nineties. Although it is dangerously simplistic to draw an analogy between the evolution of a society and the psychological development of an individual person, some aspects of contemporary Australian society suggest that Australia is passing through a period in its cultural development which has a great deal in common with adolescence.

Australia is one of the youngest societies on Earth. Most of the societies with which we compare ourselves have much longer histories and much deeper cultural roots than ours. Although various claims have previously been made about Australia attaining the status of true nationhood—especially at the time of Federation and at the end of the Second World War—it may be the case that Australia is only now approaching the threshold of its cultural maturity.

If Australia is, indeed, passing through a kind of ado-lescence, this would help to explain why the Age of

Redefinition has been so vivid and so disturbing for so many people.

Three classic symptoms of the adolescent phase of personal development have emerged in Australian society in the last quarter of the twentieth century.

## THE IDENTITY CRISIS

At the deepest level of emotional development, adolescence *is* an identity crisis. Caught between the relative simplicity and security of childhood and the unchartered territory of adulthood, the adolescent experiences an often frightening sense of uncertainty about his or her own identity. Am I a child? Am I an adult? What does it mean to be an adult? How will being an adult feel different from being a child? Why can't I just be myself? Why are people expecting so much more of me? Why is everyone telling me to grow up?

These are the standard questions of adolescence, because adolescent behaviour often appears so erratic, confused and undirected—even to adolescents themselves. They are often perplexed by their own lack of a clear sense of identity, and their parents and friends are often at a loss to identify the 'real' person.

At one moment, adolescents long to be allowed to remain dependent on their parents; at the next, they wage a furious battle for independence. They are caught between the desire to retain the comfort and security of simply being part of an established family, and the desire to assert an identity which is quite independent of that family: they will often dress, speak and act in ways which are deliberately designed to emphasise the differences between them and their parents . . . even though they have a sneaking sense of their own absurdity as they strive to make symbolic gestures of independence.

Of course adolescents feel insecure; of course adolescents have difficulty in coping with the momentous changes which are occurring in their lives; of course adolescents are fearful of the future, because they realise that the time has come to stand on their own two feet. The period of being nurtured and supported is over, giving way to the need to take responsibility—and that changes everything. It is no longer good enough to be seen as a clever, cute, wayward but lovable kid; the time has come to function in the world of grown-ups.

And so it is with Australia. Moving through the 1990s, Australians are becoming much more focussed about our national identity, as we realise that the 'good-hearted larrikin' image can only carry us so far in the international community. We are beginning to confront the reality of multiculturalism and its implications for the definition of what it means to be Australian; we are facing the possibility that our economic luck has run out, and that we will have to look for new ways of surviving independently; we are torn between our desire to remain loyal to Mother England and our impatience to cut traditional ties to a monarchy which has become remote and irrelevant.

Like the adolescent, Australians seem committed to the idea of remaining within the family of the British Commonwealth, but we want to assert our own separateness and to move beyond an identity which feels like a relic of our colonial past.

According to this interpretation, the present wave of nostalgia could be seen as more than a simple desire to retreat into the past as an escape from the uncertainties of the present; it could also be part of the adolescent urge to cling to the security and identity of childhood, as a last-ditch defence against the onrush of the demands and responsibilities of adulthood. The challenge of a grown-up future has its appeal, but so does the comfort of an immature past.

Many other countries are experiencing the impact of the Age of Redefinition, but they are not generally caught up in an identity crisis comparable to Australia's. The Japanese, for example, are not to be found at conferences discussing their national identity. The Americans may be confronting the complexities of multiculturalism, but they are quite confident about what it means to be an American. Even the Germans, economically and politically destabilised by reunification, know who they are.

Australia's identity crisis is further compounded by the sense that we are in a state of transition from our traditional alignments with Europe to new economic and cultural associations within the Western Pacific rim: in both cases, of course, we are relating ourselves to cultures with ancient traditions and national identities which no amount of regional cooperation (such as the European Economic Community) will dislodge.

The tentative shift in Australia's focus from Europe to Asia—with the USA being a consistent underlying influence on Australians' view of themselves—may coincide with a more fundamental shift. As part of its move towards economic and cultural maturity, Australia may at last be beginning to understand its place in the world as a small nation in its own right, rather than continuing to see the world as a threatening and inhospitable place where great and powerful friends (just like parents) are needed to hold our hand. The projected removal of protective trade barriers may turn out to have a symbolic significance which transcends its economic significance.

## THE MOOD SWINGS

Another of the most easily recognised symptoms of adolescence are the violent fluctuations in mood which beset teenagers and often have a destabilising effect on their concentration, their relationships and, in turn, their sense of identity. In the case of the adolescent person, mood swings can easily be attributed to hormonal activity; in the case of a society, mood swings might be attributable to the lack of a sufficient depth of history or breadth of cultural heritage to enable us to take unexpected events—both positive and negative—in our stride.

One of the characteristics of the immature person—or the immature society—is that confidence is quickly eroded by a negative experience; that hyper-sensitivity limits the capacity to absorb criticism; that small successes are over-interpreted as justification for a swaggering arrogance.

All of these characteristics can be observed in Australian society through the twentieth century. Our well-documented 'cultural cringe' sometimes shows up as a massive inferiority complex, and sometimes as an over-blown sense of our own importance compared with other countries. Indeed, Australians' own judgments about the strengths and weaknesses of their society are riddled with paradoxes which reflect the mood swings of the adolescent.

On the one hand, Australians are fond of describing the 'typical Aussie' as a battler with an infinite capacity to overcome hardships; on the other hand, the typical Aussie is frequently characterised as an easy-going, apathetic person who lets other people (especially foreign investors and migrants) walk all over him/her.

Even as Australians mention matters for national pride, they often hasten to note the dark side of what they are saying. They praise our natural landscape, and then recall how hostile it has been to explorers, pioneers and farmers. They praise our mineral wealth, and then wonder whether we have 'sold out'. They praise our sporting heroes, but then turn their backs on them if they fail to win. They praise Australia as the land of opportunity, but then comment sadly that foreigners are often better at seizing those opportunities than Australians are. They praise our freedom, and then wonder whether Australians have had too much freedom for their own good, leading to laziness and complacency. They praise our impressive history of establishing an outpost of European civilization, and then reflect mournfully (and sometimes guiltily) on our treatment of Aboriginal Australians.

Just like the adolescent, Australians' chests swell with pride at any opportunity, but this pride is very easily deflated. We want to believe in the brightness of our own future, but doubts persistently cloud our vision. Like the adolescent whose fear of the future may cause a retreat into grumpiness, so Australians are inclined to grizzle about the things which displease them rather than constructively discussing strategies for improving them.

In some ways, our attitudes to the performance of Australians in international sporting contests most graphically symbolise our capacity for breathtaking swings of mood. During the 1992 Olympic Games in Barcelona, the Australian champion swimmer, Hayley Lewis, remarked that, 'It's funny about the Australian public sometimes. If you're not winning, then no-one gives a damn about you'. Of course, the problem is not just that Australians are too ready to criticise individuals or teams who fail to win; the problem is also that, with the insecurity characteristic of adolescence, we invest too much emotional energy in the fleeting prospects of sporting triumph. *The Australian*'s no-nonsense sports writer, Jeff Wells, made the same point when, in writing about the Australian swimmers' performance at Barcelona, he referred to 'unwarranted hype followed by unwarranted moaning'. When Alan Bond won the America's Cup in 1983, the hysterical enthusiasm which accompanied national celebration was a poignant reminder of just how deep our national insecurities must run if such a victory could be taken so seriously.

Some of the same kind of immaturity emerges in Australians' 'gee whiz' approach to science and technology. Australians take pride in the fact that some of the world's leading scientists and inventors have come from Australia, but they resign themselves to the myth that Australians are so innocent and naive that they are unable to capitalise on their own cleverness. Indeed, Australians seem to revel in the view of themselves as easy-going larrikins who, though blessed with great intelligence, are too reckless to make the most of their opportunities. Even when it comes to consumer behaviour, Australians fluctuate wildly between their belief in the proposition that they should buy Australian-made products in order to support the local economy, and their belief that Australian-made products are likely to be inferior to imports—either in quality or value, or both.

Evidence of emotional instability can be found in the big swings which occur in political opinion polls—particularly those relating to voting intentions and attitudes towards political leaders. If the figures are to be believed, almost from week to week, Australians undergo quite significant changes of heart about their political masters. To some extent, that is a reflection of the nature of Australian politics; to some extent, it is a function of the style of mass media reporting of politics; to some extent, it is a reflection of the polling process itself. But it also reveals the instability of Australians' attitudes which is part of the larger picture of an adolescent phase of attitude-formation.

It is easy to push the adolescent analogy too far. Nevertheless, when Australians are capable of saying 'Aren't we clever!' in one breath, and 'Aren't we hopeless!' in the next, it is hard to escape the conclusion that we are still in the process of coming to terms with our sense of national identity and that, for the time being, we are capable of quite dramatic contradictions in our view of ourselves.

## THE 'HAVE IT ALL' MENTALITY

One of the most painful aspects of growing up is the gradual realisation that difficult and often irrevocable choices have to be made. In childhood and early adolescence, it is easy to believe that anything is possible and that all options may be enjoyed—either simultaneously or eventually. The adolescent often retains an unrealistic innocence which permits the belief that big decisions can be almost indefinitely postponed; that life can simply be enjoyed; that people can generally have what they want.

For many people, the beginning of maturity can be marked by the point at which they realise that they will have to *give something up*. Adults recognise that they can't 'have it all' when 'all' involves too many contradictory or incompatible bits. Adults realise that choices have to be made and that the consequences of those choices must be accepted. Adults realise that disappointment and failure are absolutely integral to the process of living and that they are essential to any realistic understanding of what it means to succeed.

One of the heartening signs that Australia's adolescence may soon be over can be found in the fact that some of us are beginning to realise that we can't 'have it all' in the simplistic way we had fondly imagined might be possible in the Sixties, Seventies and Eighties. As we move through the Nineties, we are beginning to understand that decisions do have consequences, and that only some options can be exercised.

Nevertheless, many of us are still clinging to the dream that, in the end, we may not have to give anything up. We might be able to combine low inflation with full employment and still maintain record levels of foreign debt. We might be able to combine low taxation with generous welfare and social security provisions. We might be able to restore Australian manufacturing to a healthy state *and* freely exercise our right to purchase imported products. We might be able to receive high rates of interest on savings and investments *and* pay low rates of interest on borrowings. Women might be able to enjoy the satisfaction of combining work outside the home with their responsibilities for raising a family, without carefully negotiating such an arrangement with their male partners. Men might be able to enjoy the extra income and stimulating companionship provided by a working partner, but still enjoy the benefits of treating that partner like an unpaid domestic servant. We might be able to enjoy the enrichment of Australian society through immigration, but still have migrants leave big chunks of their cultural heritage at home and be prepared to act like the rest of us.

The 'have it all' mentality may be waning, but it still emerges in many of the paradoxes and contradictions which pepper Australians' dreams of a better life. Even the vacuous catch-cry 'the clever country' has slowed our progress towards maturity by implying that, if only we could all somehow become a little more intelligent or creative (or, perhaps, a little more employable), we could still have whatever we wanted.

The Australian national anthem encourages us all to rejoice because, among other things, we are 'young and free'. And so we are. The relative youth of Australian society is one of its most attractive features, and one of its greatest sources of potential. By comparison, countries like Britain, France, Germany or Japan make no reference in their national anthems to the fact that those societies are young because they are not: they draw their own particular strength from the depth and maturity of their respective heritages. Even America had achieved its independence from England before Australia began to be colonised.

It is unrealistic to expect Australian society to act as if it is a mature society. It is unrealistic to expect our national parliament to behave as it might if it had hundreds of years of unique tradition. It is unrealistic to expect Australians to have a fully mature world-view when we are only now beginning to come to terms with the nature of our own national identity.

But, under the influence of the Age of Redefinition, Australians are being forced to grow up very quickly. So many questions of identity—both personal and societal—are being raised that, as we find answers to them, we will begin to shed the uncertainties of adolescence and find a new sense of maturity. The 'Who are we?' questions are coming thick and fast. Who are we, culturally? Who are we, ethnically? Who are we, politically? Should we compare ourselves with Europe or Asia, or both, or neither? Can a multicultural society work (and do we want it to)? Should we remain a monarchy—even if only in name—or should we become a republic (and, if so, what kind of a republic)? When questions as fundamental as these are being asked all over Australia, it is unwise to make any glib generalisations about the Australian identity. In the short term, it is hardly surprising that Australians are inclined to cling to some of the emotional and cultural comforts of our national childhood. In the longer term, we know that too many things are changing for life to go on in the future as it has, even in the recent past. In his 1987 Epilogue to *A History of Australia*, Manning Clark put it this way:

> This generation has a chance to be wiser than previous generations. They can make their own history. With the end of the domination by the straighteners, the enlargers of life now have their chance.

Putting it another way, the Nineties present us with the opportunity to move beyond our national adolescence.

# 4

# MASTERING THE NINETIES

After 20 years of living in the Age of Redefinition, Australians are developing a survival mentality. Exposure to sustained change and a prolonged sense of uncertainty has led to a perfectly understandable concern with getting life back under control.

Indeed, *control* is emerging as one of the key words of the Nineties: 'we must take control of our environment; we must get our economy back under control; we must exert more control over business practice in order to avoid repeating the recklessness of the Eighties; we must control the rising tide of crime in our society; we must get a greater sense of control over our own lives.'

Two other key words are *confidence* and *contact*. As we move through the Nineties with sagging morale, we long for something which will inspire hope in us and restore our belief in our own future. And, as we struggle to deal with the stress in our lives, we realise that we have lost touch with each other and that it would be comforting to restore a stronger sense of community in our lives through greater personal contact with family, friends, neighbours.

If we are coming to the end of our national adolescence, then we are bound to find ways of getting our anxiety under control and of adopting a more positive and more mature approach to our problems. By the end of the Nineties, Australians will be much more confident of how to live successfully in the Age of Redefinition; how to cope with discontinuity; how to adapt to the new social, cultural and economic patterns which are emerging.

The following chapters identify the emerging signs of three strategies which Australians are going to use to help them master the Nineties.

# 4.1

# WAYS OF ESCAPE

It is fundamental to our emotional health that, from time to time, we should escape from the sources of stress in our lives. At a time when Australians are coming to regard stress as a central fact of existence, it's no wonder that their preoccupation with finding ways of escape is also growing.

For escapism to be effective as a form of therapy, two conditions must be met. First, it must have the capacity to transport us into a temporary reality which contrasts with whatever aspects of our everyday life create stress in us. Second, it must be sufficiently harmless to allow us to return to everyday reality without having been damaged by the escapist experience: we must be free to escape from escapism.

If the primary source of our stress is that we feel powerless, then the ideal form of escape is something which makes us feel powerful: anything from whacking a squash ball around the court to identifying with an irresponsibly violent character in a movie. If the grind of daily routine has robbed our lives of romance, then the ideal escape may range from a candlelit supper to the purchase of silk lingerie (which is not, as some feminists have suggested, always a capitulation to male fantasies, but is sometimes simply a flight to self-indulgence or escapist romance).

If the primary source of stress is that life seems to be so grimly serious, then the ideal escape might be into a sitcom on TV, or some mildly irresponsible indulgence in alcohol.

If feelings of pointlessness, inadequacy or futility create stress, then the escape into a hobby or into a passionate commitment to recreation—owning a boat or following a particular code of football—might do the trick. If it is the relentlessness of the demands of work which has become unreasonably stressful, then literal escape might be called for: a weekend away or the escape into long-term planning of the ideal holiday.

The point is that in the increasingly dour and conservative climate of Australia in the 1990s, 'escape' does not need to be justified—as long as it can be easily recognised as simple fun, harmless fun or affordable fun. Some escapist self-indulgence is being used by most Australians as a necessary form of therapy (though they do not want to veer too close to anything which smacks of the materialistic excesses of the 1980s).

Indeed, 'fun' is bound to become a very big industry in the Australia of the 1990s. The more we face the realities of the Age of Redefinition, the more we will need to break out occasionally and have fun. Among the rising generation of young Australians, there is a growing sense of urgency about the need to have fun. The more life appears to be serious, and the more the future appears to be uncertain, so the pressure to have fun is increased. One of the most widespread and trenchant criticisms of their parents by young Australians is that 'they don't seem to have much fun' and this is a mistake which young Australians are determined to avoid making, for as long as possible.

Fun, to young Australians, is the ultimate antidote to pessimism, anxiety, pressure and boredom. There are as many definitions of fun as there are young Australians: it can range from the most innocent pastime to the most destructive vandalism. But if an activity can be described as 'fun', then that is all the rationalisation and all the justification it requires. Drug-taking can be dismissed as fun; shop-lifting can be excused on the grounds that it is mere fun; graffiti-writing and other forms of vandalism are regarded as acceptable as long as they are interpreted as fun rather than aggression or destruction; even random and casual sex can be justified on the grounds of fun.

For adults, all the classic, time-honoured sources of fun are going to be increasingly important as we come to terms with life in the Age of Redefinition. Sport, recreation, entertainment, travel, romance, fantasy and—true to the Australian tradition—gambling, will all play their role in offering harmless escape from the pressures of redefining our identity, our culture and our way of life.

In the depths of our worst recession for sixty years, we made a record plunge on the 1991 Melbourne Cup. Was that responsible? The question doesn't arise: it was an effective form of escape for people who were trying to relieve their anxieties. In the depths of a retail slump, we spent a record amount on St Valentine's Day in 1992. Could we afford it? The question didn't arise, because romance offers itself as a classic form of escapist relief.

Food is another classic form of escapist therapy. When the going gets tough, the appeal of reliable 'comfort food' grows correspondingly stronger. Chocolate, biscuits, snack foods, ice cream, casseroles, soup and junk food all offer the opportunity for mild self-indulgence which provides temporary relief from stress and anxiety—especially if those foods evoke nostalgic recollections of a childhood when life was simpler and more certain. Indeed, some of the most reassuring and comforting rituals of escape involve self-indulgent eating and drinking. 'That time out with a cup of coffee and a copy of *New Idea* is a life-saver for me in the middle of the day' and 'A packet of chocolate biscuits helps me get through the ironing when I've finally got the kids into bed and the washing-up out of the way', are two heart-felt comments from mothers which capture the therapeutic value of escapist food. People who live alone often report that it is a particular form of food or drink which eases the difficulty of coping with the early moments of 'coming home to an empty house'.

Nostalgia is also a favourite escape route. The rose-tinted rear vision mirror offers an appealing view: after all, we *know* we can cope with yesterday because we've already been there. Selectively recalled scenes out of a fondly-remembered past provide welcome relief from the insecurity and complexity of the present and the uncertainty of the future. There seems little doubt that the nostalgia wave of the early Nineties will continue to build and that, in response to our voracious appetite for sanitised glimpses of the past, the time lapse between now and then will shorten. At any moment, we are likely to experience an outbreak of nostalgia for the Eighties, complete with 'greed-is-good' parties and entrepreneurial fancy dress. (The probability of a burst of Eighties nostalgia is increased by the fact that our feelings of embarrassment about the excesses of the Eighties have distanced us from that decade in a way which makes it seem longer ago than it actually was. It's already starting to seem safe to go back there.)

But the standard, traditional escapist fare to which Australians have always turned for relief from stress is only part of the story. As we come to terms with the fact that the pressures of the Age of Redefinition are not likely to be relieved in the foreseeable future, some new escape mechanisms are emerging.

## THE GROWING OBSESSION WITH THE SYMBOLS OF 'THE COUNTRY'

Australians have always enjoyed the rather romanticised and unrealistic view that our heritage springs from the bush. We are proud of 'the outback' as a unique symbol of Australia, and as a reminder of the bravery of Australian explorers and pioneers. The fact that Australia is one of the most urbanised societies in the world has not deterred us from carefully preserving the myth that we somehow belong in the bush.

Henry Lawson and Banjo Paterson played a significant part in establishing the fiction that *real* Australians are to be found outside our major cities and that the *real* Australian values are somehow located in rural rather than urban culture.

As we move through the 1990s, Australians seem more prepared than ever to turn to the country as a source of comfort and reassurance: increasingly, the country is providing not only a source of physical escape, but also the inspiration for urban escapist behaviour.

The prospect of having 'a place in the country' is stronger than ever. The dream of 'bringing up the kids in the country' is more appealing than ever. The idea that country people are healthier, saner and wiser than urban Australians is a pleasing fantasy. Although growing numbers of Australians are choosing to holiday in the countryside—and there are signs of a new boom in the modern equivalent of country guest-houses—most escapist thinking associated with the country does not involve actually going there. The country has become an inspiration for urban domestic architecture, for furnishings, for kitchen design, for cooking utensils and dishes, for cookbooks and for fashion:

increasingly, the goal seems to be to create the impression that one's *heart* is in the country, even if one's life is firmly based in an urban environment. To look as if one has just returned from—or is about to leave for—rural pursuits has become the height of urban fashion. (Country Road picked a perfect Nineties name for their brand of casual clothing.)

One of the most potent symbols of Australians' growing obsession with things rural is the fact that, per capita, this is the largest market in the world for four-wheel drive vehicles. For years, Range Rover has been among the top-selling luxury cars in Australia and, at a time when the car market is generally depressed, the four-wheel drive segment of the market has held up better than most. The question is: why do Australians buy (and dream of buying) four-wheel drive vehicles in such numbers when, in fact, most of those vehicles will rarely, if ever, leave the bitumen?

The answer is to be found in the appeal of rural symbols as a means of escape from anxiety. The average four-wheel drive vehicle drives around the suburbs of our major metropolitan areas; it takes the children to school; it goes to the local shops; it has a busy time ferrying members of the family around to their various sporting and other activities on the weekend; it occasionally tows a boat, a trailer or a caravan; once or twice a year it is loaded up for a holiday excursion. All of these functions could be equally well performed by a conventional family car, but four-wheel drive vehicles such as the Range Rover, Toyota Land-cruiser, Nissan Patrol, Mitsubishi Pajero and Holden Jackaroo possess a symbolic value which the family car lacks: they appear to be cars which are uniquely equipped to tackle the Great Australian Outback. They also carry the promise that, one day, we will pack up a tent and all the camping gear we dream of owning, load the kids into the back seat and set off for Kakadu to do our duty as real Australians.

More than any other symbol of country life, the four-wheel drive vehicle forges a tangible link between city and country: it actually has the capacity to carry us into the countryside and beyond, into the rough terrain of the real bush.

So the four-wheel drive vehicle is a symbol of adventure—real or potential—and adventure, in the minds of most Australians, is likely to be found at its escapist best in the country.

(The escapist appeal of four-wheel drive vehicles actually goes beyond their rural association. Because they are big, high and powerful, they imbue their drivers with a sense of authority which is itself a potent antidote to insecurity and anxiety. They also make an escapist statement about the car itself: the decision to buy a four-wheel drive vehicle is a decision to step outside the boundaries of conventional, mainstream motoring. The same kind of symbolic declaration explains the spectacular success of the 'fun car' segment of the car market—characterised by cars such as the Suzuki Vitara and Mazda 121—which position their drivers as having escaped from the conformity of standard saloon cars. In the rebellious 1960s, the Mini Moke performed a similar function.)

The urge to go camping, to 'rough it', or to commune with nature are all classic forms of the urban fantasy that an escape into the rural environment will not only be therapeutic in the recreational sense, but will also symbolise a return to the innocence, the purity, the simplicity of 'the country'.

One appeal of bucolic escapes (whether in reality or in fantasy) is that they allow us to return to the comfort and security of life in the city. In this sense, country-based escapism is one of the healthiest of all forms of escapist fare because it is the one least likely to disrupt the return to normal life. Whereas some other forms of escape (such as the escape into addictive drugs) can actually create an alternative reality which may come to seem preferable to normal life and from which it becomes increasingly difficult to return to normal life, the country escape fantasy tends to remain just that—a fantasy.

## THE RETREAT TO THE DOMESTIC CAVE

If the growing obsession with the country implies 'getting away from it all', then the second of the new-found escape mechanisms works in the opposite way: rather than flee-ing—actually or symbolically—from the stressful urban environment, this strategy involves 'holing up' in the middle of that environment. This is an ultimately defensive form of escapism: a retreat to the comfort, privacy and, above all, security of home base; an escapist response to our ancient urge to seek the shelter and protection of a cave.

'Caving' has been given a number of names by various observers of our socio-cultural evolution. Many years before the currently fashionable American trend-spotter, Faith Popcorn, coined the term 'cocooning', the astute Melbourne market researcher, Brian Sweeney, had been noting a kind of fortress mentality in the way in which Australians were beginning to think about home.

There is nothing surprising about the trend to which these various labels have been attached. As household size shrinks, as family life becomes less stable, and as the Age of Redefinition takes its toll on our confidence and sense of security, it was inevitable that home itself would come to serve as a focal point for the urge to escape. The Mackay Report on *Australians at Home* (1986) put it like this:

> When middle-class Australians speak of their desire for home ownership and of the pleasure they take in owning their own homes, they are speaking about the sense of power which home ownership gives them—not only to express their own values and personalities, but also to control the extent of their own privacy. Particularly in the major metropolitan centres, home is becoming something of a fortress—a private zone which is fenced off from the rest of the world and which is, increasingly, being seen as a base from which to carry on the struggle . . .

Brian Sweeney was right: homes are certainly becoming fortresses as our fear of assault and invasion grows and our corresponding obsession with privacy increases. The market for domestic security systems continues to burgeon; bars are appearing on domestic windows; suburban fences which were torn down in the more open and trusting Fifties and Sixties are being re-erected; electronically controlled front gates are being installed in some of the most genteel suburban streets; the household dog is being doubly valued as a pet and a guardian of domestic property.

Inside this increasingly secure domestic environment, big changes are taking place. There is growing emphasis on entertainment and recreation equipment being installed in the home, to minimise the need to go out to be entertained or to relax. Australians' growing fear of urban violence has repositioned home as a safe haven. And, as the sense of a neighbourhood community gradually broke down during the Seventies and Eighties, we developed a compensatory obsession with the notion of privacy which, in turn, further fuelled the domestic fortress mentality.

The increasing availability of home-delivery food and other products may be a particular convenience to the working mother, but it also appeals to the cave instinct. Phoning for a pizza is yet another symbol of the fact that we have retreated to the safety of our cave, and we do not even have to go out to hunt. (The next step, no doubt, will be the re-introduction of serveries in homes and apartments, so that food can be received, and money paid, without actually having to open the front door to a stranger.)

The trend towards shopping from home which will undoubtedly gather momentum during the 1990s is not just a response to the convenience and time-saving of telephone and computer-based shopping systems: it is also a response to the urge to escape into the domestic cave, and to keep the world at bay while respite is sought.

'Caving' as an escape mechanism carries some dangers, however. Whilst it is itself a response to feelings of nervousness and anxiety, the person who adapts too well to the caving strategy may find those feelings of nervousness and insecurity are actually increased when, for whatever reason, the time comes to leave the security of the cave. As long as one cowers inside the domestic fortress, visions and fantasies of wild animals loose in the outside world are likely to become more vivid and fanciful. Caving also creates some practical difficulties. What happens when the technological links with the outside world fail? What happens when, in the case of a fire or some other emergency, a quick exit must be effected from a house which is thoroughly locked and barred? What happens when, in the case of serious illness, a person living alone in a well-secured cave is unable to answer the door to the doctor or to some other person offering needed help: how will entry be gained to a cave which has been so deliberately secured against unwanted entry?

But such problems seem less significant to the cavers than their need to escape into a domestic environment which is not only as safe and secure but also as complete as they can possibly make it. And so the trend towards total equipping of the cave continues: the home entertainment centre, the home computer, the billiard table, the exercise bike, the spa, the flotation tank, the weights, the library of video-tapes, the growing list of delivery service numbers by the phone . . .

Of course, many cavers are also perfectly sociable beings. They may be quite happy to talk to their neighbours, to go out to work and to shop, and to lead a normal social life. But, when they return to the cave, it is not simply 'coming home': it is a retreat, and the stone must be firmly rolled across the entrance.

## THE ESCAPE INTO THE INFORMATION CLUB

One of the best-disguised escapes from anxiety is the escape into information—and the mass media of the 1990s supply more than enough material to satisfy the demand of those who have chosen this particular pathway to escape.

As an escapist strategy, the immersion in information works very well. The signs of this strategy are to be found in those who can't get enough news and information about what is loosely described as 'current affairs'. They are people who hunt the news bulletins, the current affairs programs, the talk-back radio shows, the news up-dates in a quest for so much information about what is going on that they never have the time to process it. They are so busy learning what is going on that they rarely need to interpret it: indeed, because they have committed themselves to keeping so closely in touch with unfolding events at home and around the world, their capacity for judgment—for interpretation—may actually be dulled by the sheer volume of information which they have elected to take on board.

Some members of the Information Club are not bent on an escape strategy, of course: they are using information as a source of power and as a means of reducing their anxiety by developing a clearer sense of what is going on (see Chapter 4.3). But the information junkies are of a different sort: they are not using information as a means of better understanding the world; rather, they are addicted to information as a means of keeping the world at bay. As long as there is another news item, another world crisis, another rape, another political scandal, they can be fully occupied in keeping up with what is going on, never having to confront it or respond to it at any deeper level than mere possession of the information.

The proliferation of news and current affairs programs in Australian radio and television during the 1980s was a direct response to the insatiable demand from people who had seen the opportunity of escaping from their own anxieties into the fathomless sea of information about other people's lives, other people's worries and other people's business.

The same proliferation of programs more or less guaranteed that the content of those programs would become softer and more diffused as the demand for information exceeded the supply of what would have been traditionally regarded as 'real news'. Thus, on commercial television, the top-rating *A Current Affair* looks more and more like tabloid television, where a story about a shonky tradesman is as likely to dominate the program as any serious analysis of political or other events. Even ABC TV's *7.30 Report* is dropping its original commitment to trade in the currency of serious news analysis: it, too, is tending to join the TV equivalent of the tabloids in treading the populist and sensationalist path of satisfying those who are escaping into information.

News has become entertainment. The TV industry has already acknowledged this by coining the word 'infotainment', and by recognising that *any* information will apparently do to satisfy the large audience of people who are using information largely as an escape from their own anxieties.

Some viewers have even blurred the distinction between soap opera and current affairs, believing that programs like *A Country Practice* (the country again) and *Neighbours* deal with social issues in a way which is quite as helpful as any more 'serious' or documentary-style discussion of those same issues (abortion, homosexuality, drug abuse, sexual permissiveness, social conscience, etc). Perhaps that is always true of popular drama and fiction, but the screening of the BBC production, *Sylvania Waters*, has further clouded the viewer's judgment about what is 'information' and what is 'entertainment': increasingly, an escape into one is indistinguishable from an escape into the other.

Talk radio has responded brilliantly to the needs of those who wish to escape into information, and who wish to tune in to an incessant flow of talk about almost anything: today's crisis will be forgotten tomorrow, but there will be another crisis to deal with then. The information junkie will swallow anything that passes for news and current affairs, and yet is never satisfied. A famine in Somalia? A woman who has locked her keys in her car and doesn't know what to do? A man who has received rough justice from the Department of Social Security? An enquiry into corruption among senior police? An unexpected shortage of bream at the fish-markets? A caller who reports that she will go mad if she hears another politician say 'at this point of time?' Talk radio will supply all this, with equal seriousness and intensity, to the avid listener intent on escaping from the frustrations, insecurities and anxieties of daily life into the warm bath of undemanding information.

As each new guest enters the studio, a fresh source of interest arises and a new topic of transient concern provides a vaguely satisfying focus for our latent feelings of anxiety, or, more simply, a distraction from more immediate difficulties.

None of this is to deride the importance of tabloid television or talk radio: both types of program perform a valuable community function for those whose 'fix' is information, but it does mean that other members of the Information Club who are not wanting to use news and current affairs as a means of escape will have to look elsewhere for their information. It also means that, when it comes to television at least, the term 'current affairs' is itself in need of being redefined.

As the technology advances, the escape into information (broadly defined) will become even more attractive and even more engrossing. The sophisticated electronics of 'virtual reality' will push back the barriers between life and art even further, allowing us to enter into the illusion of experiential, three-dimensional reality of whatever kind we choose. Compared with *virtual* reality, the *total* reality of some people will come to seem very dull and a new hazard of escapist addiction will confront us.

## The Serious Holiday

There is nothing unusual about holidays being used as an escape from the humdrum, the pressure or even the routine of daily life. Australians have always taken their holidays seriously and recognised the restorative power of a change of pace and a change of scene.

One of the traditional charms of a holiday has always been the homecoming: the sense of relief which accompanied the return to home and family and to the security of a stable existence. But for those Australians whose homes and families are in some disarray and whose daily lives are destabilised by the tensions and insecurities of the Age of Redefinition, coming home from a holiday is not quite the pleasure it once was.

In fact, a new dimension is being added to the value of holidays: for Australians most deeply affected by anxiety and insecurity in their personal and working lives, holidays are beginning to appear not so much as an escape *from* a stable routine as an escape *to* a stable routine. The Mackay Report on *Holidays* (1983) identified 'reliability' and 'predictability' as key words in the planning of a holiday for those Australians who are now looking to a holiday as a means of taking control, rather than losing control. Such words imply the desire for holidays to have a structure which will be a welcome contrast to the lack of structure in everyday life; to provide some repetitive rituals which will have a re-stabilising effect; to create an opportunity to get things right.

For those Australians who are looking to holidays to provide this additional dimension of escape from chaos into order, and from unpredictability into predictability, holidays assume enormous emotional significance. They are often anticipated as a kind of cocoon of perfection in which shortcomings in everyday life—particularly in the management of time and personal relationships—can be overcome. Harassed working mothers will look forward to a holiday as a time when they can be more single-mindedly devoted to their families than is possible during the rest of the year. Fathers who are guilty about the amount of time they spend at work may approach a holiday as an opportunity to undertake some repair on their marriages, and on the quality of their relationships with their children.

The Marketscan Report on *The Holiday Market* (Mackay Research, 1988) identified the particular appeal of repeating the same holiday experiences for people whose everyday lives are characterised by uncertainty and insecurity:

> As the pace of life accelerates and 'the old values' seem harder to retain [people] are, once again, turning their attention to quite conservative and nostalgic holiday opportunities. For them, a holiday is a very precious opportunity to enact their own version of how life (especially family life) should be: holidays are a time to recreate the sense of an extended family, the community, or even the sense of 'who I really am'. [Such people] will frequently be looking for repetitions of old and satisfying holiday experiences.

For Australians who suffer the vague sense of insecurity (or even dread) which is characteristic of The Big Angst, one of the primary values of a holiday lies in the opportunity it provides to compensate for the unsatisfactory aspects of daily life, and to fence off a little piece of 'super-realism' which is a reassuring reminder that life could be more enjoyable; that relationships could be more stable; that stress could be reduced. For many Australians, holidays offer the promise of a self-contained exercise in taking control: a carefully designed tract of existence in which, above all else, we escape from the sense of being victims of our circumstances.

For this reason, some Australians report that they have a stronger sense of being part of a community when they are away on holiday than when they are at home in their own neighbourhoods. Those who take the same bus tour each year, or visit the same caravan park or camping area each year, or who rent the same holiday house or stay at the same guest house each year, place very high value on the stability of relationships with fellow holiday-makers— relationships which are typically renewed annually, and which involve no contact during the rest of the year. For Australians who are suffering the sense of loneliness and isolation associated with unstable families and shrinking households, holiday friends are very special friends indeed: they come into our lives at a time when we feel much more positive about our sense of control over our lives, and they do not see us during the rest of the year when we are trying to cope with the complexities and uncertainties of life in the Age of Redefinition.

Discovery tours are all very well, but in the 1990s the holiday emphasis will be on self-discovery. When so many Australians are wishing that they could slow down the pace of change and regain the sense of mastery over their own lives, 'time out' created by a holiday is more precious than ever.

## YOUNG AUSTRALIANS: WAIT AND SEE

One way of escape from the pressures of the Age of Redefinition is to hang back from making any kind of commitment which might then be eroded by the pace of change. Among today's crop of young Australians, the withholding of commitment has become an attractive means of escape, at least in the short term.

The tendency to postpone marriage or to by-pass the institution of marriage altogether is a symptom of the emerging 'wait-and-see' mentality; so is the reluctance among so many young Australians to make a political commitment, to register for the electoral roll or to join a trade union.

Among young Australians who face the bleak prospect of long-term unemployment, the lack of a commitment to a particular course of training or a particular career direction is perfectly understandable. Yet it feeds the tendency to mark time, to 'see how things turn out', and to escape to a condition of mental and emotional limbo which is based on 'keeping your options open'.

Although it is popularly believed that the rising generation of young Australians is more conservative than their parents, the picture is actually more confused than that. Although there are certainly signs of a conservative trend among young Australians (which may be nothing more than an echo of their parents' swing in a conservative direction), what passes for conservatism is sometimes simply a lack of commitment. When people observe that the current generation of tertiary students seem to be less radical and more apathetic than generations who passed through universities in the Sixties and Seventies, this does not necessarily mean that today's students are single-mindedly devoted to study and to getting ahead: in many cases, the lack of activism is a symptom of a generational desire to hang back from full participation in the debate of political, social and cultural issues, precisely because those issues seem to be so complex and the lines of debate seem to be so blurred.

Postponed commitment can offer a pleasant state of suspension: idealism may be alive and well among the young, but it is more likely to be scepticism and agnosticism which they idealise, rather than the more predictable passionate idealism of those who are driven by a commitment to an idea, a cause or an issue.

None of this is to deny that there are many committed idealists among Australia's youth. The point simply is that, coming into a society which is obviously in a state of flux, growing numbers of young Australians are content to remain as spectators, in the hope that, when things settle down they will more easily be able to define a role for themselves. Meanwhile, with youth unemployment running at around 50 per cent in parts of Australia, who can blame them for feeling rather tentative?

## THE PRISONERS OF ESCAPISM

An escapist strategy loses all its therapeutic value, of course, if the escape hatch snaps shut while we are trapped on the outside. The relaxation, the distraction, the stimulation, the solitude or the restoration of an escapist experience will be pointless if we are not easily able to return, enriched and refreshed, to the existence from which we sought temporary relief.

For Australians who are still trying to come to terms with the Age of Redefinition and who are suffering deep-seated anxieties and insecurities in their everyday lives, the seductive appeal of escapism can be overpowering. When normal life is devoid of a sufficient sense of substance and purpose, escape can begin to appear as a permanent alternative. In its most extreme form, the quest for permanent escape may lead to suicide and, among the most desperate young Australians, this has become an increasingly attractive option: between 1970 and 1990, the suicide rate for males aged 15 to 24 years has more than doubled.

But even for those who choose a less permanent form of escape, the return trip may be approached with great reluctance: for a person addicted to the escape into the effects of mind-altering drugs, the worst nightmare is having to crash-land back in a world of harsh reality where unresolved problems, hopelessness and despair make the state of permanent hallucination seem very appealing: whether the hallucinatory experiences are themselves always pleasant or not, they are at least ethereal.

Similarly, the extreme form of escape into alcohol can easily lead to alcohol abuse for those who gradually discover that they prefer inebriation to sobriety, because their view of the world when sober is too frightening, too demanding or too tedious.

Even the occasional lapse into violent behaviour or vandalism can lead to a sense of power and purpose which becomes addictive: violence and vandalism can become attractive as a permanent way of life, rather than an escape, when the alternative is to face the daily challenge of trying to fill in time.

The compulsive shopper, the compulsive gambler, the compulsive eater, the compulsive traveller, the compulsive drinker—even the compulsive romantic—are all prisoners of their own forms of escapism. Finding that the gratifications they receive from their escapist behaviour are more reliable and more satisfying than gratifications available from their everyday lives, they retreat permanently into aberrant and potentially neurotic behaviour—partly because they will attract welcome attention, but partly because it simply feels better.

A housewife who is bored or ground down by the daily routine of her domestic existence may find a welcome and harmless escape in a weekly game of tennis or bridge. But if the life from which she has escaped into her therapeutic tennis game feels no better when she returns to it, she may begin to play tennis daily, to become obsessive about tennis and, finally, to live for tennis and cease to function effectively in the routines of her domestic life. Similarly, the person who can only cope with life seen through the roseate haze of being in love may seek an endless series of romantic liaisons as a means of escaping from the demanding commitment of a lasting relationship.

The therapy of escape is only likely to be helpful and reliable when it is safe; it is only likely to be safe when it is not approached in a spirit of yearning and despair. But some of the reluctant pioneers of the new Australian way of life in the last quarter of the twentieth century have miscalculated the depth of their yearning for escape and, rather than seeking therapy of a more conventional kind (such as counselling), have prescribed their own escapist therapies and, to their own dismay, become addicted. The journey towards social maturity involves the discovery that the therapy of escape only works when we don't need it too badly.

# 4.2

# FINDING OUR BEARINGS

Because the Big Angst seems to have more to do with fear of charting a course through the future than with a fear of what the future itself may hold, it is not surprising that one of the strong emerging trends in the 1990s is the urge to find our bearings. One of the most painful lessons we have learned from living in the Age of Redefinition is that reference points which depend on previously stable social conventions and political or economic institutions can become notoriously unreliable, and that values which focus on the material and the external are unlikely to endure. If we are going to value ourselves in terms of our prosperity, or identify ourselves by a job description, or even define ourselves in terms of our racial origins, then, in the Nineties, we're going to be in deep trouble.

It has gradually dawned on us that, if our chosen reference points keep moving or disappearing, we can't easily make sense of our lives or develop a vision of who we want to become or where we want to go. A confused and dispirited middle-aged man in a recent research project put it like this: 'You can't rely on women to act like women any more; you can't rely on banks to act like banks; you can't rely on politicians to be true to the parties they belong to; you can't even rely on a Holden being made in a Holden factory . . . what can you rely on?'

It's a good question. For those Australians who have begun asking it, the most compelling answer seems to be that reference points will have to be found 'in here' to compensate for the unreliability of those 'out there'. The idea of Australia's assured prosperity is no longer a reliable landmark; the institution of marriage is an increasingly insecure basis for developing a sense of personal identity; there is no cosy and coherent description of *the* Australian way of life; the myth of the 'Australian character' has been exploded by multiculturalism.

As a direct result of the disappearance or redefinition of so many of our cherished social, cultural and economic icons, the quest for personal values is back in fashion. At a time when it is beginning to look as though 'she'll be right' may be just another set of famous last words, Australians are waking up to the idea that some debate about ideals, convictions and principles might help to generate the emotional and intellectual resources necessary for life in the Nineties. Who are we, really? What do we want out of life? What do we want to become? What kind of society do we want to bequeath to our children and grandchildren? Is this all there is?

For 20 years or more, such questions have been largely off the agenda, pushed aside by an unprecedented binge of materialism. In one of the great ironies of social analysis, Australians' confidence in the long-term prosperity of Australia was boosted by their mass misinterpretation of Donald Horne's warning, 30 years ago, that we had survived for too long on the basis of a series of lucky breaks. Instead of heeding his warning, Australians adopted his book title, *The Lucky Country*, as a kind of self-congratulatory assurance of perpetual good fortune which helped to convince them that this was a society in which, without much effort, things would always come right in the end; something would always turn up. If wool or wheat lost their power to support our economy, then the mining industry would take over (a proposition strongly promoted by the mining industry itself through an advertising campaign which assured us that mining was 'the backbone of the country'). If all else failed, tourism promised a new source of endless income . . . again, relying on the lucky country's natural charm and beauty to attract the eye of the international tourist trade.

The rapid slide into extraordinary levels of foreign debt took most Australians by surprise. It was not until the early 1990s that they began to realise that Australia's obsession with consumption was not matched by the means to finance its national—or its personal—spending spree. The harsh facts of economic life in the 1990s have presented the first really compelling evidence for Horne's assertion that, unless we changed our ways, our luck would inevitably run out.

But it wasn't only materialism and our faith in our own economic good fortune that distracted us from any serious engagement with philosophical questions about the nature of Australian society. We were also distracted by the need to cope with the pace of socio-cultural change. For many Australians, life in the Seventies and Eighties seemed like a roller-coaster—complete with unpredictability and more than a tinge of excitement—and it was easy to ignore serious questions about the future.

Nevertheless, it was inevitable that, sooner or later, we would decide that it was time to take stock; to evaluate; to question whether we actually wanted all the changes which were reshaping our way of life. Finally, it has become necessary—for emotional as well as economic reasons—to switch from a mode of constant reaction to a mode of more reflective thought. That switch could hardly be described as a mass movement in Australia, but the early signs suggest that Australians are beginning to catch on to the idea that, if we are to regain a sense of control over our lives, we must begin to develop some strategies for doing so. Strategies demand a sense of purpose and that, in turn, demands some definition of the values—or even the ideals—which we wish to embrace.

To some extent, an emerging interest in values, vision, meaning and purpose is the common characteristic of societies facing the end of a chronological era; every New Year's Eve brings its spate of resolutions for the following year; each new decade is approached as if it holds some new promise. History suggests that the turn of a century has a great impact on people's willingness to think about the kind of society in which they want to live, and to embrace new strategies for achieving those goals. (It was probably no accident that Australia became a Federation in 1901 as a direct consequence of the burst of visionary energy and zeal which was unleashed by the approaching end of the nineteenth century.) As we move through the 1990s, we are approaching not only the turn of a century but the dawn of a new millennium, and that is undoubtedly one of the influences on the emerging Australian pre-occupation with the idea of 'getting back to basics'.

But the magnetic pull of the year 2001 is a relatively minor influence on Australians' current quest for a new set of bearings: the major influence has been the instability and insecurity resulting from the turbulence of the last 20 years. Recognising that discontinuity will be with us for a long time—and perhaps forever—Australians are deciding that it is time to build up the personal resources which are required if we are going to do better than merely cope with contemporary life, and do more than simply react to events as they unfold.

The cry of 'back to basics' is being heard everywhere—in education, in politics, in management, in religion, in marketing, in the health professions, in the entertainment industry . . . and certainly in the conversation of ordinary Australians who are trying to find pathways to a more secure future. Precisely what is meant by 'basics' varies from person to person, but the underlying message is clear: Australians are on the lookout for some set of principles, some ideas, some values, some beliefs which will imbue them with a renewed sense of confidence and purpose. Australians who have felt themselves adrift express admiration for those who seem to have a clearer sense of direction and a more definite point of view. Indeed, the urge to 'find our bearings', or to 'get back to basics' is itself a recognition that there is power in a point of view—whether that point of view is religious, philosophical, political, cultural or racial. Australians are beginning to envy those who seem to have 'answers': they may not admire what they see as the extremism of some religious, political or ethnic groups, but they do have a sneaking envy for the certainty, the passion and the sense of direction which such people seem to evince.

In many ways, their envy is justified. Those who have dwelt in the world of ideas, or who have retained strong religious faith, a clear ethical position or a set of established political convictions generally do appear to have been less troubled by the Age of Redefinition, simply because the foundations of their personal belief systems have not been shaken by the changes taking place around them. As usual, the most thoughtful, the most committed (and, it must be said, the most prejudiced) are best equipped to cope with turbulence—because they are philosophically inclined to welcome new ideas, or because they have a world-view which helps them to interpret (and therefore to understand) what is going on around them, or even because their convictions allow them to remain comfortably resistant to new ideas. It is those who lack the power of a strong point of view who are most likely to feel destabilised and victimised by the pressure of their circumstances.

Australia is not about to become a community of contemplatives and yet, as the kaleidoscope of social change continues to turn, we are beginning to realise that we will have to make our *own* sense of what is happening. The meaning is not in the events themselves, but in our interpretation of them. In our rush to try to keep up with social change, many of us lost our capacity to interpret. Now we are beginning to realise that we will have to create our own answers to the questions posed by the Age of Redefinition.

The inward journey may be painful and complex—to say nothing of its emotional and philosophical hazards—but it is the essential next step for a society which has been exploring so much new territory without the aid of a conceptual compass.

## A MID-LIFE CRISIS FOR THE 'ME GENERATION'

The growing sense of powerlessness in the Australian community has been felt with particular poignancy by those Australians who passed through adolescence and early adulthood during the buoyant and optimistic years of the 1960s. That group (like similar groups in other Western societies) became known as the 'Me Generation', a label which reflected their aggressive obsession with personal gratification, personal freedom and personal power. They were the generation who challenged many of the post-war values and conventions of Australian society and, in so doing, paved the way for the Age of Redefinition.

Rebelling against what they saw as the cultural boredom and moral strictures of the 1940s and 1950s, they frightened their parents (to say nothing of educational authorities and employers) by the radical tone of their thinking and by their willingness to flout long-established conventions in behaviour—symbolised by a departure from previous codes of dress and language. This was the generation who used blue denim (and, fleetingly, the mini-skirt) as a statement of their refusal to conform to the expectations of an older, more formal, generation. With the same motive in mind, they incorporated 'shit' and 'fuck' into the parlance of the Australian middle class, leaving the great Australian adjective as a relic of the culture from which they were determined to break away. They fell enthusiastically upon the savage satirical work of Barry Humphries, because they were determined not only to create new symbols of Australian culture but also to rubbish and belittle the old (and, in the process, to render plaster ducks and names like Beryl and Edna a source of humiliation and embarrassment to those who had previously been quite comfortable with them).

The Me Generation saw themselves not only as radicals but as idealists. They were intent not merely on shaking the foundations of the culture they had inherited from the Forties and Fifties; they were determined to create a new world of their own. They were strongly reinforced in the belief in their own power to change the world by the ultimate success of their opposition to the Vietnam War: from anti-war protestors, they slipped easily into the role of protestors against anything of which they didn't approve. They became the generation who, liberated by the contraceptive pill, overturned the conventions of sexual morality. They were the generation who responded to the emerging musical idioms and rhythms of rock and roll and adopted them as the standard genre for transient music. They were the generation who created a sub-culture based on hallucinogenic drugs; the generation who saw 'dropping out' as a virtue; the generation who fell for every fad and fashion as a substitute for more enduring beliefs, and who, in an attempt to substitute the immortality of the body for the immortality of the soul, developed food and health obsessions which frequently made them a laughing stock to their own children. They were the generation who thought they had discovered Peace and Love but who seemed to be less attracted to other high-sounding concepts like Commitment and Work.

The Me Generation saw itself as idealistic but, in the end, generally settled for only one ideal: self-fulfilment. Encouraged by the economic and cultural optimism of the 1960s, these Australians embraced a hedonistic self-centredness which may have sounded and felt to them like idealism, but which lacked the complexity or sensitivity which any value-system was going to need if it was to be an effective resource for coping with the pressures and uncertainties of the Seventies and Eighties.

That rather vacuous idealism was brilliantly exposed and chronicled by David Williamson in his early plays—plays which were enthusiastically received by the Me Generation themselves: the reflection of their values appealed to their narcissism but did not, until the Eighties, come to be fully recognised as an attack on the superficiality of those values (partly because, in mounting such an enthusiastic assault on what they saw as the hypocrisy and complacency around them, the Me Generation failed to notice their own slide into self-importance).

Living through the 1960s, the Me Generation had come to believe that the ball was at their feet, the world was their oyster, and personal power was indeed within their grasp. Many of them mistook self-indulgence for freedom, and assumed that 'personal power' simply meant the ability to 'do your own thing'. Indeed, 'doing your own thing' became the distinguishing characteristic of the Me Generation and a reference point and justification for many of the extra-ordinary changes in attitudes to marriage, parenthood, family life and work which followed.

None of this is to deny the positive contributions made to Australian culture by some of the iconoclasts of the Me Generation. They were influential in forcing Australians to broaden their cultural focus and to become more open to cosmopolitan influences. In some cases, at least, the early self-centred idealism did lead to a more mature idealism in favour of social justice, equality between men and women, and a healthy scepticism about some conservative aspects of Australia's cultural and political heritage which seemed to be inhibiting its development as a nation.

Thirty years on, the Me Generation are in their forties and early fifties, and they are experiencing a full-blown mid-life crisis. Paradoxically, the very generation for whom the term 'generation gap' came into common usage are now experiencing a particularly painful generation gap between themselves and their own offspring. In their idealism of the 1960s, they had not expected to breed the yuppies of the 1980s: they had not realised how easily 'do your own thing' could transmute into 'greed is good'. In their rejection of many of the religious and ethical ideals of their own parents, they had not intended to raise a generation of little materialists. In their commitment to Peace and Love, they had not intended to create such awkward complexities in their own personal lives, nor such emotional hazards for their own children. Coming out of stable home and family backgrounds in the 1950s, the Me Generation have found themselves unable to provide the same kind of stability and security for their own children, and they are beginning to have second thoughts about the wisdom of 'doing your own thing' as an adequate principle for regulating a life.

The Me Generation are beginning to acknowledge that the process of value-shedding through the Sixties and Seventies has left them with a vague sense of emptiness—a feeling that life lacks some of the meaning and some of the sense of purpose (and even some of the simple pleasure) which they observed in their own much-maligned parents and grandparents. Facing their mid-life crisis, the Me Generation are beginning to have some regrets about their marital instability, their failure to devote sufficient time to the nurturing of children, and their lack of a coherent framework for dealing with the uncertainties of life in the last decade of this century.

Put simply, the Me Generation thought that, 20 or 30 years on, they would feel better than they do. They thought that the sense of freedom and excitement which they experienced in early adulthood would become characteristic of their lives, but it doesn't seem to have turned out that way.

As they reappraise their lives and confront their mortality, some of the idealism associated with the Sixties begins to re-emerge in a new, surprisingly conservative guise. Their new enthusiasm for environmentalism, for example, has its roots partly in the spirit of the 'flower children' of the Sixties. Some of the tension about emerging redefinitions of gender roles reminds members of the Me Generation of the ideals of sexual equality which they debated but never quite embraced in the Sixties. The early emphasis on the group (or even the commune), which was characteristic of young people in the Sixties is now being revived as the Me Generation deals with the problems of loneliness and isolation created by its subsequent determination to act alone.

Once again, the Me Generation is in the spotlight. Representatives of that generation are now holding positions of significance and influence in politics, in journalism, in business and the professions. Their mid-life crisis is bound to have an impact on the values of society at large: indeed, much of the current push to redefine our values and ideals comes from the members of the Me Generation who, having felt themselves adrift for 20 years or more, are now determined to recapture some of the sense of purpose and direction which was so characteristic of their parents' generation. They are facing the possibility that everything from the hole in the ozone layer to our crippling levels of foreign debt (to say nothing of the disintegration of stable personal relationships) may be due to an uncritical commitment to the principle of 'doing your own thing'. The dawning recognition that personal goals may have been pursued at the expense of the community is a painful reminder that, when tribal creatures lose their tribal sense, personal as well as social difficulties usually arise.

## THE NOSTALGIC QUEST FOR 'TRADITIONAL VALUES'

The Me Generation may have a particular role to play in the current search for a new set of bearings, but this time they are likely to find themselves in step with the community at large. The Me Generation haven't coped any better than anyone else with the Age of Redefinition and so they, like the rest of the community, have entered a period of reflection, re-evaluation and consolidation.

When a society comes to feel that it has lost its bearings, it is probably inevitable that the first inclination is to look back, to see whether the values of the past might have something to offer—either intact, or in recycled form. This explains the recent surge of interest in the idea of returning to 'traditional values' (by which is usually meant either a set of values associated with a more conservative period in our socio-cultural history, or values which may seem to be enduring and stable). Suddenly, the certainties and simplicities of the 1950s begin to look attractive—even though contemporary Australian society has so little in common with the society which spawned those values. Much of the current interest in so-called 'traditional values' is simply a form of nostalgia in common with the nostalgia for the fashions, the music, the politics, the sporting heroes and the relative homogeneity of Australia in the 1950s.

(There seems little doubt that one of the things which attracts older Australians from Sydney and Melbourne to Queensland is not only the warmer climate but also the sense that Queensland society retains many of the characteristics of Australian society before it entered the Age of Redefinition: multiculturalism, for example, is regarded by Queenslanders as an essentially southern pre-occupation, and Queenslanders will often claim that they have managed to cling to a way of life and a set of values which are harder to sustain in the southern states.)

As we move through the 1990s, certain words and themes are attracting increasing attention and support because they are so easily associated with the values of earlier times.

Australians may not wish to turn back the clock, but they are certainly interested in finding ways to incorporate what they see as traditional values into their contemporary way of life. So we are going to see a growing emphasis on words and concepts which seem to be connected in some way to the idea of getting 'back to basics'. Words like these:

| | |
|---|---|
| Responsibility | Balance |
| Restraint | Safety |
| Moderation | Purity |
| Heritage | Loyalty |
| Conservation | Decency |
| Morality | Discipline |
| Integrity | Motherhood |
| Simplicity | Domesticity |
| Nature | The Family |

In most cases, these words are capable of almost infinite shades of interpretation, but they have become popular as signposts which might lead us out of the confusion and complexity of the Age of Redefinition.

The push towards 'better' behaviour (that is, behaviour linked to the sort of concepts listed above) will not only come from a re-think about values: various environmental factors will push us in the same direction. Fear of AIDS will push us towards the development of a new emphasis on sexual morality. The need, for purely economic reasons, to boost Australians' personal savings will coincide with our rediscovered belief in the *virtue* of saving. Health problems arising from excessive consumption of processed food will reinforce the idea that more natural foods are not only better for us but *inherently* better. Our inability to afford many of the luxuries and material self-indulgences which seemed so important during the 1980s will fuel the development of an anti-materialist mood in the community. The shortage of work will mean that many people—both men and women—will be forced to spend more time at home and so, in turn, they will come to appreciate family life and the role of the domestic arts in personal fulfilment.

The recession of 1991–92 has already provided a telling example of the inextricable link between experience and attitudes. Even while suffering the damaging consequences of the recession, some Australians were beginning to identify ways in which they thought the recession was bringing benefits to Australian society. 'It's an ill wind that blows no good' is a proverb which acquired a certain piquancy during the recession: because Australians were desperately *hoping* that the effects of the recession would not turn out to be entirely negative, they were actively looking for signs of positive effects. For example, under the impact of the recession, many Australians were reporting that they had begun rethinking some of their values—especially those which relied on material prosperity. Others claimed that they were forced, because of retrenchment or a cutting back on the available hours of work, to spend more time with family and friends and so, in turn, they were beginning to attach more importance to the role of personal relationships in their lives. Others had found that their sympathy for disadvantaged and under-privileged people was enhanced by their own experience of the recession.

Indeed, by the middle of 1992, a quite general sentiment was emerging which suggested that, not only was the recession bringing some emotional and social benefits to Australians (particularly in the area of 'getting our priorities straight'), but also that a mere 'bounce-back' from the recession could even be a bad thing because it would imply an accidental recovery rather than one which was hard-won through the development of strategies for long-term economic health.

Many of the emerging social and emotional concerns of Australians in the 1990s will coincide with some of the economic and environmental pressures upon them. It is not necessary to disentangle cause from effect in order to see that we are entering a period of great conservatism. In the short term, things may get a bit dull (and we may, indeed, find that we are hearing some cultural echoes from the 1950s) but Australians have decided that, for the time being, they prefer a bit of dullness and predictability to what they now see as the recklessness, irresponsibility and indulgence of the 1980s.

The real danger here is that Australians could feel that past answers to past questions may serve, intact, as answers to present questions. When the morale of the community is down, the mood may become not only conservative but dangerously open to promises of simple answers and the illusion of simple certainties. The urge to find a new set of bearings will ultimately be satisfied only by an inward journey, involving the creation of a set of ideals and values appropriate to the realities of the new Australia. A nostalgic journey into the past may be a useful preliminary exploration, but it can easily become a substitute for the real thing. If we become hooked on recycled culture because we associate it with more positive or more enduring values, we may simply recycle our myths as well, and dwell in perpetual adolescence.

## HERE COME THE FUNDAMENTALISTS!

If being caught in a cultural time warp is one of the hazards of the quest to recapture 'traditional values', another big hazard is the temptation to settle for simple answers to complex questions. The turbulence of the past 20 years has led to a craving for simple certainty which can lead, all too easily, to the delusion that simple certainty is justified—even when it is not.

The present climate of instability and insecurity creates the very real danger of gullibility and, in turn, leaves the way open for a dream run by fundamentalists of all kinds—religious, environmental, political, cultural, astrological, and economic. After all, nothing builds morale like the confidence that we have cracked the code, discovered the formula, and understood the meaning of life (or, at least, an interpretation of the meaning of life which begins to make sense of the chaos). The appeal of fundamentalism is the appeal inherent in any point of view which offers the conviction that 'I'm right . . . and you're wrong'.

Strictly speaking, fundamentalism refers to the branch of religion whose faith is rooted in a simple set of absolutes (in the case of Christianity, for example, an acceptance of the literal and historical truth of everything in the Bible). But the term can be applied beyond the realm of religion, to include all those systems of belief which consist of a set of absolute, immutable propositions in which their adherents have complete faith.

Fundamentalism has particular appeal to Australians in the early 1990s because it seems to be in accord with the 'back to basics' movement. The appeal of the fundamentalists in all their guises is that they claim to have had the answer all along; they have maintained a strong conviction that they knew where society was going wrong; they have retained their faith in dogma which they believe would ultimately relieve us of our woes if only it were more widely embraced.

The essence of fundamentalism, then, is belief in a number of absolute propositions or principles which, while not capable of being proven, appear self-evident to those who believe in them and form the basis of a complete (and generally static) system of belief. Not surprisingly, such belief engenders a great sense of confidence and can easily lead to smugness and elitism. Typically, the fundamentalists are not content to enjoy the feeling of power which flows from their faith in their own convictions; they are generally anxious to assert the wrongness of alternative points of view and, wherever possible, to try to recruit converts to the rightness of their position. Fundamentalists tend to have a low tolerance of ambiguity, an impatience with the notion of compromise, and an unwillingness to accept the possibility that there may be some legitimate grey areas between the extremes of black and white. (The staunch resistance of Anglican fundamentalists in 1992 to the ordination of women priests was a case in point.)

There is nothing mysterious about the appeal of such certainty—and even smugness—in the current social, cultural and economic climate. It provides access to precisely the kind of confidence which Australians feel themselves to be lacking. It supplies a ready-made vision of the future which relieves a great deal of the pain of trying to work out what to do next. It provides a framework within which failure can be attributed to human folly, and in which otherwise impenetrable meanings can be easily explained and corrective action proposed.

The rise of fundamentalism in the Christian churches

around Australia is undeniable. Particularly in the outer suburbs of our major metropolitan areas, the booming churches are those which tend towards the simple certainties. The mystics are out of fashion; the most appealing forms of religion in the early 1990s appear to be those which offer certainty rather than mystery.

Given the appeal of simple certainty, it is not surprising that Australians' belief in astrology has increased dramatically in the recent past. Dr William Grey, a philosopher at the University of New England, has conducted some research in association with the Australian National University's National Social Science Survey in which he has found that, in the period from 1987 to 1991, the number of Australians who actually believe in astrology has risen from 16 per cent of the population to 29 per cent. For those who embrace astrology, belief that people's personalities, attitudes and behaviour are ruled by their star signs creates a pleasant sense of fatalism, and a powerful capacity to understand and explain the behaviour of other people. 'Of course he would do that,' says the astrological fundamentalist, 'he's an Aries', as if that's where the matter ends and nothing more needs to be said.

Such belief not only provides a reassuring basis for understanding the nature of the human condition, but it also purports to supply a key which will at least partially unlock the door to the future. Those who believe that the position of the planets at the time of their birth has exerted a major influence on their destinies are understandably willing to extend that belief to include some anticipation of what those destinies will bring: no wonder they regard the rest of us as being rather obstinate and pathetic in our failure to accept the illuminations of our understanding which astrology promises to supply.

Fundamentalism has also emerged in the debate about the environment. For many Australians, environmentalism has had some of the appeal of religion: it has emerged as a contemporary form of pantheism, arriving on the agenda just at the time when our insecurities were at their greatest and when our corresponding need for a new world-view was beginning to be felt. In some ways, the green movement of the late Eighties stole the churches' thunder by offering a new form of religion which seemed to be based on purely rational data and which promised its own version of 'peace on earth' in response to fear of a new unknown. Belief in the inherent goodness of Mother Earth (and even, as in some manifestations of environmentalism, belief in the planet as a vast organism) has led to belief in a series of environmental propositions which have the force of fundamentalist faith.

For some Australians, environmentalism has thrown up a new ethical code, quasi-religious in character, which—like fundamentalism in any form—provides a set of criteria against which everything can be judged to be right or wrong. To environmental fundamentalists, plastic is an evil substance; developers are satanical; every tree is a good tree; rainforests are sacred sites; recycling is an inherently virtuous (rather than merely sensible) activity, and so on. Like all forms of fundamentalism, environmental fundamentalism leads to an utter conviction of the rightness of the self-defined 'green' position, and brooks no argument. Alternative positions are regarded as either malevolent or uninformed, and debate about the subtleties of the links between ecology and economics are swept aside in an evangelical frenzy.

Like so much simple certainty, the certainty of new converts to environmental fundamentalism is not always based on a full understanding of the issues: zeal is a sufficient boost to confidence, even in the absence of adequate knowledge. When people can talk about the 'greenseas effect' or the 'ozone-free layer',or declare that they have given up pouring oil down the sink in favour of pouring it down the toilet, it's a fair assumption that their position may not yet have been fully thought through. It is easy to understand the phenomenon noted by Phillip Adams that, when zealous environmental fundamentalists are faced with new information which might challenge some of their most dire predictions for the future welfare of the planet, their disappointment is palpable.

This, of course, is the real hazard for fundamentalists: subtlety, complexity, ambiguity and mystery are unwelcome intruders into their cosy fortress.

Fundamentalism can even emerge when there is an appearance of utter rationality. Humanists would generally claim that they have logic on their side, but some of them take up anti-mystical positions with an irrationality worthy of the religious zealot. Humanistic fundamentalism is often associated with an atheism which is as cocky (and as hard to justify) as the position of any theistic fundamentalist.

In economics, so-called 'wets' and 'dries' can develop such absolute faith in the correctness of their own position that, not only do they exclude alternatives, but they may come to feel that those who hold alternative views are under-informed, pig-headed or simply stupid. The 'economic rationalists', for example, do not easily acknowledge that there may be alternative pathways to an economic Nirvana: their faith in the dogma of the free market is absolute: privatisation, deregulation and opposition to any government intervention in market operations are the fundamental tenets of their faith. Like all other forms of fundamentalism, the purity and simplicity of this position has its charms, but history would caution us against accepting *any* dogmatic view of the 'one true way' when it comes to the operation and interaction of human societies and systems.

Feminists, too, can slip into a kind of fundamentalism: in their enthusiasm for the rightness of their position they can lose sight of the fact that there are many shades and varieties of 'feminism' and that to introduce a single standard of political correctness into the feminist debate is to miss the whole point of creating a diverse, complex plurality of choices for contemporary women.

The appeal of all these forms of fundamentalism— whether they emerge from humanism, feminism, religion, astrology, economics, politics, culture or environmental-ism—is that they imbue their adherents with *the power of a point of view*. After 20 years of turbulence and insecurity, the promise of certainty becomes very attractive and, for those who embrace fundamentalism, the sense of relief is indeed very welcome. Whatever the sceptics may say, fundamentalists do experience a powerful sense of purpose; they do sleep well at night; they are motivated to act on their convictions. The passion of fundamentalists can unleash tremendous energy—they are equally capable of changing the world or of resisting change. The question for Australia in the 1990s is whether the issues—from morality to ecology, and from unemployment to gender roles—are as simple as the fundamentalists would have us believe.

## THE REGULATION OF CONSCIENCE

It is a very small step from fundamentalism to a form of puritanism which demands that, since we now know what is right and wrong, or good and bad, we should impose that knowledge on the behaviour of others. One of the big dangers for Australia in the 1990s is that, in a well-intentioned quest for new certainties, we may fall for the trap of excessive regulation and, in turn, insidious erosion of personal freedoms.

This problem does not just rest with those who have moved to the extremes of fundamentalism. It is a more general social problem: because so many Australians feel that 'things have got out of hand' (whether in relation to personal morality, corporate behaviour, economic planning or the physical health of the nation), there is a widespread tendency to support regulations which will compel people to behave more responsibly, more morally, or even more healthily.

The current surge of interest in ethics is easy to explain in terms of Australians' growing feeling that the 1980s was a period of unacceptable recklessness and general excess. But in our enthusiasm to re-establish some moral principles and to find our ethical bearings, there is a real risk that we will confuse ethics with regulation and, instead of stimulating the moral sense of Australians, we may actually inhibit and stifle it. Ethics is about choices which we are free to make: if the choices are subject to regulation, they are no longer free choices. The very imposition of regulation reduces freedom and, by definition, reduces the need for individuals to exercise moral judgment.

The proposals for new regulations governing the behaviour of company directors which surfaced in 1992, for example, were a perfectly understandable response to mismanagement and irresponsibility among business leaders—and those who advised them—during the 1980s. But a desire to clean up the corporate act carries the inherent risk of going too far: the more regulations we impose on company directors and managers, the more we limit their freedom of choice and the more we discourage the operation of individual conscience. As regulations become more numerous and complex, the automatic response is to assume that 'if it is not prohibited by the rules, it must be OK'.

But the pro-regulation lobby is riding high, buoyed by community sentiment in favour of a greater sense of certainty and a greater sense of control over events of all kinds. Thus, the advertising industry finds itself under increasing pressure to modify—or even abandon—advertising for alcoholic beverages, on the grounds that advertising may encourage irresponsibility. Similarly, advertising for cars, financial services and confectionery is bound to come under increasing scrutiny, as the pro-regulationists seek ways to eliminate any advertising messages which could be construed as encouraging reckless behaviour—on the roads, in the management of debt, or even in the mouth.

The same mentality is to be found in the area of public health. The discovery that smoking is associated with a range of physical ailments has led to widespread banning of tobacco advertising and the prohibition of smoking in various public places and in a growing number of workplaces as well. As a society, we have decided that informing people about the risks of smoking is not enough: we must begin to regulate their behaviour in ways which will prevent them from smoking conveniently or comfortably.

The pressure to consider tougher censorship regulations is mounting. Older Australians who assumed that the censorship debate was settled in the 1960s are now alarmed to find that all the old arguments are being revived because of a growing fear in the community that increasing violence and sexual permissiveness may be attributed, at least partly, to exposure to explicit sexual or violent portrayals in the mass media. Discussing the move by the Victorian Attorney-General to examine the possibility of censoring mass circulation magazines like *People* and *Picture*, the Melbourne journalist and broadcaster, Terry Lane, referred in one of his columns in *The Sunday Age* to 'that neo-wowser movement, constantly on the alert for people who might be enjoying themselves, and ready to stamp out untaxed pleasure wherever it raises its seductive head'. Harking back to a vigorous debate about censorship in Victoria in the Sixties, Lane went on: 'Arthur Rylah had no right to impose the scruples of church-going puritans on society, and Mr Kennan has no right to impose the scruples of radical feminists on the community today. Censorship was stupid and hypocritical then, and it is now—the entry of new agents of repression into the fray does not make what was wrong in the '60s right in the '90s.'

Terry Lane's argument may be powerful, but the opponents of censorship (and of over-regulation in other forms as well) are likely to find the going tough in the mid-1990s. Back in 1983, The Mackay Report on *Power & Responsibility* reported a growing tolerance of government regulations, but a corresponding concern that increased legislation could make us less, rather than more, responsible citizens. That early concern appears to have been overshadowed by our desire to 'take charge' of a society which seems to be getting out of control. But, if we continue along the path of increased regulation, we will inevitably reach the point where our anxieties about the loss of freedom surface again.

Already, some Australians are beginning to wonder whether we have gone too far in the restriction of smokers' freedoms. Already, some consumers are beginning to wonder whether unhealthy products will be banned, as another means of controlling our behaviour in preference to alerting us to the hazards of using those products. Will cholesterol become a prohibited substance? Will fat-reduction in food become an obsession, to the point of regulation? How firmly are we to draw the line between telling people what is unhealthy or dangerous, and prohibiting them from behaving in unhealthy and dangerous ways?

For people who feel a strong need to take greater control over their own lives, the appeal of increased regulation of others is obvious: it reduces uncertainty and, because pathways of action are more clearly defined, promises less unpredictability and less irresponsibility. History does not favour that promised outcome but, in the new mood of conservatism, Australians seem willing to give it another go.

It will be a pity if Australians decide that laws, rules, regulations and codes are the only satisfactory way of defining a new set of bearings. After all, regulations and codes generally express some deeper set of values and ideals. Because we believe in the ideal of justice, we legislate in ways which will express that ideal. Because we accept the idea of temperance as a virtue, we look for ways to regulate our lives in order to increase the probability that our behaviour will be temperate.

If Australia is, in fact, on the threshold of a serious debate about our identity, our national goals and our values,then it is important to begin the debate by examining the *underlying* ideals rather than simply rushing into a set of regulations which are assumed to express an ideal which was never itself properly articulated. Renewed interest in ethics and morality may well lead to the idea of 'cardinal virtues' coming back into fashion as a proper subject for public debate. Perhaps Australians are about to confront ancient ideas like courage, temperance, justice and mercy in a way which will ultimately lead to a more enlightened understanding of the kind of rules and regulations which might encourage—but not prescribe—the expression of such virtues.

If we regulate tolerance, is it really tolerance any more? If we create laws to prohibit the expression of bigotry and racism, have we addressed the vices of bigotry and racism? If we legislate for non-sexist language, have we solved the problems of sexism (or might a term like 'chairperson' be used in a spirit of derision—either by men who employ it as a sarcastic expression of their lingering chauvinism, or by those who object to the artificial distortion of language which it involves)? If we legislate in the area of diet and health to the point where intemperate eating and drinking became very difficult, have we made a mockery of the notion of temperance as a virtue? If we simply banned all environmentally insensitive products, would we have heightened our environmental sensitivity and encouraged people to appreciate the need for greater care?

Of course, Australia is a long way from any of those extremes, but the contemporary mood seems to favour increased regulation in a way which can easily discourage debate about the underlying 'virtues'. It is all too easy for those who believe they know what is good for society (whether in terms of people's physical health and safety, mental well-being, cultural enrichment or economic prosperity), to feel that the processes of debate and education are too tortuous and time-wasting, and to believe that legislative action is the only worthwhile goal. But we shall have to decide whether freedom is more important than fat in the diet; whether justice is always best served by involuntary obedience; whether cost-benefit analysis is all there is. We are already being swept along by developments in genetic engineering and by the uneasy sense that some regulation of the inventiveness of the scientist would be appropriate. But what are the *principles* which would inform regulation of genetic engineering?

Similarly we are being confronted by the need to decide to what extent working mothers and fathers should have their family responsibilities taken into account by their employers. In the early stages of that debate, emphasis has been placed on the possible economic (especially productivity) benefits of management policies which are more sensitive to employees' family contexts. But what are the underlying *principles* involved? Might there not be ethical issues as well as economic issues involved in such a question? What about circumstances in which we deliberately decide to be inefficient because of the claims of a virtue which we rate more highly than efficiency (for example, when we decide *not* to replace six workers by a machine)? What about the people who rate some virtues more highly than health? Might they be permitted to have a say in this debate as well?

This is a critical moment for us because we may not yet have realised that the difficulty with the pro-regulation mentality is that it will fail, at the deepest level, to satisfy our urge to find a new set of bearings. Because so many Australians feel that the reference points for defining the Australian way of life have become either invisible or unreliable, they are bound to find something plausible about the idea that more rules and regulations will provide an alternative set of reference points. It is almost as though Australians, shaken by the events of the 1980s, are wondering if they can be trusted to regulate their own lives, to clarify their own moral principles, or to define their own goals. The vacuum thus created can easily be filled by the willing acceptance of tougher external regulations (whether in the form of censorship, health and safety legislation, or the codification of ethics), without realising that an externally imposed framework may begin by creating a sense of security, but end by stifling personal freedom, courage and initiative.

Our experience with protective trade barriers provides a partial analogy: under the protection of tariffs, creativity and innovation in Australian industries appears to falter, because the sense of security created by tariffs leads to a kind of complacency. Precisely the same thing can happen when a society allows too many rules and regulations to be imposed upon it. The belief that 'everything is under control' can easily stultify the development of an active moral sense.

Australians are generally cynical about the idea of self-regulation when it is applied to industries or commercial organisations. There is a deep mistrust in the Australian community of the idea that powerful organisations could be expected to behave with responsibility and restraint. Part of the current feeling of hostility towards the banking sector is based on the belief that, under the influence of the deregulation of the banking market, the banks behaved irresponsibly and recklessly. Such cynicism is linked to a widespread fear that we may be incapable of regulating our own lives. Again, the characteristic insecurity of the adolescent emerges: Australians still seem to lack confidence that, without having their consciences regulated, they could be trusted to behave sensibly.

The regulation of conscience may solve our short-term

sense of insecurity, but consciences which are agressively regulated ultimately become inactive. At a time when Australians are waking up to the need to articulate their values and aspirations—and to talk about matters of principle as well as practice—it would be a pity if they chose to short-circuit that process by simply settling for another set of external reference points to replace the previous set. If we are serious about debating the question, 'What do we want to become?', then part of the point of that debate will be to decide whether we want to be regulated by experts who claim to know what is good for us, or whether we want to become involved in *deciding* what is good for us on the basis of better public access to the relevant facts. In other words, if we are going to devise a new compass, we had better first decide which virtues, which ideals, which values are going to exert the magnetic pull which will give the new bearings their orientation.

## KNOWLEDGE IS POWER

For some Australians engaged in the quest to find a new set of bearings, the most urgent need is simply to *know more about what is going on*.

In consumer research, one of the strongest emerging themes from the early 1990s is that consumers want to know more about the products they buy, so that they will feel better equipped to make increasingly complex purchase decisions. This explains the strong demand by consumers for more information on product labels, for more inform-ative advertising content, and for more access to consumer advisory services.

In politics, similarly, Australians are beginning to tire of what they perceive as the increasing trend towards personality politics and showmanship, and to demand something more philosophically substantial from the parties who seek their votes.

In relation to the environment, Australians are becoming confused by claims and counter-claims which make it hard for them to feel that they fully understand the situation, and to doubt whether anyone else does, either—a feeling which may well lead to a decrease in their conviction that environmental issues are really serious. Even some of the original converts to environmental fundamentalism are drifting away from the fold, feeling that the early power of their convictions has not been reinforced by adequate information.

In the same way as the fundamentalist looks for the sense of power which comes from having a clearly defined point of view, so other Australians are hoping to acquire a comparable sense of power through heightened understanding. 'Tell me what is really going on' is a demand which is increasingly being heard by politicians, by economists, by marketing companies, and by scientists: Convince me; prove it; show me!

One reason for the attraction of the fundamentalist position (based, as it so often is, on an *absence* of knowledge) is that Australians' faith in the ability of experts in all fields appears to have taken a battering during the unstable and unpredictable years of the Age of Redefinition. Economists routinely disagree about the correct interpretation of economic events in their prescriptions for a brighter economic future. Educationalists disagree about the best way of educating our children. Nutritionists and other health professionals disagree about the components of a healthy diet. In the face of all this disagreement, the ordinary citizen feels increasingly uneasy about his or her own ability to make sensible decisions.

This explains why so many Australians are interested in getting 'the inside story' on any subjects which concern them. Australians' almost insatiable appetite for news and current affairs information via radio and TV is a symptom of an underlying thirst for knowledge as the pathway to security and stability. In Chapter 4.1, the yearning for information was identified as one of the ways of escaping from the complexity and insecurity of everyday life but, at the same time, many Australians are seeking information as a means of better understanding and interpreting everyday life. While information is a form of escapism for some, it is a source of power for others.

## COUNTERPOINT: 'GO WITH THE FLOW'

Not all Australians are ready for a debate about ethics, values or a vision of Australia's future. There is a strong current of opinion which regards all of that as an irrelevance and a waste of time. For some Australians, innovation—especially in science and technology—is the key to Australia's long-term salvation. Their view is that, given enough time, everything will come right because the scientists and technologists will find a way of solving whatever problems beset us. Meanwhile, the only thing to do is react and adapt.

This is really just another manifestation of the 'lucky country' syndrome. Those who place their faith in science and technology are generally doing so in a 'she'll be right' spirit: by some lucky break, a boffin in a laboratory somewhere will hit upon an invention of a process which will take the world by storm and, incidentally, help to solve our balance of payments crisis; science will find a solution to global pollution which will absolve individuals of the responsibility of having to be more environmentally sensitive; in the end, medical science will find solutions to most of our health problems and so, in the meantime, we shouldn't worry too much. As each new life-saving drug comes on to the market, so the need to maintain personal health and fitness seems, to such people, to recede.

Of course, there are other Australians whose faith in science and technology is more realistic, and who believe that scientists have a legitimate role to play—along with everyone else—in shaping Australia's future. But the most ardent believers in the proposition that 'everything will be alright in the end' invest scientists with almost mystical powers and assume that, right now, the solutions to most of the world's problems are being worked out. It is a short step from blind faith in science to fatalism.

Faith in the future does not only rest on faith in science and technology, however. For some Australians, the future is simply an intriguing and exciting alternative to the present, and they can't wait to get there. These are the compulsive futurists who always want to be on the leading edge of change—whether technological, cultural, intellectual or simply culinary. They are the experimenters, the pace-makers, the innovators: the people who believe that 'new' is an almost transcendental condition; the people who believe that, in the face of rapid social change, the thing to do is to jump in and go with the flow.

For such people, the search for 'enduring values' is a fruitless quest. Nostalgia does not interest them, nor does anything which suggests an urge to turn back the clock. If life were a videoplayer, their finger would constantly be on the 'fast forward' button.

Loyalty, for them, is an outmoded concept because transience is the name of the game. In marriage, in other personal relationships, in ownership of possessions and in employment, their eye is constantly on the next opportunity, the next attraction, the next phase. They have a short attention span, but a low level of anxiety. They are not troubled by change, because they welcome it; they are not made insecure by unpredictability or impermanence, because they have accepted them as the very essence of contemporary life. To the futurists, the most attractive slogan of all is this: 'The only constant is change'.

The compulsive futurists are almost exclusively interested in the short term; are attracted to quick-and-easy solutions and want instant gratification. Debt is fine, because credit is the magic mechanism for bringing tomorrow into today. For them, tomorrow is almost here, and yesterday is dead and gone.

It is important to appreciate the futurists' response to the Age of Redefinition, because they represent one of the possible directions for Australian society. As we move through the Nineties, we may well decide that the only constant is change and that the most appropriate response to that is simply to react and adapt to every new event with no underlying sense of vision or purpose beyond a constant willingness to experience the new. In many ways, that was the course which Australia seemed about to set for itself during the Eighties.

Such an orientation has obvious appeal—especially in times of economic buoyancy and high morale. But the compulsive futurists appear rather out of tune with the conservative mood of the mid-nineties. Many of them are quite overtly impatient with it, seeing an increased interest in intangible concepts like values and morality as mere philosophical and ideological lead in the saddle. Rather than trying to create a framework for understanding and interpreting the events going on around them, the compulsive futurists are simply saying that the best way to cope with the rate of change is to make the most of it: resistance, for them, is pointless.

In the end, of course, the compulsive futurists are victims of the changes they so enjoy. By their pre-occupation with what is round the corner, their focus remains external rather than internal; their values tend to remain grounded in the material; their reference point continues to be the self and its gratification. The thrill of the new tends to obscure the lessons of the past.

The pull of the year 2001 will undoubtedly induce some millennium madness in Australia (as in other societies whose calendar we share). Once that begins to happen—probably around 1997–98—the time for a reflective debate about Australia's future will have passed. The futurists will have come into their own. The conservatism of the mid-nineties will be swept aside by a new radicalism. Almost regardless of our economic circumstances at that time, the emphasis will be on the new, the daring, the experimental, the adventurous.

The mood favouring consolidation will give way to a renewed emphasis on growth and development. Bold initiatives will be called for; grand schemes proposed. The calm voice of discourse will be drowned out in enthusiastic shouts of anticipation.

So the middle years of the Nineties offer a unique opportunity to respond to the present urge to take stock of our situation and to open up the debate about who we are and what we want to become. If that happens, Australia will be the arena for some classic confrontations. In the process, we may finally come to value the currency of ideas.

# 4.3

# BACK TO THE TRIBE

It is no accident that the resurgence of interest in values and morality coincides with a desire to recreate a *sense of community* within Australian society. The rising level of concern about standards of ethics—in private life, in business, in politics and government—is directly related to concern about fragmentation of traditional Australian tribal groupings.

Ethics is, after all, a social sense. There is scarcely an ethical issue—or a question of value—which does not, in the end, depend upon the individual's sense of being part of a community. The framework for discussion of values and ethics is the social group; the concept of morality arises directly from our relationships with each other; the sense of duty and obligation is an inherently social sense. All the moral questions which confront us arise from relationships between ourselves and others (involving, in particular, the extent to which we are prepared to take the rights, needs and welfare of others into account).

Every group develops its own set of values, conventions, ideals and virtues. 'Honour among thieves' is a concept which recognises that even those who reject the code of the wider community are bound to develop their *own* code: every sub-group constructs a moral framework to protect its identity and to regulate the behaviour of its members. Families, neighbourhoods, clubs, work-groups . . . communities of all kinds create the climate within which the moral sensibilities of their members develop and in which codes of acceptable behaviour evolve. Ethics are formed out of human networks: disintegrating networks gradually kill off our ethical sensitivities.

The process of developing and passing on a system of values is generally unspoken: it happens by example rather than by spelling it out (partly because, in many cases, the *real* convention is different from what it is said to be: actions speak louder than words). But any development of an ethical framework depends upon the members of the group having a sense of *belonging* to the group. Personal relationships are the medium through which ethics, ideals, values and virtues are transmitted and shared.

The story of Australia in the past 20 years has been a story of declining emphasis on personal relationships; a declining importance attached to being part of a family, a neighbourhood, a community; a declining awareness of *shared* culture.

There have been many powerful reasons for this decline in a 'tribal' sense in the Australian community; in fact, the Age of Redefinition itself is the primary cause. What is particularly significant, in the present context, is the extent to which social, cultural, economic and even technological change has had the specific effect of fragmenting social groups and breaking down the sense of social cohesion:

The struggle between men and women over the redefinition of gender roles has led, for the time being, to a more wary, more adversarial approach to relationships between the sexes, replacing the traditional acceptance of pair bonding as the basis of our social structure with greater emphasis on the individual;

The rising divorce rate has fragmented family life to an extent which has forced many Australians to search—often fruitlessly—outside the family for a group, a herd, a tribe to which they might belong;

The 'personal growth' movement which gained so much momentum during the Seventies and Eighties encouraged egocentricity and, for many people, led to an obsession with personal gratification to the exclusion of traditional concepts of social cohesion;

Multiculturalism has seemed, in the short term, to place more emphasis on diversity than unity;

Politics has become virtually synonymous with economics and has, in the process, seemed to many Australians to have retreated from a concern for human values and social justice;

In corporate life, information technology has become so sophisticated that data transfer is often confused with communication, and personal relationships within organisations have suffered directly as a result. Sending and receiving disembodied information is increasingly allowed to occupy time which used to be spent in keeping closely in touch with each other;

Even on the domestic front, technology has played its part in fragmenting the herd: the dishwasher replaces an episode of personal interaction during the washing-up; the microwave oven reduces the need for the family to eat at the same time.

Under these and similar influences (such as the depersonalisation of financial transactions and the rising popularity
of electronic games in which children interact with a screen
instead of each other), the feeling that we belong to an
identifiable community has been under threat. History
suggests that it is virtually an axiom of human nature that,
when the tribal sense is in decline, the moral sense is
similarly threatened.

Given this inextricable relationship between personal
values and group cohesion, it was inevitable that, as
Australians began to return to some of the basic questions—Who are we? Where are we going? What do we want
out of life? What should we do next?—we would simultaneously look for ways to re-establish some tribal connections. The signs are already beginning to emerge of
Australians' desire to pay more attention to personal
relationships, to re-connect with each other, to re-establish
the sense of belonging to a neighbourhood, a community,
a society. Some of the early signs are little more than hints,
but they form a pattern.

## CONCERN FOR THE ENVIRONMENT

Although Australians' anxieties about global environmental issues (the greenhouse effect, the ozone layer) wax and
wane according to the intensity of competing issues such
as unemployment, it is clear that the environment has
become a significant focus for an enhanced sense of being
part of a community.

For the most zealous greenies, this has led to a vision
of the Human Family as a crew struggling to husband the
dwindling resources available to us on Spaceship Earth.
Less grandly, Australians of all shades of green do seem to

be responding to the idea that we should take more interest in the quality of our physical environment; that we should minimise the pollution of air and water; that we should begin to take the threat of mounting garbage more seriously.

The success of Ian Kiernan's 'Clean Up Australia' campaign (starting with Sydney's 'Clean Up The Harbour' campaign in 1989) indicates how positively Australians will respond to environmental issues which have a local focus and create an opportunity for direct action. But it indicates something else, as well: it suggests that Australians are ready to come out of hiding and to begin co-operating with each other in community projects of mutual benefit.

Community spirit is always fuelled by a crisis. When a town is flooded, its citizens come to the rescue with un-qualified support. When a suburban street is hit by a natural disaster (such as a violent storm) or a personal tragedy (such as the death of a child) neighbours tend to congregate and to support each other—even where they may previously have been strangers to each other. Australians who lived through World War II fondly recall the strong community spirit which permeated Australian society at that time.

The threat of ecological disaster on a worldwide scale may lie beyond the reach of most Australians' concerns, but more immediate and local examples of environmental degradation do have the potential to unite communities in a common fight against pollution—whether via air, water, soil, garbage or even traffic—and to draw us out of our Me-shaped cocoons.

As urban life becomes more complex and crowded, Australians will be forced to develop more co-operative ways of living together. The environment has provided a focus for the early development of that capacity.

## THE WORKPLACE

For Australians who are suffering feelings of isolation and loneliness at home, the workplace has long provided a valuable context for social stimulation and personal relationships. The work group *is* the tribe for many Australians and, even for those who are involved in other social groupings as well, the work group is one of the most reliable sources of personal identity and stability.

As we move through the 1990s, the focus on the workplace as a social environment seems bound to increase. Not only will the workplace satisfy the social needs of lonely people, but employees are already demanding a return to much more *personal* management techniques. The backlash against electronic technology is almost over, and we are ready to put it in its correct place—as servant, rather than master of the organisational culture.

Through the Nineties, we should see a return to more emphasis on consultation, personal meetings, and a more sympathetic appreciation of the employee as a total human being, rather than simply a person at work. If managers are prepared to give more attention to the workplace as a *human* setting, so the sense of people belonging to an organisation will increase and, as their community needs are increasingly met, so their job satisfaction will be enriched— with a likely commercial payoff in terms of increased productivity and loyalty.

The trend away from centralised wage fixing in favour of enterprise bargaining will further enhance the status of the working environment as a community, as workers become more involved in the negotiation of their own wages and conditions through a process of consultation with their own managers. As a direct consequence of such moves, managers and employees will become more attuned to each other's values, aspirations and motivations.

At work, as elsewhere, it is likely that an increasing emphasis on the sense of community will lead to a sharper sense of the moral and ethical issues involved in shaping a better future. Employers and employees who have a *mutual* interest in workplace reform and an enhanced understanding of each other's points of view are more likely to cooperate in the development of mutually satisfying business strategies. The converse is also true, of course: if the 1990s produce a hardening of employer/union confrontation and a declining level of mutual involvement in the community of the workplace, then the agendas, values and aspirations of management and work-force will come into debilitating conflict and industrial relations will descend once again into a moral morass.

## 'FAMILY VALUES'

It is one of the ironies of contemporary Australian life that, at the very time when, demographically speaking, the family is in such disarray, the ideal of 'family life' appears to be increasingly attractive.

To some extent, this is a normal psychological compensation for which there are many precedents. As our society becomes more intensely urbanised, for example, we dream more fondly of rural pursuits. As we come to depend more and more upon impersonal electronic technology, we try to invest machines with characteristics which make them seem more human (such as talking ATMs, and computers which we call 'user-friendly').

While some of the surge of renewed interest in the family is mere compensation, some of it undoubtedly signals a genuine desire on the part of many Australians to recapture some of the values which have been traditionally associated with family life. Again, we see the inextricable link between the idea of a group and the values which grow out of that group.

For all their enthusiasm for divorce and for individual gratification, Australians in the Nineties are beginning to recognise that some of the so-called 'family values' might stabilise their lives and reduce their levels of anxiety and stress. After all, the family is still widely recognised as providing the kind of emotional security which is hard to achieve outside a family unit: a family is expected to provide ultimate loyalty, ultimate acceptance, and the ultimate comfort of being loved without qualification. For all the cyclonic emotions and upheavals which family life causes, it is still thought to offer a guarantee of companionship, mutual support and a strong sense of identity.

Conversely, people who find themselves outside a family structure sometimes report that they have more difficulty in establishing their own sense of identity than those who can easily be defined in terms of their relationships with others. White Australians are still a long way from Aboriginal Australians in the extent to which they identify themselves in terms of group membership, but the emphasis on the individual as the social unit of our society has never quite replaced the need for people to identify themselves in terms of a relationship to someone else. One of the reasons why 'street kids' are thought to be at particular emotional risk is that they lack the sense of personal identity which flows almost automatically from being identified with a family. (Being told that you are 'a chip off the old block' is not always flattering, but it provides a reassuring sense of being part of the flow of family generations.)

None of this implies that the divorce rate is about to fall or that Australian family life is about to become more stable, or that people who prefer to live alone will find themselves drawn into family groupings. What it does imply is that people who are already living in families are beginning to appreciate more fully some of the emotional attractions of family life. Similarly, those who are in blended families, step-families or more transient family groupings are looking for ways to capture some of the sense of identity and security which flows from being a 'real' family.

The fastest-growing household type in Australia is the so-called 'non-kin household'—that is, people who have decided to live together, without any familial or sexual connection, simply because of the urge to create a 'family' and to enjoy the benefits which flow from being identified, recognised and acknowledged as part of a human herd.

Families thrive on interaction with other families. During the 1990s, we are likely to see a renewed emphasis on family group activity: backyard barbecues where the neighbours are invited in; social activities sponsored by business organisations, churches and clubs which extend to the whole family; restaurants explicitly incorporating 'family' in their names.

The family is back in fashion. The term 'family' will be defined in increasingly flexible and diverse ways, but the underlying appeal of the family—however it may be defined—is that it provides a social context in which traditional family values (loyalty, acceptance, shared responsibility, mutual support) are more likely to thrive.

## THE GANG

For young Australians, who, because of family breakdown, lack a clear sense of group identity, 'the gang' provides one option for satisfying the urge to belong to an identifiable tribe.

In our largest cities, youth gangs are on the increase, and are likely to develop more as we move through the Nineties. Although some gangs will engage in vandalism and other forms of anti-social behaviour, the primary motivation for gang formation is not violence, but the need for tribal connection. Because the tribe becomes a major source of personal identity, gangs tend to develop highly visible symbols of membership: particular hairstyles, particular styles and brands of clothing and footwear, socks worn at precisely the right height, and so on. The pastimes chosen— or eschewed—by particular gangs also help to mark out their identity, as do the territories they occupy and the slang and jargon they develop for private communication within the gang.

The peer group has always been a major source of comfort, companionship and identity for adolescents who are passing through a period of uncertainty about their own identity. The gang is simply an extension of the traditional peer group which has become more elaborate and formalised because of the need to compensate for tribal connections otherwise unavailable through the family or the workgroup.

This is not to suggest that all gangs—or all gang members—are the direct result of family breakdown or unemployment: even the relatively conservative and stable Fifties spawned bodgies and widgies. But the more numerous and diverse gangs of the Nineties seem to be symbolising a desire to conform, rather than to rebel: they form part of an emerging pattern of a society trying to relieve its insecurities by re-establishing its tribal identity.

## FORMING GROUPS

In precisely the same way as teenagers gravitate towards peer groups or more elaborate 'gangs' in search of tribal identity, so Australian adults whose herd instincts are not satisfied by family/household groupings are searching for groups which will create a sense of belonging.

We are about to witness a boom in variations on the 'encounter group' phenomenon of the Sixties but this time the goal is group membership rather than self-awareness. Everything from educational courses to aerobics classes, discussion groups, ballroom dancing, bushwalking clubs and organised bus tours can supply the need to join a herd which will provide comfort and security.

(The trend is much further advanced in America than here: reports are even coming to light of groups of Americans getting together to help each other limit their consumption of Coca-Cola. If groups are forming for that purpose, it is safe to assume that the real problem is not Coca-Cola consumption but loneliness, and the real motivator is the urge to find a herd to join.)

Churches, clubs, societies . . . associations of all kinds which offer the opportunity to join in herd-sized activity groups are likely to experience increased support during the Nineties.

## EATING OUT

The fringe benefits tax and the recession of 1991–92 have

done dreadful damage to the short-term health of the Australian restaurant industry. In the longer term, however, the tendency for more and more Australians to eat out is irreversible.

Australians have traditionally been very private about eating. The home has been the conventional location for eating, even with the extended family and with friends, and home-cooked meals have, until very recently, been regarded as the most reliable source of healthy, economical food. Australians' nostalgic reflections on ideal eating occasions still tend to focus on home cooking and on domestic eating occasions (such as the Sunday roast, the barbecue, or modest feasting associated with birthdays, anniversaries, Christmas and other celebrations).

All of that is beginning to change. Although it is true that eating habits within Australian households are increasingly individualistic and the formal family meal-time is in decline, new pressures are emerging to encourage Australians to take advantage of the growing number of facilities now available for eating out. The era of the 'community dining room' is about to dawn.

Of course, it dawned many generations ago in other cultures—notably in Europe and Asia. In those cultures, eating in restaurants, sidewalk cafes, coffee houses and other communal settings has long been regarded as an important element of communal life. But Australians, stranded in their detached bungalows, remote from the restaurants of the inner city, have been slow to appreciate the social pleasures of eating out.

In the Nineties, however, the tide is turning. The major influence on the emerging trend towards eating out is the rise of the working mother as a mainstream social phenomenon. In the early days of trying to combine domestic responsibilities with new-found work outside the home, working mothers tried very hard to use meal-times not only as a time to get the family together, but also as a time to prove that the family was not suffering from the mother's job. The evening meal was often treated like a military operation, with the object of producing the same kind of meal as would have been produced by a stay-at-home mother. In the late Seventies and Eighties, working mothers could be heard declaring that 'no-one is going to accuse me of letting my job interfere with the family' and the evening meal was often the focus of such determination.

Today, working mothers are more relaxed about their dual roles. Recognising that it will be a long time before they can recruit the routine assistance of their male partners in the preparation and serving of meals, they are beginning to realise that occasional trips to local restaurants and foodhalls are a very sensible way of killing two birds with one stone: first, by eating out, they are able to conserve their own time and energy for the many other domestic tasks which they still have to perform; second, by proposing that the family eat out, they are able to create an occasion in which the family will be able to spend time together, to catch up on each other's news, and to escape from a domestic environment which is often associated with tension and pressure.

So, working mothers see eating out as a big opportunity for some tension release—not only for themselves, but for the whole family. When we eat out, we are buying something even more precious than the food: we are buying time which can be spent together.

The second factor likely to accelerate the trend towards eating out is a significant re-thinking about the relationship between diet and health. The Mackay Report on *Food*

(1992) suggested that a growing number of Australians are coming to believe that *how* you eat is at least as important as *what* you eat. In other words, simple acceptance of dietary information as a key to healthy living is beginning to give way to a more complex conclusion that diet itself is only part of the story.

In response to the plethora of dietary messages which Australians received during the Seventies and Eighties, food acquired the status of fuel, or even medicine. With every new revelation about the goodness or badness of particular elements of the diet, Australians became increasingly uncertain about the best way to ensure a healthy diet. In response, they have begun to retreat from what they perceive as frequently contradictory information about diet, to a position where they favour a more relaxed, more moderate approach. Australians generally believe that their diet is healthier than it was 10 or 15 years ago, purely in terms of the food they eat—but they have begun to recognise that the *way* they eat is probably not conducive to health.

One popular expression of this re-thinking about the relationship between diet and health is to reflect on the habits of previous generations whose diet might be regarded as less healthy than the contemporary diet, but whose way of life now seems more likely to have been healthy than the stressed and anxious lives of contemporary Australians. Some of this way of thinking is mere nostalgic revisionism, of course, but the idea that we should regard the *eating occasion* as being a significant contributor to dietary health is an idea which is finding increasing acceptance among Australians. The emerging feeling is that food should be more than medicine; that meals should be more than a pit-stop; that eating is one of the 'simple pleasures' associated with the traditional values which Australians seem so eager to recycle in the Nineties.

Australians are still interested in dietary information; indeed, they take pride in referring to the greater diversity, lightness and healthiness of their diet. The incorporation of pasta and salads, in particular, into the staple Australian diet is thought to have significantly improved it; similarly, the swing from red meat to white is regarded as a healthy move.

But the focus is shifting away from constant modification to the diet itself towards the idea of creating pleasant, relaxed, sociable eating occasions. Even fast, frozen and processed food—until recently associated with the need to eat on the run—is being re-evaluated as a stepping stone to slow eating.

McDonalds may have established itself in the Australian market as a place which would allow us to eat and run; increasingly, McDonalds is being used as a place where families can stop and talk to each other. Again, we buy more than a hamburger: we buy a hamburger *plus time*. The Sizzler chain is a significant signpost to the future development of 'community dining rooms' in Australia: a visit to Sizzler provides the family with an opportunity to sit and talk but also reassures the mother that what they are eating is something which comes very close to the standard and style of a meal she might herself have cooked at home.

As Australians begin to discover the pleasure of eating out, so they begin to recognise the social opportunities which this creates. Meeting friends at a restaurant is less hassle than 'straightening the house for visitors'. Eating in the context of a family restaurant or the foodhall of a regional shopping centre is itself a social activity in which the sense of being part of a community is enhanced—even for people who are eating alone or in small groups.

It is probably a long time before Australians will be participating, *en masse*, in eating activities which Europeans would recognise as characteristic of their communal life, but the process has begun (and in Sydney and Melbourne, in particular, it is well advanced in some of the inner-city areas and some of the more cosmopolitan pockets of suburbia). But even the growing emphasis on *eating* rather than simply on the food itself represents part of a significant social shift. When Australians do begin to emerge from the security of their caves, it is likely to be the sociable pleasure of eating which will entice them to rejoin the herd.

## HOUSING AND THE NEIGHBOURHOOD

Particularly in Sydney, Australia Day 1988 reminded people of the extent to which they had neglected the habit of keeping in touch with their neighbours. Bicentennial activities provided a very welcome reminder of the pleasure of being part of a neighbourhood community: street parties, in particular, established a precedent for many neighbourhoods which has led to regular get-togethers (not only on Australia Day) in the ensuing years.

The tendency for local neighbourhoods to disintegrate is easy to understand. The steady increase in use of the private car as a means of transport has reduced the footpath population, and the sheer mobility of Australians works against the formation of coherent neighbourhoods: on average, we move house every six years. The cliche that 'you don't know your neighbours any more' is by no means universally true, but it is sufficiently true to be mentioned in a spirit of regret when Australians talk about the changes taking place in their way of life. As households shrink and growing numbers of people find themselves in transient living arrangements, the urge to establish some kind of neighbourhood association becomes correspondingly stronger.

In many neighbourhoods, the process has been artificially helped along by organisations such as Neighbourhood Watch encouraging people to be more aware of their suburban environment, and to be more closely in touch with their fellow-residents. In response to such prodding, urban Australians are re-learning the lesson that being in touch with the neighbours makes the neighbourhood safer—quite apart from the psychological benefits involved.

The awakening desire to re-form neighbourhoods may well erode the traditional Australian obsession with the detached bungalow on its own block of land. Medium-density housing—especially in some of its more architecturally innovative forms—has growing appeal to contemporary Australians who recognise that the medium-density option not only offers the possibility of cheaper housing, but also because the medium-density concept creates a more communal locality. Australians still resist high-rise apartment living, but the town-house concept—and other variations on the medium-density theme such as the Green Street project, involving narrower streets and smaller blocks—will become increasingly acceptable as the idea of 'safety in numbers' finds expression in new patterns of urban living.

Economic imperatives will drive the trend, but it is the socio-cultural changes which will finally encourage us to accept the development of new medium-density suburbs on a scale comparable with the original development of older suburbs such as Sydney's Paddington and Melbourne's Carlton.

Purely in terms of infrastructure, it is getting harder and harder for Australia's major conurbations to sustain the traditional pattern of house-and-garden living. Part of the process of the maturing of Australian society will be our acknowledgment of the fact that we can't have it both ways: we can't continue to live in ever-growing cities *and* cling to an unrealistic concept of what 'home' can mean.

## CUSTOMER SERVICE

Our desire to re-establish tribal connections has also surfaced in the area of consumer behaviour. Australians are expressing a sharply increasing demand for improved quality of customer service and that demand generally focusses on the need for more attention to be paid to the *personal relationship* between customer and service provider. Again, the underlying need for human contact emerges: 'treat me as if I belong here; acknowledge me as a person; let's act *as if* this commercial relationship is a personal relationship.'

Faced with poor service, Australians feel affronted because, quite simply, they assume that when the retailer, the tradesman, the bank or the professional person has not paid enough attention to the personal component of the encounter, this means that it is not the *person* who has been valued, but only the person's money.

Because so many Australians are battling with loneliness, and with the problems of identity associated with the fragmentation of their traditional family and neighbourhood groupings, every encounter with another human being (whether commercially-based or otherwise) has the potential to reassure us that our personal identity has been recognised and acknowledged. If we can't get the sense of tribal connection anywhere else, Australians seem to be saying, at least we should be able to get it when we are paying for it. The tribal link can take the form of conversation about a consumer's needs or circumstances; it can take the form of being greeted by name (even if the name is only read off a plastic credit card); it can take the form of welcoming children in a retail environment where children are often perceived as being unwelcome; it can simply take the form of a smile which seems to recognise and acknowledge the customer as a person, rather than merely a customer.

Australian consumers are saying they want every encounter with service providers to have some of the character of an ordinary encounter with another human being. 'If you expect me to maintain a relationship with you or your organisation, then act as if we have a relationship: even though we know the basis of this relationship is commercial, we should still treat each other like human beings.' That kind of remark reveals the extent to which consumers, in a purely commercial context, are beginning to demand that some attention should be paid to the social, tribal aspects of that context.

The same tendency emerges in consumer's increasing willingness to make direct contact with manufacturers through customer service 'hot-lines'; to join clubs and associations which are commercially based (Range Rover 'Connections', the Omomatic club); to attend seminars, workshops and other functions arranged by marketing organisations (such as Bank of Melbourne's seminars for women).

Commercial tribes are clearly set to take their place among the many other tribes which are forming to satisfy our urge to find a social context for our search for a clearer sense of who we are.

Tying all these threads together, it certainly looks as if the Me Generation's ascendancy is over. An identity crisis, in the end, amounts to the question, 'Do I really *belong* here— or anywhere?', and that puts renewed emphasis on the desire for membership of human herds, as a means of reassuring us about our sense of identity. The obsession with 'me' is giving way to a recognition of 'us'.

One of the hazards of the urge to re-group in identifiable herds or tribes is that, because Australia is now such a diverse society, the tribal sense is likely to be quite narrowly-focussed and regional. The real danger exists that, in the quest for a stronger sense of in-group identity, Australians will develop an equally strong sense of *out-group* identity.

Sydney already suffers from this problem on a regional basis. People from the north shore, the northern beaches, the eastern suburbs and the western suburbs are already inclined to identify themselves with those regions to the exclusion of others. It is now quite common for people in particular regions of Sydney to speak in either patronising or antagonistic terms of those who come from other regions. That tendency is likely to increase, and to emerge in non-geographical groupings as well. One of the hazards of multiculturalism, clearly, is that in our enthusiasm to protect and encourage ethnicity, we may inadvertently increase tension and rivalry between ethnic sub-groups. Similarly, the growing gulf between the haves and the have-nots in Australian society has the potential to add a new dimension to tribal identity and tribal conflict.

If our need to re-tribalise is *too* strong, we run the risk of creating further damaging divisions. The move beyond the simplistic egocentrism of the Me Generation will do us no good if we simply replace the individual with a group which is self-absorbed to an extent which further damages the fabric of Australian society.

## UNITY IN DIVERSITY?

Will we ever regain the sense of being a *community* of Australians? Will we come to accept—during the painful period of re-evaluating our economic, social and cultural directions—that we are *all* Australians and that, despite the increasing diversity of our origins and lifestyles, we all belong here? Will those who want to define more sharply their own ethnic, cultural, religious or political identities acknowledge the absolutely equal right of everyone else to define their identities differently? Will those who assert so enthusiastically that wealth must be created before it can be shared embrace with equal enthusiasm strategies for ensuring that it *is* shared?

Because the desire to establish tribal identity is, as we have seen, inextricably linked to the desire to clarify our values and ideals, the concept of 'unity in diversity' will have central importance in any debate about the emerging Australian identity, character and ethos. If we see ourselves as a community only in the sense that we tolerate anything and anybody in the name of diversity, then we will have come no closer to the goal of shared values or a shared vision. Ultimately, the sense of community—regardless of the diversity which it embraces—depends on a fundamental unity: shared culture, shared values, shared ideals are the essential pre-requisites for harmonious tolerance of diversity. They do not guarantee harmony (since an exaggerated sense of unity can very easily overwhelm tolerance of diversity) but, without an underlying sense of shared ideals, values and purpose, Australia will simply become a cultural and tribal battlefield.

The Age of Redefinition has put Australians' sense of unity to the test. However unattractive or unrealistic it may now seem, we had a strong sense of homogeneity in Australian society up until the early 1960s. From then on, we have been placing increasing emphasis on diversity. The urge to re-tribalise will only turn out to be a healthy and productive urge if it leads us to acknowledge that Australia is now so diverse that homogeneity is no longer an option; that diversity need not imply division; that our sense of community is, by definition, a sense of what we have *in common*.

Paradoxically, one of the most striking features which Australians have in common is that we live in a diverse and rapidly evolving culture. If we can learn to love our diversity, then we will have gone some way towards unifying it (without homogenising it); if we can't, then diversity will divide us.

Presumably, there is something more to being an Australian than simply living in Australia: serious discussion about Constitutional change and the gathering momentum of the push for republicanism may precipitate a wider debate about the cultural values and social ideals which can unify us without stultifying us.

Australians have always prided themselves on having a relaxed attitude towards nationalism: we have been rather embarrassed by other cultures' extravagant displays of patriotism. Now, suddenly we find ourselves arguing over the flag and considering whether we should further assert our independence from the British monarchy. Symbols are assuming new importance. We are torn between the desire to define our new identity and the desire to reassure ourselves about our heritage. In the same way as we must face the challenge of trying to find the balance between cultural unity and diversity, we must also face the challenge of trying to achieve a stronger sense of national identity and patriotic pride without losing our healthy disregard for the jingoistic excesses of nationalism.

# 5

# WHAT ARE WE WAITING FOR?

We are all prisoners of our experience, which is another way of saying that we bring all our yesterdays into today to try to make sense of what is happening to us. Our discoveries, our learnings, our decisions gradually evolve into a recognisable pattern, a framework, or a 'world view'. Once that framework has begun to develop, we tend to see the world in a highly subjective and selective way, because we see it through the filter of our own convictions, our own prejudices, our own point of view.

It is as though we are engaged in a lifelong process of constructing personal 'cages' around ourselves. The bars of our cages are all the things that life has taught us: our knowledge, our attitudes, our values, our beliefs, our prejudices. As the cage becomes stronger and more complex, we feel increasingly comfortable and secure inside it: after all, it is a cage which we ourselves have each constructed out of our own, unique life's experience. Where we have been, and what we have learned from the journey, defines who we are.

Because we look at the world through the bars of the cage, the bars impose their own pattern on what we see: our values and beliefs affect the way we perceive and interpret what's out there. The viewer is, indeed, part of the view.

(Cages are therefore the critical factor in the communication process, because they can so easily obscure and distort our view of each other, and limit our capacity to interpret each other's messages—but that's another story, and another book.)

The process of cage-building never ends, because life never stops bringing us new experiences to incorporate into the patterns created by the old. When life is proceeding smoothly and predictably, the cage gradually evolves as we add new bars to the structure and, perhaps, perform some gentle modifications to what's already there. But when, as in the Age of Redefinition, new experiences constantly *challenge* our existing patterns of attitude and belief—when the bars of the cage are rattled by continuous assault from a world which no longer supports our world-view—we experience all the anxiety, insecurity and uncertainty which has become characteristic of contemporary Australia. On the one hand, we want to satisfy our deep psychological need for secure and stable cages; on the other hand, we are forced to acknowledge the need for a demolition job and a re-building of at least part of the cage.

The good news is that reconstruction of the cage generally involves psychological growth and development. People who survive life-threatening illnesses—or other extreme personal traumas—typically report that, in retrospect, such an event was 'the best thing that ever happened to me' because of its effect on the cage: working through a trauma forces us to re-think our priorities, to re-focus on our values and to decide what kind of life we really want to live.

(More simply and less dramatically, the cliche that 'travel broadens the mind' captures the same idea: exposure to a different culture often turns out to have a cage-altering effect.)

The problem for most of us in the Age of Redefinition is that our level of anxiety hovers below the threshold of a major crisis. We are made uncomfortable by the tension between the patterns of the past and the discontinuities of the present, but we have not yet been galvanised to an extent which would force us to take decisive action—either in the way we manage our lives, or in the way we interpret the world around us. We still find ourselves, too often, trying to fit uncomfortable new experiences into the framework of comfortable old cages.

Nevertheless, the social and cultural instability of the Seventies and Eighties will undoubtedly lead to a great deal of soul-searching in the Nineties and this, in turn, will create the potential for a new confidence in Australians' view of themselves, a new self-respect, and a new determination to take control of our destiny . . . *but only the potential.* Whether we actually approach that potential will be the test of our maturity.

The temptation to settle for less than our potential will be strong. Rather than daring to dream of great Australian possibilities and setting long-term goals to achieve them, it will be easier to make escapism a way of life; it will be easier to settle for the role of victim and to blame our personal difficulties on the economy and our national difficulties on irresistible international influences; it will be easier to decide that our economy is already eclipsed by our Asian neighbours to an extent that makes Japanese economic imperialism inevitable (with us as a colony, again); it will be easier to decide to wait and see what happens and, in the meantime, to induce 'paralysis by analysis'. Above all, it will be easier to wait for a suitably messianic leader to appear on the political scene—someone who will tell us all what to do next.

The extraordinary thing is that, when groups of Australians talk to each other—at home, at work, at the pub or the club, at meetings, at leisure—these are the very hazards which they themselves identify. Ordinary Australians speak of the need for more open communication about the nature and direction of our society; the need to experiment with more imaginative redeployments of available work; the need to 'get our values straight' and to rebuild our sense of being a community; the need to take more control of our lives. Australians are not short of advice about how to reinvent Australia, but they seem curiously powerless to take their own advice. So what are we waiting for?

## TAKING CONTROL OF OUR LIVES

While it is no doubt true that great national debates need to occur about the unemployment problem and labour market reform, about immigration patterns and policies, about the restructuring of Australia's industrial base, about Constitutional reform, and even, perhaps, about our national identity, it is equally true that small, personal debates are called for. Patrick White hit the nail on the head with his assertion (reported in *The Age* of 1 June 1983) that 'Australia will never acquire a national identity until enough *individual* Australians acquire identities of their own'.

No one is going to wave a magic wand which will restore to Australians the sense that they have their lives under control: each individual has the responsibility of taking control of her or his own life.

There will be no mass movement which will resolve the conflicts between men and women over the redefinition of gender roles: individual men and women in personal relationships—at home, at work and elsewhere—must negotiate their own way through to a better mutual understanding of each other's needs and a mutual accept- ance of each other's roles. The sense of being a community will not be magically restored to neighbourhoods as a result of some official policy declaration: individuals must begin to accept that they are the community and they determine the character of that community. 'We don't know our neighbours' is a statement about us, not our neighbours. There is no point in bleating about the divisiveness of multiculturalism: if we want to integrate immigrants into our neighbourhoods, we must take positive steps to do so.

Destructive criticism is as useless as smug detachment. There is no point in grizzling about the state of Australian politics, for example, unless we are individually prepared to become more politically active: to vote more thoughtfully, to attend political meetings, to join parties, to exert some influence on the selection of candidates, to speak to our members of parliament or, indeed, to stand for political office ourselves. Politics won't magically improve, all by itself: improvement is a step-by-step, person-by-person process.

New and more creative ways of matching the work-force to the available work will not happen because of a national conference which decrees that it must happen: individual employers and employees must begin to negotiate working arrangements which suit them better than the present arrangements. There is no point in yearning for the inspiration of some 'national leadership': every chief executive, every manager and every supervisor has the potential to offer inspired leadership in a situation where real and immediate benefits can be felt.

There is no point in unemployed youngsters mooning around a video store, complaining that there is nothing to do: within a kilometre's radius of their melancholy complaint, there are bound to be enough disadvantaged, elderly or disabled people needing help to provide any amount of satisfying work (the performance of which could be regarded, if our ethical framework were different, as an obligation upon those able-bodied Australians who are being financially supported by the community).

Hopelessly idealistic? We certainly seem to be a long way from deciding to take such matters into our own hands, but this is ultimately what is required if we are ever going to regain the sense of having our lives under control. Being 'in control' doesn't mean that life will suddenly become orderly and predictable, or that everything will happen to our liking: what it means is that we have seized the initiative; that we have thrown off the victim mentality and decided to accept responsibility for our own situation; that we have been prepared to dream of a better future and then take the first tentative steps towards achieving it.

There is no mystery about the strategies for taking control of our lives: Australians talk about them every day, and are already showing the early signs of adopting some of them (as described in Chapters 4.1, 4.2 and 4.3). The critical decision is the decision to take personal and individual responsibility for our lives, rather than blaming someone else or, worse, believing that we have to get someone *else's* life under control as well. (If our happiness depends on someone else toeing *our* line, we're sunk.)

How will we take more control of our lives? What should we actually *do*?

## 1. GETTING OUR PRIORITIES STRAIGHT

It is all very well complaining about the values of Australian society, or the corruption in high places, or the materialistic excesses of various corporations and individuals. In the end, though, the values which most seriously affect our own lives are our *own* values.

The 'back to basics' movement is healthy only if it implies a sincere desire to work out what we really want out of life: to establish what kind of world we would like to create for our children and grandchildren; to re-order our priorities so they line up with our personal goals. Perhaps 'back to basics' is simply saying that we want to establish which bits of our personal cages we are not prepared to demolish or abandon; perhaps it is saying that we want to re-examine our cages to decide whether they were soundly constructed in the first place.

It is a common human experience to find, at the end of one's life, that there were few regrets about what was done, but many regrets about what was *not* done. Typically, those regrets focus on a failure to have sorted out personal priorities early enough in life to have let them determine the course and the character of life. (One of the most common regrets, for example, is voiced by people who feel that they spent too much time at work and not enough time nurturing and enjoying personal relationships in their private lives.)

The sense that we are trapped in a particular pattern of life is almost always due to the fact that we have not stepped back for a moment to consider what kind of life we really want; what kind of beliefs we really hold; what values we really espouse. The feeling of being trapped is really the same as the feeling of being adrift: in both cases, the problem is lack of control over what is happening to us. Until we have worked out our personal priorities, values and reference points, we will have no basis for taking control of our personal destinies.

A word of warning, though: mystics and philosophers through the ages have often come to the conclusion that we don't really begin to take control of our lives until we relinquish the sense of *having* to be in control. That sounds like a paradox, but it is simply reminding us that, when we finally get our values and priorities straight, it often turns out that being 'in control' isn't really one of them, after all (or doesn't mean what we thought it meant).

## 2. WORKING ON OUR RELATIONSHIPS

A critical aspect of feeling in control of our lives is the knowledge that our lives are not lived in isolation, but involve sharing in a common experience with other people. The group, the herd, the family, the tribe . . . the social context is essential for most of us to feel confident about who we are and where we are going.

This is partly because, as Chapter 4.3 suggested, our sense of values grows out of our understanding that we are part of a community. But it is partly also because the idea of personal identity actually makes no sense outside of a social context.

Our sanity—our sense of being in control of our lives— therefore rests very heavily on being part of a human network. We need the support of family, friends and colleagues in order to develop a confident sense of who we are, and in order to experience the comfort which derives from knowing that we belong to a human herd.

You want more sense of control over your life? Spending more time working on personal relationships with the people around you is a sure pathway to achieving that goal. With so much talk of 'survival' in the air, it is perhaps appropriate to draw an analogy with the lifeboat: when survivors scramble into a lifeboat, they not only experience the relief of knowing that they are, quite literally, all in the same boat, but they also find that it is helpful to have someone else to share the rowing.

Personal relationships are the only channels through which we ever really communicate with each other. Personal relationships are the channels through which we gain some understanding of who we are. Personal relationships are the only channels through which we can ultimately gain some sense of our own worth.

Solitary confinement is the worst possible punishment, short of death, precisely because it cuts us off from the channel of personal relationships. This is not a punishment which we should impose on ourselves: loneliness erodes our sense of being in control of our lives.

Australian society offers abundant opportunities for individuals to join networks. For most of us, the extended family provides a ready-made network, and we usually benefit from the time we invest in maintaining extended family relationships. Workplaces, similarly, provide an easily accessible source of human contact and personal relationships. But there are countless clubs, societies, associations and groups of all kinds which offer the opportunity to interact with other people—often with a particular focus such as recreation, education, music, religion, languages or drama, which takes the heat off our personal interactions, and allows relationships to evolve naturally in the context of singing together, acting together, playing together or learning together.

None of this is to suggest that everyone *should* link themselves to a family, a neighbourhood, a club or a work group: it is simply to note that people who aren't prepared to work at developing and maintaining a sufficient number of personal relationships to create the reassuring sense of being part of a 'network', are often the people who experience the most acute sense of their lives being out of control.

## 3. DEVELOPING THE ART OF REFLECTIVE DETACHMENT

If we want to feel in control of our lives, we need to have regular 'time out', not only to restore our energy but also to ensure that we maintain a healthy perspective on the rest of our lives.

There are many different ways of achieving the restorative sense of peace and contentment which flows from regular participation in some form of ritual detachment from the stresses of daily living. Those who adopt various forms of meditation and relaxation (such as Hindu yoga or Christian meditation) report that their strict adherence to the disciplines involved gives them a sense of tranquility which becomes a precious resource for dealing with the daily events of their lives. Those who enjoy the experience of religious worship in a carefully structured liturgical context report the therapeutic value of ritual. Those who have developed jogging into a ritualised period of detachment report that physical fitness is only one of the benefits they enjoy: time spent jogging often produces a feeling of 'cleansing' of the mind, a reduction of stress, and a clarity of thought.

Music-making can produce similar effects because of the need for intense concentration on the music and absorption in the sounds being produced (and, in the case of singing, the added therapeutic benefits of deep breathing). Other arts and crafts, similarly, can provide a feeling of 'space' into which a person can retreat for a period of reflective detachment while painting, stitching, sculpting, or gardening.

Not everyone has the urge to engage in organised recreational activities—nor to develop the disciplines of formal meditation—and many people find that regular walking provides the opportunity for reflective detachment. As long as the walking is sufficiently brisk to involve some deep breathing and to develop a rhythm of its own, walking can be an intensely therapeutic way of creating a daily 'retreat'.

Participation in active sport is more controversial. Although it is true that playing a game of tennis, for example, does involve a very concentrated focus on the ball, the degree of emotional involvement in a competitive game can easily swamp any attempt at reflective detachment. Nevertheless, many people do find that, in the afterglow of sporting activity, they experience feelings of contentment and tranquility which are conducive to reflection.

Some people use their pets as a focal point for reflective detachment. The rituals and structures associated with the grooming, exercise, care and feeding of pets can provide a welcome retreat from the demands of human society, and the highly focussed relationships which many pet-owners have with their pets are valuable precisely because they are detached from the complexities of human relationships: time with a pet can be intensely valuable 'time out'. (Indeed, research published in the September 1992 *Australian Medical Journal* reveals that, among pet owners, blood pressure, blood cholesterol and the general risk of heart disease appears to be lower than among non-owners.)

Activities which successfully create opportunities for reflective detachment appear to have two features in common. First, they involve a physical break from the mainstream activities of daily life—we have to *do* something in order to induce the detachment we require. Barracking for a football team does not qualify (and neither does flopping in front of the TV). Second, they involve a narrowing of focus (ranging from the mantra of meditation to the rhythmic breathing of controlled relaxation) which excludes any conscious concern with the wider context of our lives. Paradoxically, such narrowed focus creates the opportunity to develop a healthier perspective on that wider context when we return to it. Almost without exception, successful forms of reflective detachment involve quite rigorous disciplines: in order to obtain maximum benefit, we must 'play by the rules' of whatever pursuit we choose.

One way or another, achieving the sense of being in control of our lives seems to depend upon creating definite periods in every week when we submit to the kind of routines and rituals—ranging from the meditative to the creative—which can take us out of ourselves and fix our attention elsewhere. Sometimes, the result of such detachment is that we are able to identify tensions in ourselves created by gaps between our values and our behaviour; sometimes, the result is that we acquire a new perspective on our circumstances which leads us to accept what previously seemed unacceptable; sometimes, solutions to apparently insoluble problems emerge in the moment of retreat from them. Whatever the outcome, reflective detachment is fundamental to the construction—or reconstruction—of a well-integrated cage.

The urge to revamp our cages is undestandable and desirable; indeed, some renovation is bound to be necessary as we equip ourselves for dealing with the continuing instability of life in the Nineties. We might even decide that it is a good idea to build a little flexibility into the structure so that we are better able to cope with some of the contradictions and ambiguities which are characteristic of the Age of Redefinition.

If we are going to reinvent Australia—and that's the process we seem to be involved in—it's reassuring to know that we are all in this together. However accidentally, we are *all* pioneers. It's reassuring, also, to know that, just when we need them, the historians, social philosophers and commentators are prepared to stimulate our ideas about what should happen next. Guidance also comes—as ever— from the contemporary novelists, poets and playwrights who, in observing and interpreting our society, are often actually sending us signals from our future.

Sooner or later, though, we shall have to recognise that all the talk about the ideal of *shared* values, *shared* purpose and a *shared* sense of identity comes down to the need for each of us to explore and clarify our own individual values, purpose and sense of identity. Although we will define them in terms of the community to which we belong, the community won't define them for us. The 'meaning of life' is not waiting to be discovered by someone else and then relayed to the rest of us: we must put our own meanings into our own lives or they will remain meaningless. In the same way, Australia will become what we make it, because the matter is in no-one's hands but ours.

# Appendix:

# THE MACKAY REPORT

*The Mackay Report* is a continuous program of qualitative social research, established in 1979, which is funded by annual subscriptions from a wide range of commercial and government organisations (such as large industrial companies, banks and other financial organisations, marketing companies, advertising agencies, media organisations and government departments and instrumentalities).

Each year's research program consists of four major studies of particular aspects of the Australian way of life, which are published as quarterly reports. In addition, *Keynote* reports are published, from time to time, on topical issues as they arise. Monthly *Talking Points* bulletins are also published as a means of monitoring the ebb and flow of social issues and community concerns.

All the reports and bulletins are issued for the exclusive use of the subscribers who fund the programs, but copies of the reports are lodged in the National Library, and in certain State and academic libraries, for the use of research students. *Reinventing Australia* is an attempt to summarise the main themes emerging from this research program, and to provide a distillation of the research findings for the general reader.

# The Research Method

In social research, it is critically important to find a method which is compatible with the kind of thing we are trying to investigate. For example, if we want to know how many people visit a particular place—or how often they go there, or how much money they spend, or what they do while they are there—then a method which relies primarily on observation will be most appropriate. We can attach precise numbers to all those things, and so the observation will be *quantitative*.

If we can't directly observe what people are doing, we may have to rely on an indirect research method, such as a questionnaire-based survey, to get an approximate idea of their behaviour based on their own recollections or claims about what they did. Again, this information will be able to be expressed in numbers.

If we want to determine the extent to which certain information is known within the community (for example, the name of Australia's biggest trading partner, or the number of banks offering a particular service, or the policies of the major political parties on a particular issue), we can again measure the extent of that knowledge by means of a structured questionnaire.

But when we venture beyond the realm of behaviour and quantifiable knowledge into the more complex and subtle question of *why* people behave as they do—the area of attitudes, opinions, values and beliefs—the task is not so straightforward. Although a great deal of quantitative research is undertaken to 'measure' attitudes, it generally takes the same form as the surveys of easily quantifiable data: that is, simply asking people a series of questions designed to elicit the required information. In such cases, serious difficulties arise. For a start, every time you ask a question you are likely to receive an answer, and it is tempting to believe that the answer has told you what you wanted to know. But one of the hazards of attitude research based on structured questionnaires is that we can never be sure whether the answer was obtained only because the question was asked: does that 'attitude' or 'opinion' really exist, or does it only exist in the form of an answer to that question?

The matter is further complicated by the fact that, if we were to ask a set of questions in a different order, we would almost certainly obtain different responses. If we varied the wording of the questions, the answers would also be likely to vary. Researchers know that it is not hard to determine the outcome of a survey by controlling the way in which questions are asked. So what is the 'correct' form of any set of questions designed to elicit the attitudes we want to investigate, and what is the 'correct' order in which those questions should be asked? We can experiment with variations, but we can never be sure that we have eliminated the influence of questions on the answers we obtain.

There's another problem as well: when a set of structured questions is used to investigate attitudes, we can never be sure whether there are other attitudes present in our respondents' minds which lie beyond the scope of the questions. What *else* do people feel about a particular subject which we may have failed to elicit because we didn't ask enough questions—or the right questions?

Questions involving the use of 'Why?' are a particular hazard in surveys based on a formal structured question-naire. As soon as someone is asked 'Why?' about anything, the expectation is created that there *should* be a reason for the behaviour or the attitude under investigation. Once the expectation has been created that a 'reason' exists to explain some piece of behaviour, the respondent is likely to offer a rational-sounding response (which may be a mere rationalisation) in order to satisfy the rational demands of the question. 'Why did you marry that man?' 'Why did you stop going to church?' 'Why did you vote for that candidate?' All such questions assume that there's a reason for doing those things, yet we do many things for no 'reason' at all (at least, for no logical or easily-explained reason).

In fact, one of the controversies in social research concerns the question of whether some attitudes, beliefs and values are appropriate for measurement at all. Measurement is a rational process, after all, so research instruments which are designed to obtain measurements are perfectly appropriate for rational data (how much? how often? when? where?). But if the *explanations* of behaviour are not rational, then why try to measure them? Even if some apparently simple and straightforward attitudes are measurable, the explanation of why those attitudes are held may not be.

Some social research sets out to quantify the *extent* to which people hold certain attitudes (or, more accurately, the extent to which they agree or disagree with statements which are thought to express those attitudes) but there are still serious problems involved in first trying to uncover the attitudes in question, and then trying to express them in a measurable form. It can be done, but it is a very complex process—generally involving finding a number of *different* ways of expressing each of the attitudes being investigated.

But even then, the fundamental issue remains: might it not be possible that people have attitudes or beliefs which are not capable of being measured? Isn't it possible that the rational instrument of a structured questionnaire is an inappropriate method for investigating information which may be non-rational and highly emotional in character? Might it not be more appropriate to devise a research method which is itself non-rational, non-linear and non-structured, in order to match more closely the nature of the material being investigated?

It is that kind of concern which led to the development of *qualitative* research. Because qualitative research is primarily concerned with explanation and diagnosis, the question of measurement hardly arises. Can we measure the happiness of a child at a party? The security of a loving relationship? The ambition of a school leaver? The despair of unemployment? The private pain of divorce? All these things can be explored and understood, but trying to measure them may be an inappropriate goal.

Qualitative research sets out to investigate attitudes, values and beliefs without the use of structured survey techniques which are designed to produce numbers. Qualitative research is deliberately designed to bypass the rational; to avoid the use of direct questions, especially those questions involving 'Why?'; to minimise any pressure on survey respondents to give answers which fit a particular survey instrument. (We still want to find out 'Why?', but experience suggests that there are better ways than asking.)

A doctor will generally use qualitative data (such as a conversation with the patient, or some insight into the patient's history and circumstances) to help her/him in the task of interpreting quantitative data from medical tests, before deciding on a diagnosis and prescribing some treatment. In the same way, qualitative social research is intended to illuminate our understanding of why people behave as they do.

*The Mackay Report* employs two qualitative research techniques in an attempt to explain people's behaviour by exploring their underlying attitudes, values and beliefs in all their subtlety and complexity, without attempting to impose measurement on the exploration, and without asking any direct questions at all.

## NON-DIRECTIVE GROUP DISCUSSIONS AND UNSTRUCTURED PERSONAL INTERVIEWS

The group discussion technique was illustrated by the opening pages of Chapter 1. It involves a natural, existing social group (typically 5–8 friends, neighbours or work-mates) meeting together in their natural habitat (the home of one of them, or a work-place, or wherever the group feels most 'at home'), to engage in relaxed, informal and unstructured discussion about the topic in question. No questions are asked: no formal agenda is set. The researcher plays no active part in the discussion, beyond an introduction which explains the purpose of the study, outlines the topic and describes the way in which the discussion might proceed.

Thus, in the relaxed and permissive atmosphere of a group of people who already know each other and are used to talking to each other, the discussion ranges widely over all aspects of the subject which interest or concern the members of the group. Some people will talk a great deal; some will say very little. The discussion will proceed as any natural, normal group discussion proceeds. There will be leaders and followers; those who are dominant and those who are submissive; agreements and disagreements; side-tracking and wise-cracking.

In the ebb and flow of natural conversation, the attitudes,

values and beliefs of the group will gradually emerge. It is the dynamics of non-directive group interaction which yield the information we are seeking.

In order to be successful as a method for social research, the group discussion technique must have three features: the group must be a *real* group (that is, people who are well-known to each other and who are used to interacting with each other); the discussion must be conducted on the home ground of the group—a place where it is natural for them to be, and where they feel most comfortable; the discussion must proceed freely and spontaneously, without any interference or any structure being imposed upon it by the researcher.

Of course, the group discussion technique has its limitations. It is not a suitable technique for eliciting information from people who are generally isolated from social interaction, and it is not a suitable technique for eliciting the kind of information which people may not wish to discuss even in the company of friends with whom they are socially at ease. For these reasons, a comprehensive social research project must also employ another technique which does not rely on group interactions.

*The Mackay Report* uses, as its second technique, the unstructured (or 'non-directive') personal interview. The nature of this technique is fundamentally the same as the group discussion technique, except that it involves a private conversation between a researcher and a respondent. Again, the interview takes place on the 'home ground' of the respondent; again, direct and formal questions are avoided; again, the respondent is encouraged to ruminate extensively about the subject under review.

An important feature of both techniques is that the respondents' anonymity is guaranteed: although the information they give us is incorporated into our reports (often appearing as verbatim quotations to illustrate or support our findings), the source of that information is kept absolutely confidential.

The information yielded by the non-directive group discussion and the unstructured interview technique is subjected to extensive and rigorous qualitative analysis procedures which are in every way as strict as those employed for the statistical analysis of quantitative research data, but follow quite different principles.

Because of the nature of qualitative methodology and the aims of the research, sample sizes for qualitative social research are much smaller than for quantitative surveys where the data will be subjected to statistical processing. Because the emphasis is on diagnosis and explanation, rather than measurement, we concentrate on the *diversity* of the sample (rather than its sheer size), so that each study incorporates the widest possible range of respondents within the practical limits of the project. The fundamental rule is that each group and individual interviewee should be as different as possible from every other group and interviewee in the study in terms of characteristics such as age, socio-economic status, position in the life-cycle, geographical location etc. In data analysis, one of the primary aims is then to discern the *range* of attitudes emerging from that highly diverse sample.

In the end, of course, the integrity of social research—whether quantitative or qualitative—depends upon the interpretation of the data. All research is flawed, partly because there is no such thing as perfect interpretation, and partly because of the ever-present danger of the dreaded 'experimental effect': the possibility always exists that the data we are trying to interpret has been influenced by the methods we used to obtain that data. One reason for our heavy reliance on the group discussion technique is that, when it is carefully applied, it seems to minimise the dangers of the 'experimental effect' by providing a method of data collection which is as *natural* as we can make it. As a further safeguard against misinterpretation, the continuous nature of this research program allows us to set the data from each individual study in the context of the broad sweep of the whole program, and our reliance on the team approach (with three or four researchers working independently on each project) minimises the possibility of subjective bias in our analysis.

## THE REPORTS

Following is a complete list of the 69 Mackay Reports published up to the end of June 1993 (including nine *Keynote* reports):

1979 Mothers & Daughters
Leaders & Heroes
Saving & Spending
Television

1980 Energy
Diet & Health
Advertising
Being 19 Now

1981 Brands, Private Labels & Generics
Drinks
Australian or Overseas Control
Computers, Technology & the Future
Behind the Ratings
Retirement

1982  Radio
      Supermarketing
      Leisure
      Parties & Politicians

1983  Holidays
      Children & Television
      The Working Wife
      Power &
          Responsibility

1984  Money
      Goals
      Purchase Decisions
      News & Current
          Affairs

1985  Turning 40
      City Life, Country
          Life
      Big Business
      The Multiculture
      Singles

1986  Luxuries
      Class & Status
      Australians at Home
      Contemporary Social
          Issues
      Television

1987  Food
      Turning 55
      Newspapers
      Discretionary
          Income

1988  Being Australian
      The Point of
          Purchase
      Teenagers and Their
          Parents
      Premium Products

1989  Direct Marketing
      Australians at Work
      Men & Women
      Health & Fitness

1990  Corporate Ethics
      The Post-Election
          Mood
      The Australian
          Dream
      Sponsorship
      Privatisation
      The Environment—
          Who Pays?

1991 Advertising
     The Recession
       Mentality
     Customer Service
     Value for Money
     Our Evolving
       Relationship with
       Television
     The Family—'90s Style

1992 Food
     The Keating/
       Hewson Factor
     Creating Customer
       Loyalty
     What Do I Believe
       In?
     User Pays
     Media Roles

1993 Buy Australian
     Why Did Labor Win?
     The Grey Market

In addition to *The Mackay Report*, Mackay Research also publishes an occasional series of syndicated market research reports. Under the series title *Marketscan*, these reports explore consumer attitudes, values, motivations and aspirations as they apply to specific markets.

In *Reinventing Australia*, five *Marketscan* reports have been quoted:

     The Banking Market (1985)
     Shopping (1986)
     The Banking Market (1988)
     The Holiday Market (1988)
     The Banking Market (1992)
     The Self-Medication Market (1992)

# INDEX

# About the Author

Hugh Mackay is a social psychologist who began his research career in 1955, obtaining his academic qualifications as a part-time evening student. He established Mackay Research in 1971 and The Centre for Communication Studies in 1975. In 1979, he launched *The Mackay Report*, a continuous program of qualitative social research which is unique in the world.

Hugh Mackay is a graduate of the University of Sydney and Macquarie University, and he was elected a Fellow of the Australian Psychological Society in recognition of his pioneering work in the application of qualitative methodology to social research.

He broadcasts regularly on ABC radio and writes a weekly column on social issues for *The Australian Financial Review*.